Bristol Channel and Severn Cruising Guide

Dedication

Through the 1980s and 90s Peter Cumberlidge became a well-respected nautical writer and photographer for cruising under both sail and power. His first foray into pilotage guides was the *Bristol Channel and Severn Pilot*, published in 1988 by Stanford Maritime. It was a small book with black and white illustrations and hand-drawn charts. When Imray took the book on in 2008 it became colourful, had clear professional charts and has become the guide many yachtsmen have come to rely on.

Peter died in 2019 and this edition is dedicated to his memory. His philosophy for both life and cruising was enjoyment and in his writing he shared his love of being afloat with a good read. In doing this update I hope I have managed to retain this and that he would approve the changes that have been made.

After Peter's death many people generously sent donations in his memory which have been given to the Ellen MacArthur Cancer Trust. If you would also like to contribute to this amazing organisation you can do so through **www.justgiving.com/fundraising/petercumberlidgecruisingfund**.

Contents

Preface	vii
Introduction	1
Cruising in the Bristol Channel	2

North coast

Milford Haven	6
Tenby	18
Saundersfoot	24
The Towy Estuary	27
Burry Port	30
The Gower Peninsula	34
Swansea	36
Briton Ferry	42
Port Talbot	44
Porthcawl	47
Barry	50
Cardiff Bay	56
Rhymney River	65
Newport and the River Usk	67
St Pierre Pill	72
River Wye and Chepstow	75
Lydney	78

Upper Severn

Avonmouth to Sharpness	82
Sharpness	87
Sharpness to Stourport	91

South coast

Oldbury Pill	98
River Avon and Bristol	100
Portishead	108
Walton Bay	111
Clevedon Pill	112
Langford Swatch	114
Woodspring Bay	116
Weston-super-Mare	117
Uphill and the River Axe	120
Burnham-on-Sea and the River Parrett	123
Watchet	128
Minehead	131
Porlock Weir	134
Foreland Point	137
Lynmouth	138
Combe Martin	141
Watermouth Cove	143
Ilfracombe	146
Passage-making from Ilfracombe	151
Appledore, Instow and Bideford	152
Clovelly	158
Lundy Island	161
Bude Haven	166
Boscastle	172
Port Gaverne	173
Port Isaac	174
Padstow and the River Camel	177
Newquay	185
Gannel Creek	188
Hayle	190
St Ives	192

Key to plans	197
Index	198

Published by
Imray Laurie Norie & Wilson Ltd
Wych House St Ives
Cambridgeshire PE27 5BT England
☎ +44 (0)1480 462114
Email ilnw@imray.com
www.imray.com
2023

All rights reserved. No part of this publication may be reproduced, transmitted or used in any form by any means – graphic, electronic or mechanical, including photocopying, recording, taping or information storage and retrieval systems or otherwise – without the prior permission of the publishers.

1st edition 2008
2nd edition 2023

© Peter and Jane Cumberlidge

Peter and Jane Cumberlidge have asserted their rights to be identified as the authors of this work in accordance with the Copyright, Designs and Patents Act 1988.

© Plans Imray Laurie Norie & Wilson Ltd 2023

© Photographs Peter and Jane Cumberlidge unless otherwise credited.

ISBN 978 178679 375 1

British Library Cataloguing in Publication Data.

A catalogue record for this book is available from the British Library.

PLANS

The plans in this guide are not to be used for navigation. They are designed to support the text and should at all times be used with navigational charts.

The UK Hydrographic Office (UKHO) and its licensors make no warranties or representations, express or implied, with respect to this product. The UKHO and its licensors have not verified the information within this product or quality assured it.

© British Crown Copyright 2023. All rights reserved.

Licence number GB AA - 005 - Imrays

BEARINGS

Any bearings are given as °T and from seawards.

CAUTION

Whilst every care has been taken to ensure accuracy, neither the Publishers nor the Author will hold themselves responsible for errors, omissions or alterations in this publication. They will at all times be grateful to receive information which tends to the improvement of the work.

CORRECTIONAL SUPPLEMENTS

This pilot book will be amended at intervals by the issue of correctional supplements which will be published at www.imray.com and may be downloaded free of charge. Printed copies are also available on request from the publishers at the above address.

Printed by Short Run Press, Exeter, Devon, United Kingdom

PREFACE

Although there have been no major new developments for cruising yachtsmen in the Bristol Channel over the last few years the popularity of the area as a destination has increased enormously and facilities for anyone coming by boat have steadily improved. The much wider use of electronic navigation devices has taken much of the terror and mystique out of navigating these waters. Having said that the tidal range is just as massive and the strength of currents can test the best engines if you get your timing wrong.

Home waters cruising increased in the early 2020s, partly as a result of the pandemic, which has encouraged more yachtsmen to explore the Bristol Channel. The downside is that Peter's comments about how easy it is to find a mooring may no longer be true but it has had a positive effect in showing many sceptics what a fascinating area this is to discover by boat. Anyone coming to the Bristol Channel for the first time will find friendliness and a warm welcome wherever you moor up for the night and often a one night stop will turn into several days.

You could say that the coasts of the Bristol Channel and Severn estuary have been modernised to just the right degree, with enough new facilities to attract more boats and create more convenient stopping places, and yet not so many as to risk spoiling the special character of this unique area. Since the 2008 edition a wet basin has been developed at Porthcawl, further mooring locations have been established within the Cardiff Barrage and work is going on to improve the conditions in Burry Port. The waterfront development at Milford Haven has made this a must visit destination.

Further down the south side of the Channel little has changed along the Devon and Cornish coasts. Ilfracombe still has no marina. Strategically it might be beneficial for Bristol Channel cruising if there was a marina there, but there's something about the feel of the traditional harbour that is timeless and comforting. In 1988 Padstow was a drying harbour and at low water visiting boats settled alongside one of the quays. By 2008 its

High water in the inner harbour at Ilfracombe

PREFACE

Mumbles Head and lighthouse in Swansea Bay

picturesque locked basin was a popular port of call for cruising visitors from all around the Channel and now it is regularly used by hundreds of boats every season.

When Peter first explored these waters and wrote the original edition not only were the photos black and white but the experience felt a bit like that too. The old coal dock at Penarth was just being turned into a marina, Milford docks was not a place for yachts and there were only drying harbours on the south coast of the Channel. All navigation was with paper charts, HB pencils and dead reckoning. Pushing a tide with a low powered and unreliable engine frequently meant finding an anchorage to wait for the next favourable tide. By the last edition all manner of things had improved enormously both with boats, navigation and ashore but cruising the Bristol Channel was still thought to be an acquired taste, now it is recognised as a fascinating location to explore by boat.

The layout and content of this edition is essentially the same as the last one with updated pilotage directions where these are necessary. I have kept the short features on different aspects of the history of the area, though some topics have been changed when it seemed appropriate. Although not many boats will venture as far up river as Stourport the chapter up the Severn from Gloucester has been retained as this is one of Britain's most important navigations and a surprising number of boats live on and cruise along it.

As with previous editions, this new *Bristol Channel and Severn Cruising Guide* owes a huge amount to local boat owners and yacht club members who have read through the old text and told me about developments in their particular areas. Marina managers and harbour masters have been enormously helpful and have patiently responded to emails and phone calls and lots of people have allowed me to use their photographs. There are too many people to name individually but I would like to say a huge thank you to all of them.

Jane Cumberlidge
June 2022

INTRODUCTION

This new edition of the *Bristol Channel and Severn Cruising Guide* extends to all tidal waters east of a straight line joining St Ann's Head on the Welsh side (the west headland of Milford Haven entrance) and Pendeen Point on the Cornish side, and includes the Gloucester and Sharpness Canal and the canalised River Severn up to Worcester and Stourport. Starting at Milford Haven the book works eastwards along the north shore of the Bristol Channel up to Lydney and then westwards along the south shore from Sharpness to St Ives.

Each port has its own section, organised to make it easy to locate important information. The sections begin with a brief summary of the port, so that the navigator has a picture of the sort of place he or she is approaching, i.e. whether it is a deep water or drying harbour, whether there's a marina, when the harbour can safely be entered, how sheltered it is, where best to lie at anchor, and so on.

Immediately after each summary are the tide times and the local heights above chart datum. The times of local high water have been given as differences on both HW Dover and HW at the nearest standard port. Where applicable, port control VHF listening and working channels have been included after the tide times.

Bearings of marks ashore have been given from seaward in degrees true according to normal practice. Each port generally has a separate heading for 'Entry at night' and the more important light characteristics are included in the text. It is recommended that the lights as given in this pilot are checked against a current nautical almanac or the most recent *Admiralty List of Lights*. Most yachts will now have some form of electronic navigation equipment and before a cruise you should ensure that the latest updates have been downloaded. With the continuing move away from paper charts I have removed references to specific charts from the text and included a suggested list in a separate section at the end.

The plans in this edition are based on Imray charts which are available as a ring-bound folio, 2600 The Bristol Channel, or electronically from www.imray.com as part of their digital chart ID30. The smaller havens in the Bristol Channel are often marked and buoyed by courtesy of the local yacht clubs, and in such cases their members supply the most accurate information about entry directions and pilotage. The Bristol Channel Yachting Association produces 'The Blue Book' which includes information about cruising in the Bristol Channel, contact details for local sailing clubs and sketch charts of some of the more out of the way places. This can be purchased at www.bcya.org.uk/shop.

This edition of the *Bristol Channel and Severn Cruising Guide* includes details on changes to ports and marinas that have occurred since the last edition. The mini-features throughout the main pilotage material give some flavour of the fascinating diversity of Bristol Channel cruising and some clues to the maritime history of these shores. Peter's original pilotage directions were cautious and seamanlike but he did not want to write off the more tortuous entrances by including too many gloomy navigational provisos. For most of the entries I have not changed his directions unless I have been advised to by local yachtsmen. Almost anywhere is easy to get into near high water, given settled weather and light offshore winds, but even the trickiest Bristol Channel havens are used by local boats in a wide range of weathers. In the end, though, navigators must always trust their own judgement when deciding which places are safe to enter in *their* boats under the prevailing conditions.

With the greater use of electronic communication it is easier to make corrections and provide updates so I will be pleased to receive any corrections or suggestions from local or cruising yachtsmen, by email, text or other means to the publishers, Imray.

CRUISING IN THE BRISTOL CHANNEL

Several generations of cruising yachtsmen, particularly those from England's south coast, eschewed the Bristol Channel as a destination because of its reputation for shifting mud and silt, phenomenal tides and changing channels. Navigation was perceived to be difficult, if not downright dangerous, there were no marinas and the history of shipwrecks throughout the Channel was horrifying.

Through the 1980s and 90s developments in electronic navigation and the affordability of chart plotters greatly eased the navigators' fears. Several comfortable and accessible marinas were established, the Cardiff Barrage was built and the increasingly crowded cruising destinations on the south coast encouraged more adventurous skippers and crews to investigate the possibilities of what Peter dubbed 'The Great Western Channel'.

Of course the Bristol Channel still has the most powerful tides in Europe – the spring range at Avonmouth exceeds 13 metres and rates of over six knots are not unusual. The upper reaches also have many square miles of sandbanks, which when covered stir up eerie overfalls and when fully exposed shrink the navigable channels to narrow gullies. Many of the smaller Bristol Channel harbours dry and aren't suitable for larger boats except for quick visits near high water, but RIBs or smaller boats that take the ground safely can explore some amazing nooks and crannies. The Rhymney River, St Pierre Pill, Oldbury Pill, Woodspring Bay, are secret places only a few locals know. The creation of new marinas and improved facilities in other harbours and safe havens have helped to ensure the Bristol Channel is now taking its rightful place as an enjoyable and interesting cruising ground for many more visiting boats.

With a coastline of nearly 400 miles there's a huge choice of destinations to explore and a fascinating history that goes with it. From the fantastic natural harbour of Milford Haven, where you can easily spend a couple of weeks exploring afloat, the South Wales coast offers a varied selection of ports-of-call. Drying Tenby harbour with its colourful seafront

Dried out in Ilfracombe outer harbour

CRUISING IN THE BRISTOL CHANNEL

Fishing off St Ann's head in the entrance to Milford Haven

remains virtually unchanged while next door, at Saundersfoot, work is underway to improve the accessibility and facilities for visiting boats. The new marina management at Burry Port, the Marine Group, has invested a lot of money to address the perennial problem of sand building up in the harbour, while Porthcawl now has a wet basin so boats can stay afloat.

The well-established marinas at Swansea and Penarth have been joined by the Cardiff Marina in the River Ely. The friendly and welcoming yacht clubs long the coast are happy to meet visitors and help with advice and moorings. Further up the estuary the Environment Agency is working to improve access at Lydney.

Along the south coast Portishead is now a regular staging post on many cruises, particularly for people intending to venture up the River Avon to Bristol where the Floating Harbour is a great location for several days. The Marine Group are also tackling the silt problem at Watchet and the marina has again become a practical place to visit.

I have to confess to being quite pleased that Ilfracombe remains a traditional drying harbour and plans for a marina have still not come to fruition. The atmosphere in and around the harbour is fun and timeless and it's great to see self-sufficient yachtsmen coming in here in the tried and tested fashion. Porlock Weir and Clovelly also appear to be completely unchanged with a sense of magic and history.

The joint estuaries of the rivers Taw and Torridge are still little explored by visiting boats but you will receive a warm welcome from the North Devon Yacht Club at Instow once you have managed to negotiate your way over Bideford Bar. Further west Padstow has a well organised locked basin with good facilities for visiting boats and lots to explore in and around the town. The north Cornish coast can feel a bit exposed and hostile but for adventurous crews in suitable boats there is a lot to discover.

For fast motor boats, some crossings of the Bristol Channel are quite short, allowing you to leave one harbour and reach another on the opposite shore on the same tide. In settled weather you might head for a favourite daytime anchorage that will be sheltered around low water, when the turbulent streams are at rest and exposed banks act as natural breakwaters.

The upper reaches of the Severn estuary are accessible for masted yachts as far as the attractive dock in Gloucester, having locked in at Sharpness and followed the canal for 16 miles. The final 42 miles up to Stourport are only really practicable for motor boats but it's surprising how many sea-going vessels you can meet up here.

Skomer Island

Skomer lies half a mile off the southwest coast of Pembrokeshire, one of Britain's most spectacular National Parks. A great variety of wildlife and birds thrive in this corner of Wales, and Skomer is a carefully protected National Nature Reserve managed by the Wildlife Trust South and West Wales. The waters around the island form the Skomer Marine Conservation Zone.

A large colony of grey seals live around Skomer all year round and an estimated 350,000 pairs of Manx shearwaters nest here, the largest colony in the world. You will also see puffins, guillemots, razorbills and kittiwakes between April and July. Ashore, rabbits are numerous and the genial Skomer vole is unique to the island.

The internationally important populations of burrow nesting seabirds means the island operates strict bio-security rules to prevent the arrival of invasive species, rats in particular. Everyone who lands on the island has to check their belongings and tenders for stowaways, open bags are not permitted. Before visiting Skomer read the boat owners guide online at https://biosecurityforlife.org.uk

The island is open to private landings between 1000 and 1700 from April to September, every day except Mondays, though the island is open on bank holiday Mondays. Yachtsmen are welcome so long as they land only at North Haven and contact a member of staff at the public landing point to pay the landing fee that helps the Trust run this idyllic retreat.

Most boats visit Skomer from the splendid natural harbour of Milford Haven, starting from Neyland Yacht Haven (16 miles), Milford Marina (12 miles) or perhaps the anchorage off Dale (9 miles). You need to pick your weather and tides for the eight-mile passage from Milford Haven entrance, but in quiet conditions it's easy enough to get out to Skomer, timing your passage so as to slip through Jack Sound at dead slack water and then curving northwest to approach North Haven from due north.

Four public moorings are available during the summer months, on a first come first served basis, or you can anchor just east of the landing steps, but keep clear of the public landing steps used by the island ferry and the southeast part of the bay. In this area is a seagrass bed which is a protected feature, marked by buoys with a cross to show the part to be avoided. With any north in the wind, you'll find better shelter on the other side of The Neck in South Haven, a snug anchorage although no landing is allowed anywhere around this bay.

From North Haven, footpaths lead west across the island or skirt South Haven towards the south plateau and its spectacular views across the Mew Stone towards Skokholm. At the centre of Skomer you will find the information centre, public toilets and picnic area in the old farm. This is also where accommodation for overnight guests is located, though this must be booked in advance at island@welshwildlife.org.

From Skomer Head on a clear evening, you can see Grassholm Island out to the west horizon and the flashes of the lonely Smalls lighthouse remind you that reefs and shoals lurk up to 15 miles offshore.

Pilotage

Neap tides are best, with high water slack around mid-morning. Aim to arrive off Jack Sound at dead slack water (1 hour 45mins after HW Milford Haven or 4 hours 40 mins before). The notorious races west of Skomer and Skokholm can be dangerous.

From Milford Haven entrance, round St Ann's Head a quarter of a mile off and follow the coast NW towards Skomer. Stay half a mile off Gateholm Island, which looks like a peninsula from a distance. Continue towards Skomer until Jack Sound bears due north true, then turn towards the gap on this heading. Avoid Bench rocks off Pitting Gales Point and the nasty Blackstones two cables south of Midland Isle.

Keep to the middle of Jack Sound. Drying dangers extend from either shore – Cable Rock on the east side and the Crabstones on the west. High water slack is the best time for this passage. Once through the Sound, head northwest until North Haven is well open and approach from due north. A five-knot speed limit applies within 100m of Skomer and visitors are asked to be as quiet as possible to avoid disturbing nesting birds.

Contact

For the most up to date information about the island see www.welshwildlife.org/skomer-skokholm/skomer. To contact any of the island staff before visiting phone the Warden on ☏ 07971 114302, the Visitor Officer on ☏ 07530 796150 or the Assistant Warden on ☏ 07816 990371, VHF 74 call sign Skomer One.

Puffins on Skomer
West Coast Birdwatching

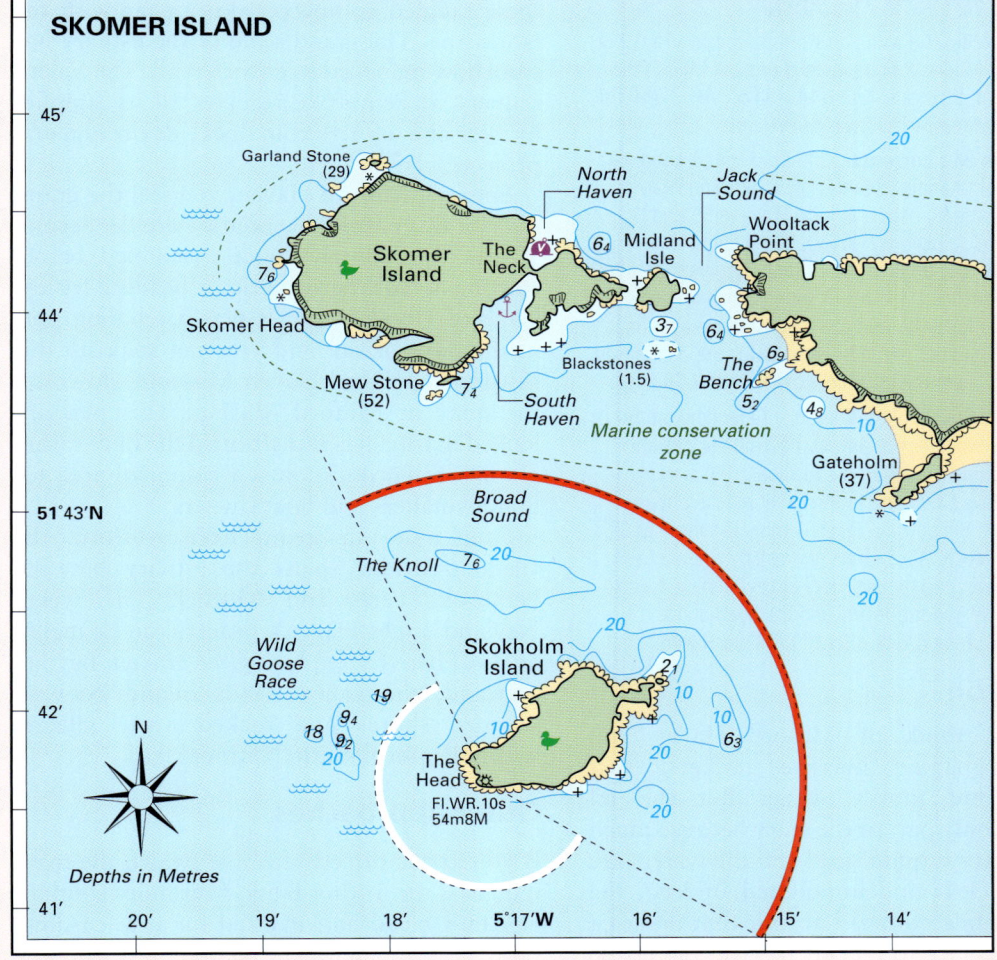

A view of Skomer looking towards the mainland and Milford Haven
Lucy Griffiths

MILFORD HAVEN

Summary

A glorious and extensive natural harbour formed by the Cleddau estuary. There are several passage anchorages near the mouth and more sheltered berths, including two marinas, further upriver. Entry is straightforward by day or night at any state of tide and the Haven makes a good port of refuge. Keep clear of large tankers in the harbour and approaches. The Cleddau is navigable by most yachts for 12 miles upstream.

Tides HW Milford Haven is at HW Dover −0500. Heights above chart datum outside Milford Docks: 7.0m MHWS, 0.7m MLWS, 5.2m MHWN, 2.5m MLWN.

Port Control Milford Haven Port Control, call on VHF 12 or 16. For Milford Marina locking instructions call Milford Pier Head on VHF 14, then call Milford Marina on VHF 37(M) for a berth. For Neyland Yacht Haven call VHF 80.

Tidal streams and currents Off Milford Haven entrance the main Bristol Channel streams flow E by S and W by N; the E-going stream begins at local HW +0455 and the W-going stream at local HW −0100. Both can reach 2–3 knots at springs. The flood in the entrance begins soon after local LW and reaches 1½ knots at springs; the ebb begins about ½hr after local HW and can reach 2 knots at springs. The streams in and out of the Haven often cause a confused sea where they meet the main flow of the Bristol Channel.

Rates in the Cleddau vary considerably, depending on the stretch of river, whether you are on the inside or outside of a bend, and how close you are to shoals. The streams are weaker above Lawrenny. In the lower reaches, near Pembroke Dock, the ebb can reach 4 knots locally at springs; the flood may reach 2½–3 knots particularly when a fresh westerly is blowing up the river. HW at Lawrenny is approx. 15 min after HW Milford Haven, and the flood above Llangwm may run for 1½ hr after HW Milford Haven.

Description

When you think of Milford Haven you probably imagine massive tankers, vast refineries and murky water. But the oil industry is only part of the story because much of the estuary is quite rural and the waters are invariably clear and unpolluted. Indeed, the Haven is a fine natural harbour that makes a fascinating place for yachts to visit and cruise – easy to enter with plenty of sheltered river to explore. The entrance is about 1½ miles wide and faces SSW between St Ann's Head and East Blockhouse Point. Inside these protecting headlands the drowned valley of the Cleddau turns east to provide a deep shipping channel up to Pembroke Dock.

Milford Haven developed as an oil port in the late 1950s and early 60s, although that boom later turned into a gradual decline and then a levelling off. The long jetties for the tanker berths reach well out into the harbour and ships are linked by a maze of pipes to refineries close inland. Strangely enough, these tangled complexes do not jar with the landscape. The grand scale of the estuary has somehow managed to absorb it all. The Valero refinery at Pembroke receives all its supplies by sea and is active in local environmental projects.

Entering Milford Haven, you feel the grand scale of this natural harbour where the Second World War convoys once assembled before starting across the Atlantic or heading for the Cape of Good Hope. It was a whaling port in the days of sail and you can soak up this history at Milford Haven Museum, down on the quay at Milford Marina. This pleasant locked marina has transformed the once rather gloomy town docks into a colourful area for holidaymakers and boat owners.

Four miles upstream from Milford, the Cleddau bridge spans the estuary between Pembroke Ferry and Westfield Pill, where Neyland Yacht Haven's peaceful creek makes an ideal base for exploring the Haven. Beyond Neyland, the valley winds inland between wooded shores and tucked away villages within Pembrokeshire National Park.

Outer approaches

If you arrive directly from seaward, the main danger is the Turbot Bank, four miles south of St Ann's Head and marked by a W cardinal buoy. Although it has plenty of depth, the

MILFORD HAVEN

Heading out past St Ann's Head

Bristol Channel and Severn Cruising Guide

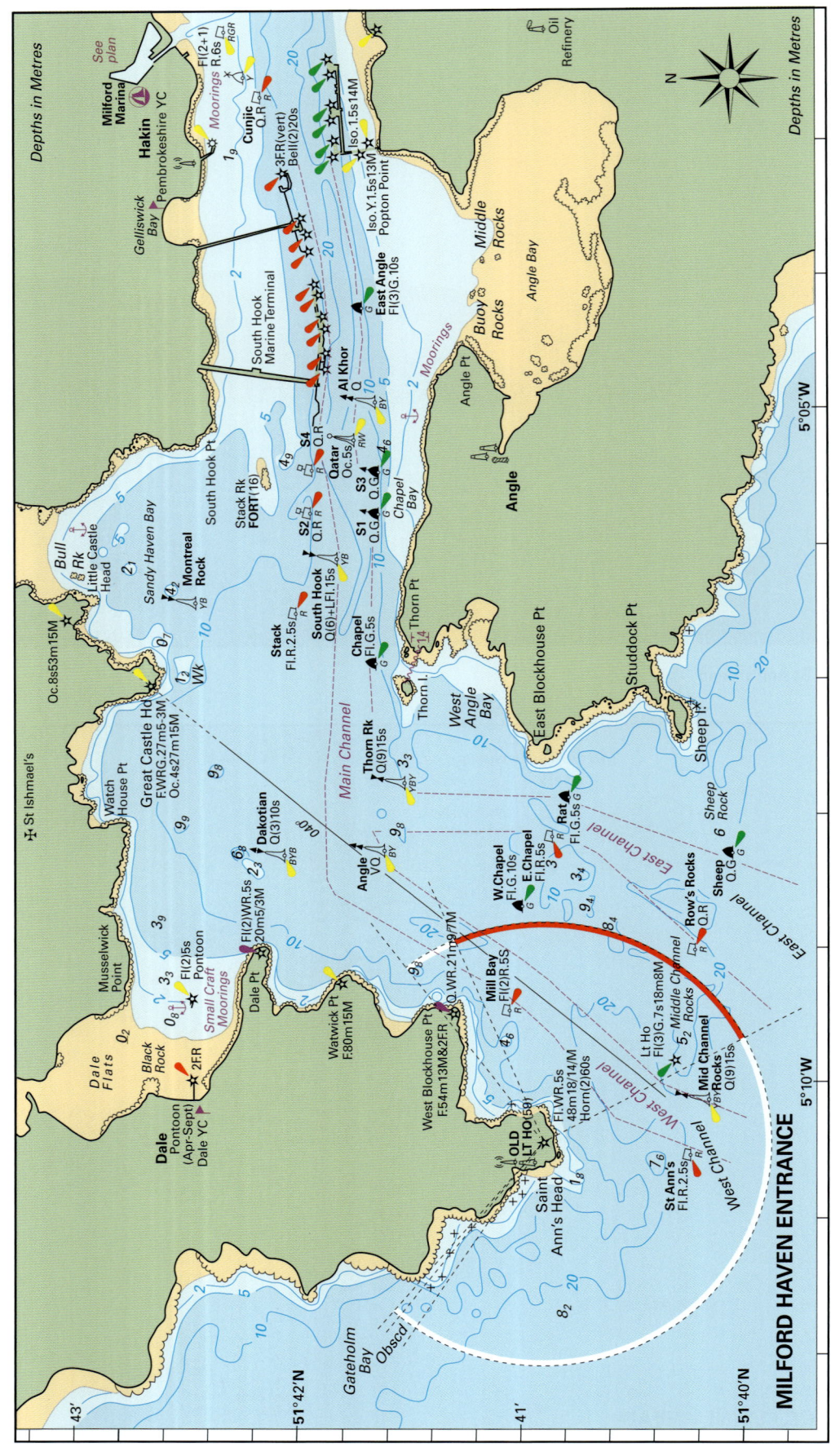

MILFORD HAVEN

Turbot can kick up a nasty sea in fresh winds, especially when the tide is weather-going. Give the bank a wide berth under these conditions.

Approaching from the east along the coast in moderate weather, the shortest route is between St Govan's Head race and the overfalls over St Gowan Shoals. Keep about 1½ miles off the headland, especially on the ebb stream in a westerly wind. Although the shoals have a least depth of 6.4m, the sea often breaks over them and tide rips may extend up to five miles east of this area. As you near Milford Haven give the rocks off Linney Head a wide berth.

When approaching Milford Haven from westward, avoid Wildgoose Race just west of Skomer and Skokholm, by keeping about two miles seaward of both islands. Further out, note that overfalls can extend to over a mile southeast of Grassholm.

MOD firing ranges at Castlemartin and Manorbier

On weekdays from 0900–1630 there is usually practice firing in the range between St Govan's Head and Linney Head. If approaching this area you can expect to be hailed by one of the patrol launches or called on VHF 16/12 and directed some miles offshore. To avoid such a detour, stay a good five miles off in the first instance, outside St Gowan S cardinal buoy. The precise area depends on the type of weapons being fired and can range from 3 to 12M. For firing times call Milford Haven Coastguard on VHF 16/67, telephone Castlemartin Range ☎ 01646 662367 (recorded message for firings on the current day). The Castlemartin Range Officer, ☎ 01646 662496, can advise on future firings and the best passage plan. Online information **www.gov.uk/government/publications/castlemartin-firing-notice** or Manorbier Range Control ☎ 01834 871282, **www.gov.uk/government/publications/manorbier-firing-flying-notice**

Entry

St Ann's Head forms the west arm of Milford Haven entrance, a flat-topped promontory with a conspicuous white lighthouse and cluster of coastguard buildings at its south tip. On the east side of the entrance is East Blockhouse Point, with Sheep Island half a mile south of it.

There's plenty of room to work into the Haven under sail; both shores are steep-to and yachts need not keep to the buoyed channels. However, Middle Channel Rocks (with 5m over them) and Chapel Rocks (with 3m) should both be avoided in heavy weather. The leading marks on Great Castle Head and Little Castle Head provide a useful reference.

There are two buoyed shipping channels into the Haven. West Channel is entered half a mile south of St Ann's Head, between St Ann's red can buoy and Middle Channel Rocks W cardinal buoy which is close south-west of Middle Channel Rocks lighthouse. From this gateway, West Channel leads 040° as far as Angle N cardinal buoy. The fairway then turns east and is wide and well marked up to Hobbs Point.

East Channel is entered a little over half a mile WSW of Sheep Island, leaving the Sheep green conical buoy close to starboard. Thereafter the buoyed channel trends NNE and north as far as Thorn Rock W cardinal. Although West Channel is the deeper of the two, East Channel can be a better bet in strong south-westerlies, particularly during gales when the ebb is running. Under these conditions a confused sea builds up in the vicinity of the ledges south-west of St Ann's Head. **Caution:** If using the East Channel you may see local fishing boats cutting between Thorn Island and Thorn Point. This passage saves no great distance and the overhead cables that supply power to the island's hotel give a least headroom of only 14m at MHWS.

Once inside the entrance follow the buoyed fairway more or less, but remember that

A pleasant morning sail in the Haven

NORTH COAST

Colourful houses climb up from the waterside in Milford Haven

yachts can use large areas of water outside the buoys. Indeed it is often safer as well as considerate to stay out of the main channel when tankers are under way. Keep well clear of oil jetties, the many large mooring buoys and any manoeuvring ships and tugs. The bylaws give right of way to commercial traffic.

Milford Haven town and Milford Marina are on the north shore just beyond the Puma Energy terminal. Having passed Milford and the Valero terminal opposite, keep over to the north side of the river. Off the south shore, the shoal area known as Pwllcrochan Flats dries at LAT to well over half the width of the Cleddau – visitors are apt to disbelieve the chart at this point! Beyond Pwllcrochan, work southwards to leave Wear Spit beacon to port. The channel then follows the north shore again past Carr Rocks and Dockyard Bank.

Entry at night

The West Channel is better lit than the East. St Ann's Head lighthouse has an 18M range Fl.WR.5s; a red sector covers St Gowan Shoals to the SE and the intense red covers the unlit rocks off Linney Head. Middle Channel lighthouse has an 8M range Fl(3)G.7s. Approach from the SSW with St Ann's Head white sector to port and Middle Channel light to starboard. The first set of leading lights bearing 022° brings you in as far as Middle Channel W cardinal buoy; the front light is on West Blockhouse Point F.WR and the rear light on Watwick Point (F).

The second set of leading lights then take you into the Haven; the front light is on Great Castle Head Oc.4s and the rear light on Little Castle Head Oc.8s. Follow this transit, bearing 040°, to just beyond Angle N cardinal buoy. Then turn east along the well-lit fairway that leads up the harbour, or head northwest to round Dale Point Fl(2)WR.5s if you are bound for the Dale anchorage. In the latter case note the Dakotian E cardinal buoy Q(3)10s 3½ cables east of Dale Point, which marks a wreck with 2.3m over it.

To enter the East Channel at night, first make for the Sheep buoy and then follow the fairway as by day. Once inside Thorn Island it's preferable to stay within the buoyed channel in order to avoid the numerous large, unlit mooring buoys in the Haven.

There are often several small tankers anchored in Dale Roads, with bright and confusing deck lights. This can make it difficult to pick out some of the inner navigation marks from the outer approaches between St Ann's Head and Sheep Island. Keep in mind, however, that the pilotage into the Haven is not at all critical, and the lights will become clear as you get further in.

Berths and anchorages

Dale This friendly village lies near the mouth of Milford Haven, at the head of an attractive bay just inside the entrance on the west side. Dale offers a convenient passage anchorage in westerly weather and you can stay afloat at all states of tide so long as you bring up well outside the local moorings. The silty sand bottom shoals towards the village, so watch the echo-sounder as you come in and before you settle down for the night. During the summer, a visitors' pontoon is moored in the middle of the bay south of Musselwick Point, more or less on the two-metre contour.

In southwesterlies, you can anchor off the south shore close under the steep-to arm of Dale Point. If there is much north in the wind, tuck under the opposite shore for shelter. Avoid Dale in easterlies, when there's a long fetch across the lower reaches of the Haven. Dale Flats, the inlet northwest of the moorings, dries out to stony mud and is only suitable for bilge or lifting keel boats.

Coming ashore, it's best to land at the beach near the Dale Yacht Club, which always welcomes visiting yachtsmen. Dale is a picturesque place where sailing dinghies tack about and walkers stride along the cliffs towards Dale Fort. The Griffin pub is handy on the waterfront and there are shops nearby.

Sandy Haven A couple of miles east across the Haven from Dale is Sandy Haven Bay, at the head of which is Sandy Haven itself, a secluded wooded creek which makes a perfect hideaway for shallow draft boats that can take the ground. Deeper draft yachts can anchor near the creek mouth over a sandy bottom, as tide permits. In northwesterlies there's a good spot about two cables northeast of Little Castle Head in about 1.5m.

However, be careful to avoid Bull Rock (dries 1.5m) a cable east of Little Castle Head and some other rocky patches nearby. Clear out of this anchorage if the wind shifts to the south.

Angle Bay A wide, shallow inlet on the south side of the Haven directly opposite the South Hook LNG and Puma Energy terminals. It is entered between Angle Point and Sawdern Point and a large refinery dominates the east shore. Although most of Angle Bay dries to soft mud, there are some local moorings in the northwest corner just opposite the Old Point House Inn. The pub has changed hands and is now run by the Pembrokeshire Beach Food Company, well known to locals and visitors alike for Café Môr which started life as a beach shack in 2011. This exciting enterprise specialises in local seafood including lobster, crab and seaweed, if you are in the area don't miss it. At neaps, yachts of moderate draft can stay afloat close to the east of the moorings. Shoal draft boats can take the ground at anchor, but note that parts of the foreshore around the bay are rocky.

Keep to the west side on the approach to Angle Bay, cutting close to the disused slipway on Angle Point. Thus you will avoid Buoy Rocks and Middle Rocks in the mouth of the bay, two drying patches which are unmarked. Angle is a sheltered spot in westerlies but is open to the north. The village is a short walk away along the beach.

Near LWS you won't be able to stay afloat in Angle Bay, but there's a deep-water anchorage over sand, close off the south shore of the Haven anywhere up to half a mile west of Angle Point. You'll find reasonable shelter here in winds between south-west through south to southeast.

Milford Marina Converted from the old dock basin, Milford Marina has matured over the years and is now an attractive place to lie, with the town close to hand and, if you need to change crews or leave the boat for a while, reasonable rail connections eastwards via Swansea. You can enter the dock basin via the entrance lock between HW –0400 and HW +0315 and locking follows a published in/out timetable. During the 'free flow' period, both lock gates are open for the two hours before high water and movement is generally unrestricted. Locking is available either side of this period, according to the timetable available from marina control. Contact Milford Pier Head on VHF 14 before entering the dock basin or leaving a marina berth.

The waterfront has been greatly developed over the last few years and offers a range of good shopping, restaurants and pubs a short stroll away. It's not far to walk to a big supermarket.

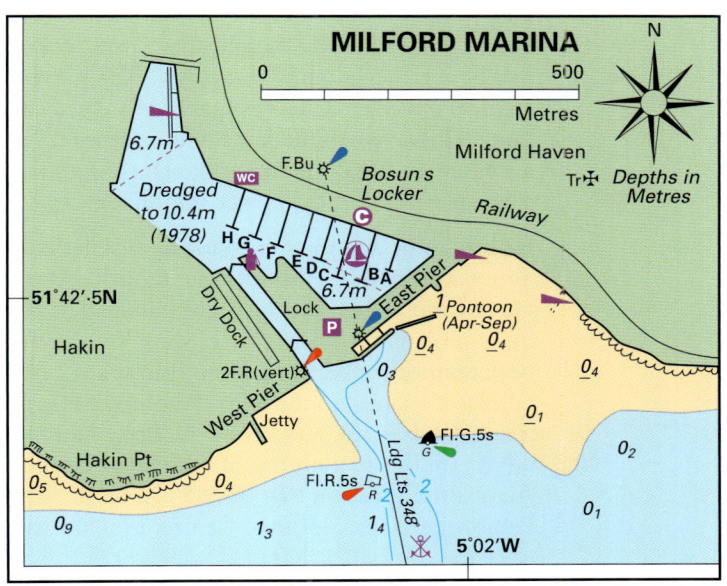

NORTH COAST

MILFORD HAVEN MIDDLE REACHES

There is diesel and petrol alongside, inside the marina basin near the lock. Milford Marina can be contacted on ☎ 01646 696312, VHF 37 or via www.milfordmarina.com.

Gelliswick Bay This shallow bight three quarters of a mile west of Milford Marina entrance offers a fair weather neap anchorage off the Pembrokeshire Yacht Club. The bay dries right out to sand at LAT.

Pennar Gut You can anchor just inside the mouth of this shallow inlet in three to four metres depth, a couple of cables due south of East Pennar Point. There is good shelter here except in northerlies, though the power station makes a rather gloomy backdrop. The narrow channel into Pennar Gut is marked by a red can buoy (Fl.R.2·5s) off the south shore of the Haven a mile or so WSW of Pembroke Dock. Landing is not permitted at the power station jetty.

Hobbs Point On the south side of the Cleddau, about seven miles above the mouth of the Haven and just below the high road bridge, the quay and wide slipway at Hobbs Point offer only temporary berthing alongside at a council pontoon secured to the quay. Pembroke Haven Yacht Club is set back from the quay and can advise on the availability of moorings, contact Alan Pritchard on ☎ 07785 764271. The Pembroke Dock Heritage Centre, in what was once the dockyard chapel, is well worth a visit. It tells the fascinating story of the development of the town as a naval dockyard from the early 1800s until 1922. From the 1930s and during World War II the RAF had a flying boat base here and in the centre you can read the story of the Sunderland flying boats.

Neyland Yacht Haven This restful marina occupies a sheltered creek on the north side of the Cleddau directly opposite Hobbs Point. The marina is divided into two basins and the lower (outer) part is accessible at any state of tide. The upper basin has a sill and is normally accessible from HW ±0330hrs. The sill has a tide gauge at either side and has about five metres depth at MHW.

A dredged channel leads into the creek, marked by two port and two starboard hand buoys. It carries a least depth of 2m at LAT. Pass outside the old pier stagings on entry and not through the small-boat mooring area north of these stagings. A limited number of visitors' berths are available during the season and they are sheltered from all quarters. Advanced booking is recommended. Use the outer pontoons first upon arrival, unless directed otherwise. The maximum length that can be accommodated is 80ft; the maximum draft is 2.0m in the lower basin at lowest springs, and slightly more in the upper basin.

The marina maintains 24hr listening watch on VHF 37(M1) and 80, or ☎ 01646 601601

MILFORD HAVEN

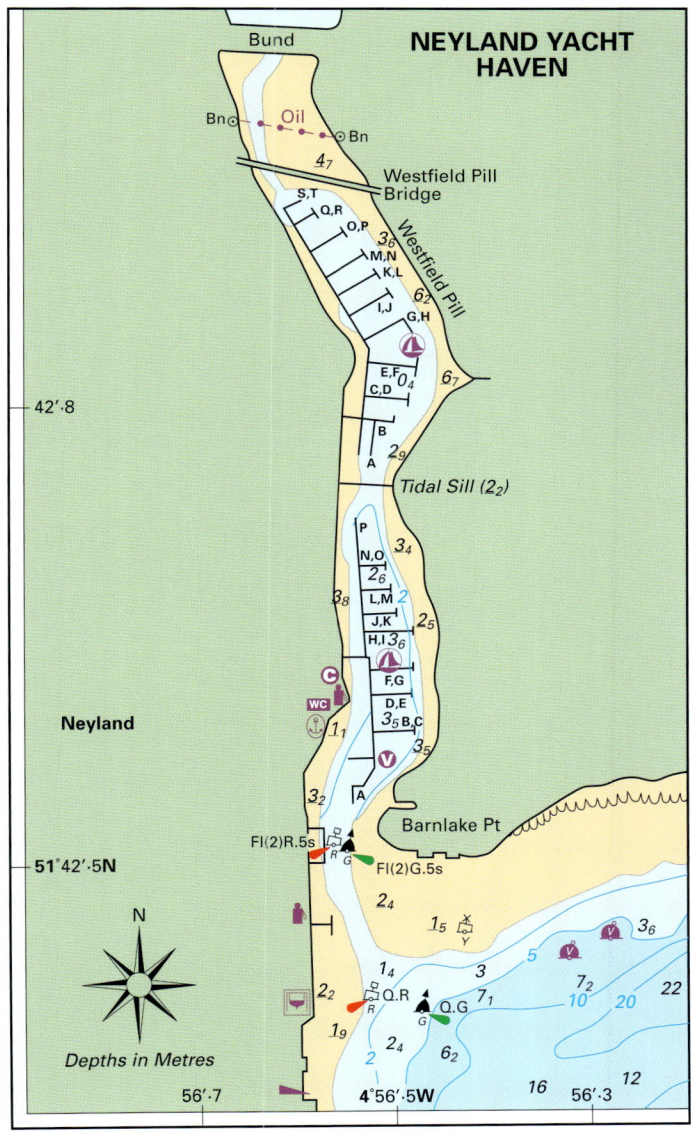

between the hours of 0730-0130 7 days a week. Services ashore with Dale Sailing including lifting out, storage, chandlery and all repairs ℡ 01646 603100. Diesel and petrol pontoon at the south side of the marina entrance. Neyland town centre is five minutes' walk from the marina, with a few useful shops.

Just above the bridge on the port hand, where a ferry used to operate between Burton and Pembroke Dock, you might spot a pontoon which belongs to the Jolly Sailor. The beer garden has spectacular views of the Haven and it's a great place to stop on your cruise up the Cleddau. You can watch all the comings and goings on the river as you sample the interesting menu.

Top: Neyland Yacht Haven *Neyland Yacht Haven*

Bottom: The lower basin at Neyland Yacht Haven *Neyland Yacht Haven*

NORTH COAST

Lawrenny Quay About 2½ miles above Neyland Yacht Haven the Cresswell and Carew Rivers flow into the Cleddau from the east. On the north shore of this confluence is the long-established Lawrenny Quay, previously called Lawrenny Yacht Station, ☎ 01646 651212 a kind of nautical country and caravan park which has some deep-water moorings, a pontoon, chandlery and a small boatyard with a slip. Diesel and petrol are available alongside the pontoon. The moorings are sheltered, the surroundings attractively rural and the Lawrenny Arms has its own pontoon where you can tie up to stop for a great meal or just a glass of something. This is an interesting place to stop if you plan to explore the upper reaches of the Cleddau.

The Upper Cleddau The peaceful and unspoilt upper stretches of the river offer various anchorages depending on your draft. A good deep-water spot is just opposite Lawrenny in Castle Reach, presumably named after Benton Castle, conspicuous on the west bank high among the oaks. Castle Reach turns into Beggars Reach at the mouth of Garron Pill and then you come up with the picturesque village

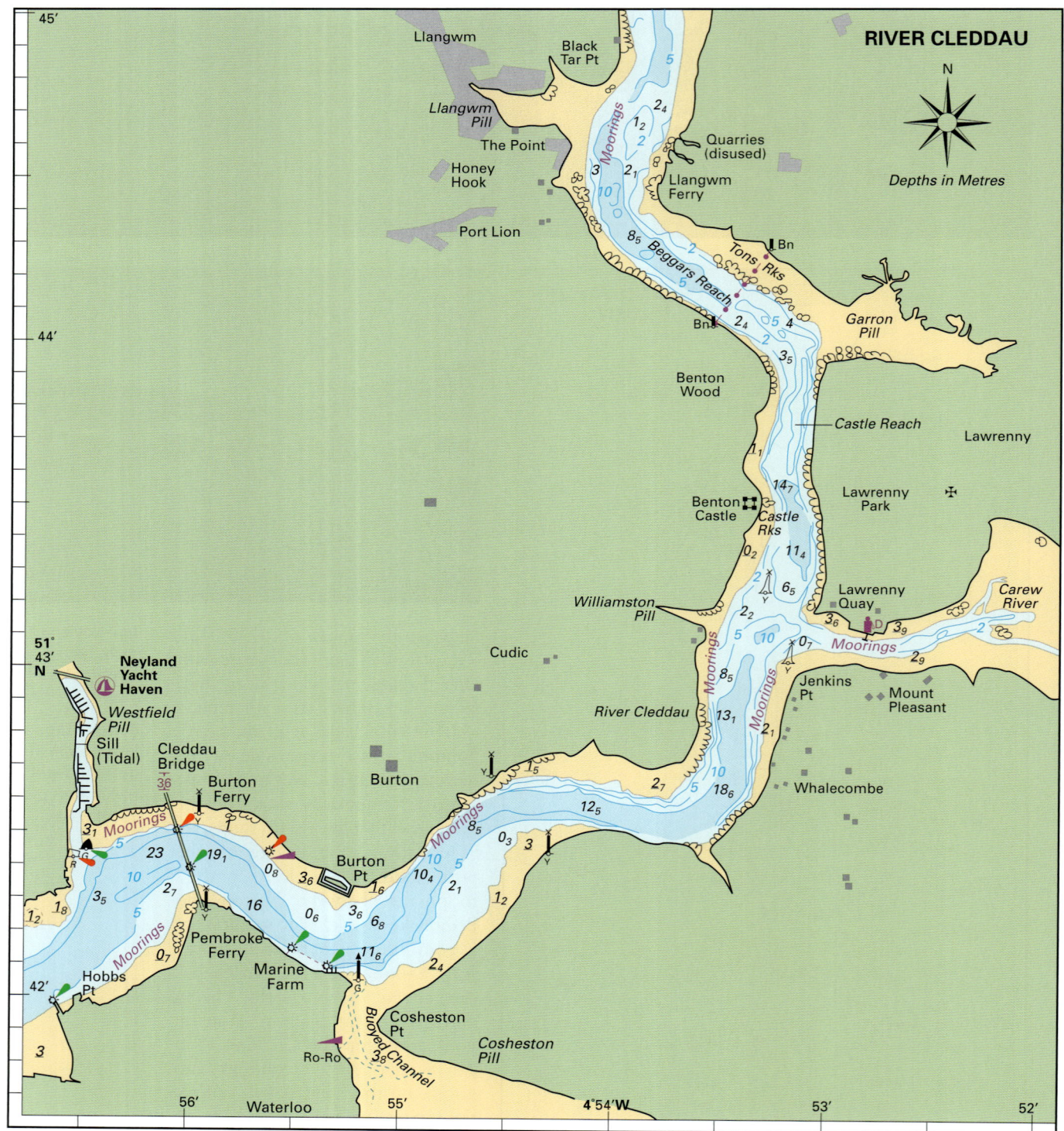

14 • Bristol Channel and Severn Cruising Guide

of Llangwm on the west side of the river where you will find a post office and stores and the Cottage Inn. There's a pleasant anchorage off Llangwm Pill and a landing slip at Black Tar Point.

There are no navigation buoys or perches in these higher reaches, so keep an eye on your echo-sounder and plotter. Off Black Tar Point the river is relatively deep and narrow and there are some moorings close under Knap Wood. Then a broad mud flat pushes the fairway over to the east past the ruins of Landshipping Quay and the river divides at Picton Point. More moorings are laid in the lower part of the East Cleddau, where there is limited room to anchor.

The West Cleddau leads another three miles up to the old market town of Haverfordwest. Intrepid adventurers would find a stores and post office at Hook, on the south shore. The channel is shallow, unmarked and should only be negotiated by boats of less than 1.2m draft that can take the ground easily, preferably on the last of the flood. The banks close in considerably above Hook. Four sets of high-voltage power cables span the river on the outskirts of Haverfordwest, with clearance between 9 and 11m; these dictate the limit of navigation for most sailing yachts. Motor boats can almost reach the town, but the channel vanishes to a trickle among the reeds and there's no convenient place to berth.

A Milford Haven pilot heading out to meet a ship

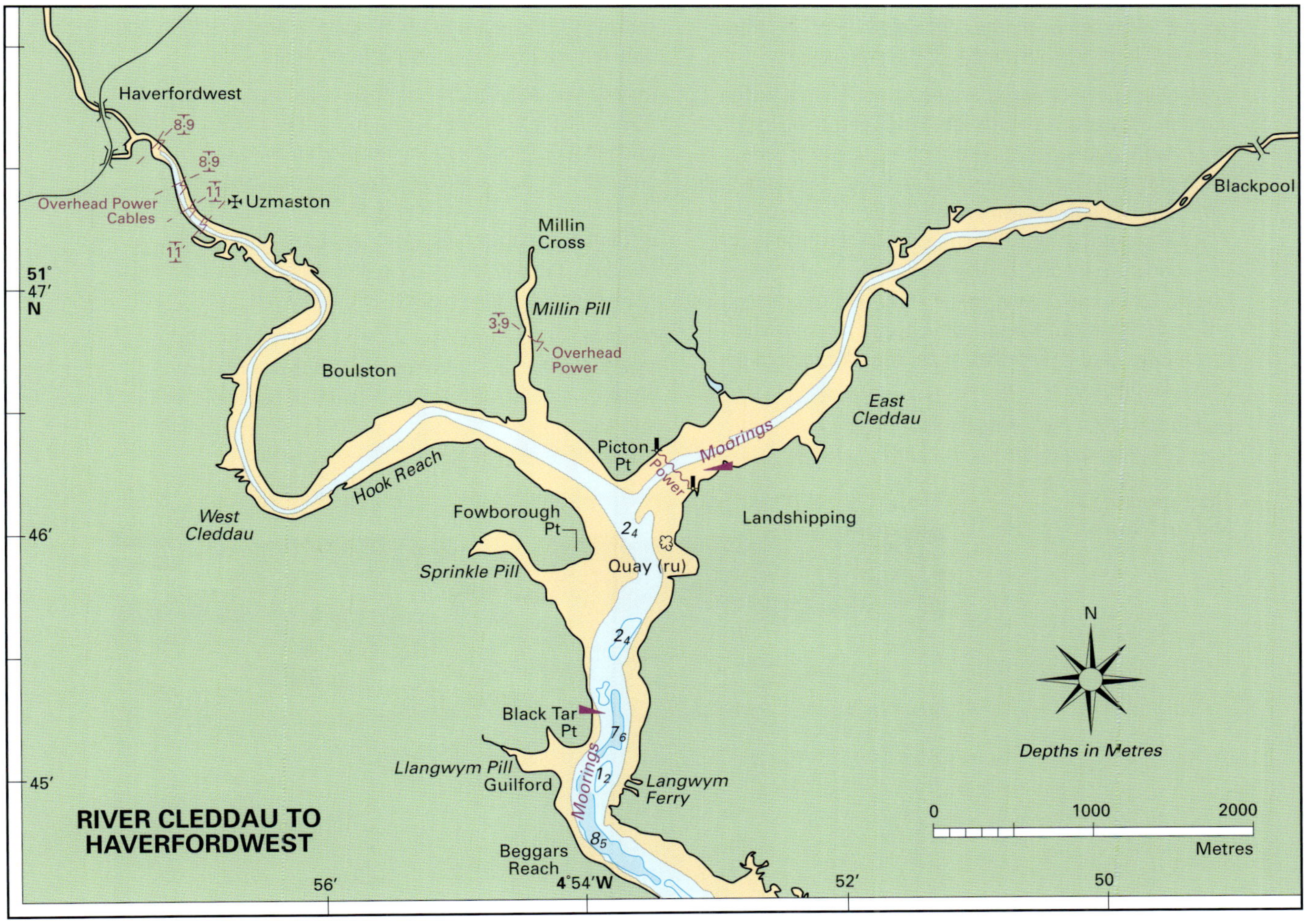

RIVER CLEDDAU TO HAVERFORDWEST

Milford Haven through the ages

Even a quick glance at the chart shows that Milford Haven is a superb natural harbour, strategically located for the Western Approaches and with deep water reaching well up the estuary to provide complete shelter for large ships. Geologically the Haven is a ria or drowned valley which was created at the end of the ice age and it is one of the deepest natural harbours in the world. Even Shakespeare sang the praises of the Haven in the play *Cymbeline*, when Innogen, King Cymbeline's daughter, escapes to Wales.

It has been used for trade and invasion for millennia. In the 9th and 10th centuries the Vikings used it regularly and Hubberston village is named after the Viking chieftain Hubba whose forces wintered in the Haven in the mid-800s. The name Milford actually derives from the Norse words melr, meaning sandbank, and fjord. Ships mustered here on several occasions ahead of invasions to Ireland and Henry Tudor returned to Britain from France, landing in the Haven to gather troops before marching to meet Richard III at the Battle of Bosworth in 1485.

In 1649, Oliver Cromwell sailed from Milford Haven to Ireland with a sizeable army that he claimed, somewhat prematurely, could deliver the 'final settlement of the Irish problem'. At the end of the 18th century there was an attempt to develop Milford as a whaling port but this failed and then the Navy Board, encouraged by Nelson, started building warships in the Haven. Naval ships were first built at Hubberston Pill, then at Milford Docks and later at Pembroke Dock. The Lord Nelson Hotel in Milford's Hamilton Terrace is a reminder of this connection.

Fishing had been an important activity in Milford Haven through the ages, but in the late 19th century Milford Docks were developed specially for the needs of the fishing industry. Ice factories and smoke-houses were built, along with a quayside fish market. Before the First World War Milford Haven was Britain's sixth largest fishing port and soon after the Second World War was landing up to 60,000 tons of fish a year. In the 1940s Milford Haven was a base for American troops, about 1,000 being billeted in the town, and it played an important part prior to the D-Day landings.

During the 1950s, the fishing business declined, while the Suez Crisis had sharpened the demand for huge oil tankers and associated oil terminals in deep sheltered water. It's not surprising that the Haven became so important as a tanker port during the 1960s and by the mid-1970s Milford had become the second largest oil port in Europe. The development of Britain's own North Sea oil fields shifted the energy focus and Milford Haven's Esso refinery closed after less than 20 years' operation. The oil business is notoriously fickle and will relocate on a grand scale when the commercial need arises. In February 1996, the 148,000-ton tanker *Sea Empress* ran aground in the entrance to Milford Haven and leaked 72,000 tons of crude oil and 480 tons of fuel oil into the sea, an early and damaging oil spill though the recovery from it has proved to be very good. As oil refining in the area declined facilities have been developed for handling liquefied natural gas.

After the *Sea Empress* incident there was much debate about the possible risks associated with the location of oil refineries and a tanker port in such an environmentally sensitive area, particularly as the Pembrokeshire Coast National Park was established in 1952. Pembrokeshire attracts huge numbers of visitors, especially bird watchers, walkers and naturalists. There are plenty of organised activities for tourists to enjoy, not least boat trips out to see puffins, porpoises and seals around the coast.

New enterprises are flourishing in Milford Haven, much of it based around renewable energy and environmental developments. On the Pembroke Dock side of the waterway new opportunities are being pursued to encourage these exciting technologies. Pembroke dock is also the site of the busy ferry terminal connecting Wales and Ireland.

Milford Docks were turned into a locked marina basin in 1991, initially with 225 berths. Today it is a hive of activity offering moorings to visiting boats from all round the UK and much further afield. The waterfront has seen a huge investment over the last few years and now has bars, restaurants, shops, crafts, gyms and the Milford Haven Museum. There is self-catering accommodation and a new hotel overlooking the marina and the Haven.

Meanwhile, the Haven is a superb sheltered cruising area for yachts and motor boats, with plenty of deep water, two good marinas and a range of peaceful creeks and anchorages with a seclusion that is now becoming extremely rare on England's busy south coast.

The approach to Milford Marina

TENBY

Summary

Tenby is one of the most attractive havens on the South Wales coast, huddled in the southwest corner of Carmarthen Bay, two miles north of Caldey Island. Easy to approach, it makes a useful staging post between Milford Haven and Swansea. The small harbour is accessible about 2½ hrs each side of HW, dries to firm sand and is sheltered from most quarters, although fresh winds between northeast and southeast send in a swell. Visiting yachts lie alongside the breakwater inner wall, close to the town. There's an outer anchorage 2–3 cables NNE of the lifeboat slip, sheltered from northwest through west to SSW.

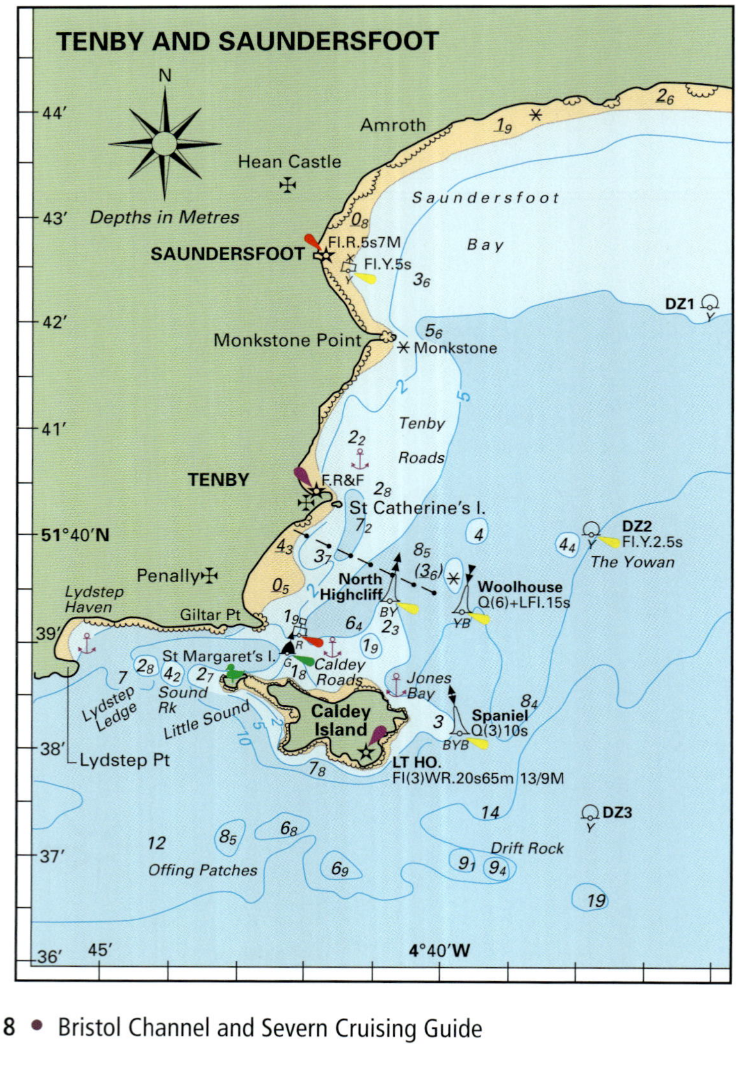

Tides HW Tenby is at HW Milford Haven –0010, or HW Dover –0510. Heights above chart datum: 8.4m MHWS, 0.9m MLWS, 6.3m MHWN, 3.0m MLWN.

Port Control Harbour Authority (Municipal), Pembrokeshire County Council. The Harbour Office is in Castle Square 01834 842717. Listening watch VHF 16, working on 80, 37 (M1) and M2

Tidal streams and currents NE of the harbour in Tenby Roads streams barely reach a knot at springs. Stronger rates occur between Tenby and Caldey Island; 1½ knots at springs in Caldey Roads and up to three knots in Caldey Sound. In Caldey Sound the ebb flows WSW from one hour before to four hours after HW Tenby, and ENE from five hours after to two hours before HW.

Description

Facing broadly east across Carmarthen Bay, Tenby is a popular seaside town that has kept much of its traditional charm. Colourful terrace houses look down across the picturesque drying harbour towards Castle Hill and the lifeboat slip. St Catherine's Island with its old fort lies close southeast of Castle Hill and is connected to it by a drying ridge of sand. From the harbour breakwater, on a clear day, you can see right across Carmarthen Bay to the high ground of the Gower Peninsula.

Tenby harbour dries to firm sand, joining with North Beach at LW, but within two hours of high water you can lie alongside the breakwater quay. The local moorings are closely laid and visitors normally take the ground alongside the breakwater inner wall – there are ladders here and it's a handy spot for the town. The harbour is liable to swell in any easterly wind, although Castle Hill and the breakwater protect Tenby from direct onslaught. The approaches are straightforward, but Woolhouse Rocks (drying 3.6m) lie 1¼ miles southeast of Castle Hill. Tenby Roads are shallow and the outer anchorage is a good quarter of a mile northeast of the breakwater at springs.

Tenby Sailing Club welcomes visitors at their premises on the west quay. Fuel is not available near the harbour and involves a fair hike with a jerry can, though there's a chandler in town and water at the breakwater. You'll get a good breakfast at the Harbour Café, while Fecci & Sons fish and chip restaurant in Lower Frog Street is a local institution. Tenby station connects with Carmarthen and thence east or west via the main coast line.

Two miles south of Tenby, Caldey Island is a green and pleasant retreat for a community of Cistercian monks, whose Italianate abbey has views across the island and back to the mainland. In quiet weather you can anchor off Caldey's north shore but you are only allowed to land at the slip if you come on a recognised tripper boat.

Outer approaches

When approaching Tenby from the westward, Caldey Sound is the most direct route – given daylight and moderate weather. Enter the Sound from the WSW between Lydstep Point and St Margaret's Island, steering for Giltar Point and leaving St Margaret's at least two cables off. Note Lydstep Ledge (2.8m) just over half a mile east of Lydstep Point, and Sound Rock (4.2m) a cable further east. There are overfalls near these two shoals in a weather-going tide.

Caldey Sound carries a least depth of three metres in the buoyed channel. Pass between Giltar Spit red can buoy and Eel Point green conical buoy, and then head northeast keeping Eel Point buoy just open of Caldey Island astern to avoid the northeast extremity of Giltar Spit. When North Highcliff N cardinal buoy bears roughly SSE and Tenby promenade

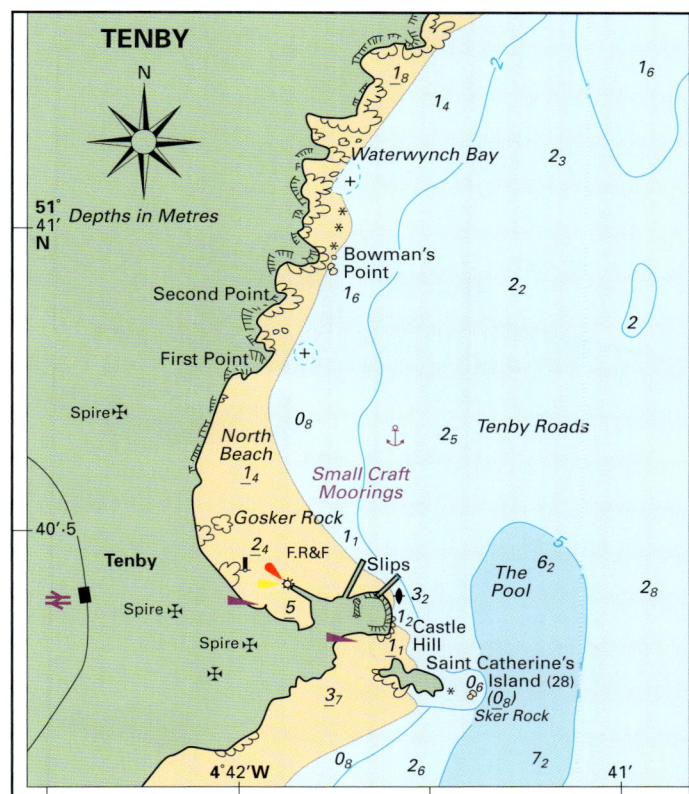

begins to open up behind Castle Hill, alter to the north for Tenby Roads. Leave Sker Rock, off St Catherine's Island, a cable to port.

At night, pass south of Caldey Island staying at least half a mile off in a weather-going tide. Heavy overfalls can occur up to half a mile southwest of West Beacon Point. Drift Rock (9.4m) is one and a quarter miles southeast of Chapel Point and the west-going tidal stream can kick up a nasty sea in its vicinity. Spaniel Shoal (3m) lies half a mile east of Caldey, and yachts can normally pass either side of the Spaniel E cardinal buoy.

Safely dried out in Tenby harbour

NORTH COAST

Tenby harbour, lifeboat station and the castle

Floating wind

The idea of floating wind farms sounds as if they are in perpetual motion but actually it just means the wind vane structures are anchored to the seabed rather than being permanently fixed. At the western end of the Bristol Channel the Crown Estate has put forward proposals for five possible initial locations to test the idea. In February 2022 the Crown Estate held a stakeholder workshop to give presentations and allow opportunities for interested parties to discuss a range of topics. These discussions included environmental, fishing and navigation concerns as well as looking at the impact of exclusion zones, shipping routes and the effect on flora and fauna.

As part of the UK Government's clean energy transition there is a commitment to generate 1GW of energy from floating offshore wind by 2030 and the Welsh government is working towards 70% of its electricity demand from renewable resources by the same date. The proposals for this development are moving quickly with plans to offer the first Agreements for Lease by the end of 2023.

The five projects that are being proposed at present have the potential to supply 400MW of test-scale wind projects but will also be important in testing and developing new technologies. Three of the sites have to undergo Habitat Regulations Assessments before they can be confirmed and the site off the north coast of Cornwall will convert from a Wave Hub to a floating wind farm.

As well as the actual off-shore sites themselves the project will offer opportunities for jobs onshore in the development and construction of the hardware. There will also need to be significant development to ports in the area to enable the floating structures to be produced and moved to site.

The whole area of the Celtic Sea is one with little industry and the coastlines, towns and population derive a substantial part of their income from tourism. There is something of a balancing act to ensure the peace and beauty is not impaired while, at the same time, investing in this fascinating new technology.

20 • Bristol Channel and Severn Cruising Guide

Woolhouse Rocks, drying 3.6m, lie one and a quarter miles northeast of Caldey Island. Avoid Woolhouse, either by staying close to the east of North Highcliff N cardinal buoy, or else by skirting well to the east of Woolhouse S cardinal buoy.

Approaching Tenby from the east, say from Burry Inlet, make directly for Castle Hill by keeping Tenby church spire just open north of St Catherine's Island. This line passes close north of DZ2 yellow spherical buoy and leaves Woolhouse Rocks half a mile to the south.

Coming from the southeast round the Gower Peninsula, either make for the east side of Caldey Island and thence to Castle Hill via the North Highcliff buoy, or else head up to DZ2 yellow spherical buoy and come north-about Woolhouse Rocks. Approaching from the ENE and the Towy estuary, head straight into Tenby Roads by making for the north side of Castle Hill.

Entry

Having reached Tenby Roads, approach the harbour from the northeast giving a good clearance to the end of the lifeboat slip. Head first for an iron beacon post standing on an isolated drying rock about 150m northwest of the breakwater head. A similar distance NNW of this post is the conspicuous Gosker Rock, an islet close off North Beach. As the harbour begins to open up turn to port round the breakwater and come alongside its inner wall.

Entry at night

The only light on Caldey Island is the main lighthouse above Chapel Point on the southeast corner of the island (Fl.3.WR.20s). This light has two red sectors – one shining NNE to cover Woolhouse Rocks and one at just north of west to guard West Beacon Point and its off-lying ledges.

From the west through Caldey Sound

The various buoys around Caldey Island are all lit, so in clear visibility and quiet weather you can come in through Caldey Sound by GPS if arriving from the west, keeping in the wide gap between Lydstep Point and Saint Margaret's Island. Once well into Caldey Sound, make good just north of east to pass between Giltar Spit red buoy (Fl.R.2.5s) and Eel Point green buoy (Fl.G.2.5s).

Having come through this gateway, turn north-east to make good 030° for 1½ miles. This track leaves North Highcliff N cardinal buoy 4 cables to starboard and brings you up safely abreast of Saint Catherine's Island and Castle Hill. From here curve to port to come round Castle Hill and the two lifeboat slips towards Tenby, keeping well off the shore until the harbour pier head light (FR and FW) bears less than 230° and you can turn south-west to approach the harbour.

From the west round Caldey Island

If you are arriving from the west and decide to go south and east-about Caldey, keep at least half a mile south of Chapel Point and its lighthouse before turning north-east to leave the Spaniel E cardinal buoy reasonably close to port. From here the most direct route to Tenby harbour tracks at 336° for about 2¾ miles, leaving North Highcliff N cardinal buoy a cable to port. As you approach and pass this buoy, Woolhouse Rocks (drying 3.6m) and their S cardinal buoy lie only half a mile to starboard, so be careful not to get set to the east if the tide is still flooding well.

The 336° track leads you a cable east of Sker Rock (dries 0.8m) off Saint Catherine's Island and then on past Castle Hill and the two lifeboat slips. Stay on this track until the harbour pier head light (FR and FW) bears less than 230° and you can turn south-west to approach the harbour.

Checking the menu in one of Tenby's narrow streets

Top: Tenby lifeboat and a trip boat at the landing stage

Bottom: The fort on St Catherine's Island can be visited at low water

From the east Coming from the east or south-east, say from Burry Port or from the Gower, make for the DZ2 yellow buoy first (Fl.Y.2.5s), to be sure of passing safely north of Woolhouse Rocks. If approaching from the north-east from well inside Carmarthen Bay, make straight for the Tenby pier head lights (FR and FW).

Berths and anchorages

Tenby Harbour Moor alongside the breakwater inner wall, drying out on firm sand. There is good shelter in most conditions, but easterly winds may send in a swell.

Tenby Roads Anchor 2–3 cables NNE of the lifeboat slip. There is reasonable holding and good shelter in winds from northwest through west to SSW, limited shelter from due south, but the anchorage is exposed to easterlies, particularly between east and southeast.

Caldey Roads Anchor in Priory Bay on the north side of Caldey Island, which has fair holding in sand. Keep clear of the ferry moorings but edge in as far as draught and tide permit. This anchorage offers reasonable shelter from southeast through south to WSW, although it is rarely perfectly calm.

Jones Bay There's an attractive temporary anchorage in Jones Bay, on the northeast corner of Caldey Island, sheltered from south through west to northwest. Tuck as close in as depths allow.

Lydstep Haven This wide sandy bay is just north of Lydstep Point and a mile due west of Caldey Sound. The bottom is gradually shelving sand and the bay offers good shelter from the west. Edge as far in as your draught and the tide allow.

Caldey Island

Lying just three miles off the Welsh coast near Tenby, Caldey Island's lighthouse stands on Chapel Point, not far from the old priory. Built by Trinity House in 1829 at a cost of £3,380 11s 7d, nearly 100 years later, in 1927, the light was automated so there were no more lighthouse keepers. Caldey was the last Trinity House light to be powered by acetylene gas and was only converted to mains electricity in 1997. The rather stubby but striking white tower is 65m above sea level and the three white flashes of the main light have a range of 13M.

Caldey Island has been a monastic settlement for over 1,500 years. The Welsh name of the island is Ynys Byr, after the 6th century abbot, Pyro. This settlement was probably destroyed by Vikings in the 10th century and the name Caldey has Norse origins. Henry I granted the island to Robert fitzMartin with an unusual clause giving possession down to the low water mark which still exists today, so the beaches really are private. In 1131 the island was given to French Benedictine monks from the Abbey of Tiron. During Henry VIII's arguments with the Pope all monasteries were dissolved in 1536 and the monks were expelled from the island.

From the mid-1500s to the 20th century Caldey had several owners and farming and quarrying were the main activities. In 1906 the island was bought by a community of Anglican Benedictine monks who had the present rather grand, Italianate abbey built in 1910. The design was by the Penarth architect John Coates-Carter and its distinctive red tiles were also used to replace slate on cottages on the island. In 1925 the abbey was sold to the Order of the Reformed Cistercians, a rather stricter community of monks who still live there today on this truly green and pleasant retreat.

Wildlife conservation is an important part of life on Caldey and, after a successful rat eradication programme, red squirrels have been reintroduced to the island. The individuals came from a varied gene pool and seem to be thriving and breeding. Hedgehogs are also present in healthy numbers and it is hoped that the absence of rats will enable puffins to breed here. Hardy Soay sheep have been introduced and they graze mostly in the west part of the island.

Caldey is a delightful place to visit for a day. The monastery has its own dairy farm producing milk, butter, ice cream and clotted cream. There's also a very successful perfumery that makes soaps, bath essences and perfumes inspired by the wild flowers of the island. At the Post Office you can buy mouth-watering chocolates and shortbread made by the monks, as well as all the perfumery products. You can also send a postcard franked with the island's own imprint. Just west of Caldey is its tiny sister St Margaret's, which is a seal and bird sanctuary.

Although there are some pleasant anchorages around Caldey you are not allowed to land on the island unless you come by a recognised trip boat, so if you want to stroll the island you need to leave your boat elsewhere and arrive from Tenby. There is no pub, shops or fuel on the island.

Caldey Island lighthouse

SAUNDERSFOOT

Summary

Saundersfoot is just over two miles north of Tenby in the northwest corner of Carmarthen Bay. This small seaside town is not as picturesque as Tenby and tends to become more crowded with tourists. The enclosed harbour is accessible about two hours each side of HW, dries to firm sand and is protected from all quarters, although prolonged easterly winds send in a surge. The harbour is safe but usually full of local boats and has limited space for visitors. The outer anchorage is further offshore than at Tenby, but well sheltered from NNE through west to SSW.

The harbour was built in the 1830s to export coal and later iron ore and pig iron. Coal had been shipped from the area for many years, loaded onto boats from the beach. During the 19th century business was active in the harbour with tramways bringing coal from the mines to the quayside. In the early 1900s activity declined and gradually a few fishing boats started using the harbour before its use moved towards leisure.

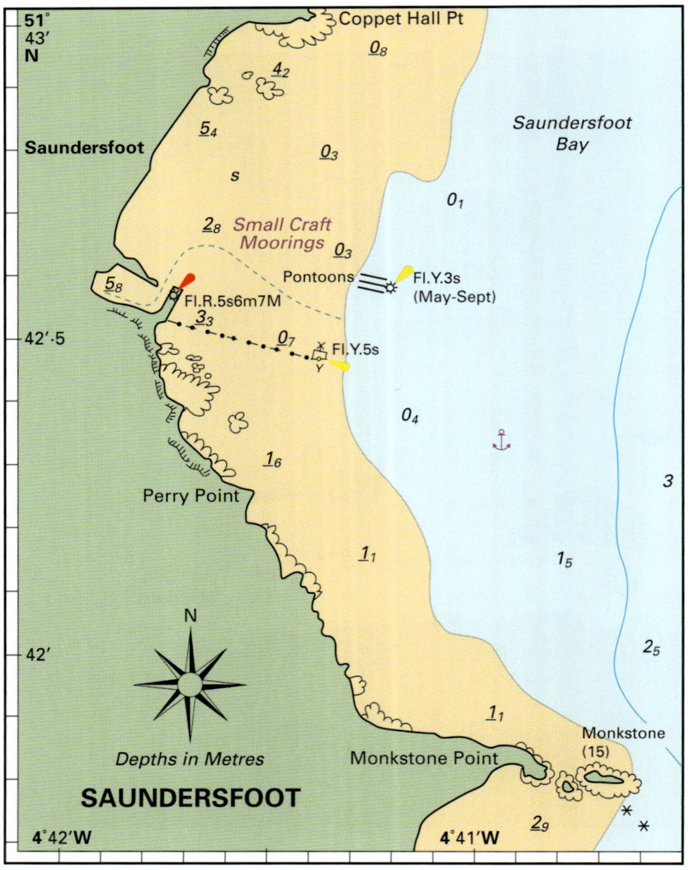

There is an ambitious development plan to improve facilities for visitors afloat and ashore. The Wales International Coastal Centre has already provided dry stacking for smaller boats and improved access on the outer harbour slipway from 2 hours either side of HW to 4 hours. Further developments will see the restoration of disused buildings to new uses and the provision of interpretation and visitor centres.

Tides HW Saundersfoot is at HW Milford Haven –0010, or HW Dover –0510. Heights above chart datum: 8.4m MHWS, 0.9m MLWS, 6.3m MHWN, 3.0m MLWN.

Port Control Saundersfoot Harbour Commissioners. For the Harbour Office ☏ 01834 812094, office hours, VHF 11.

Tidal streams and currents Streams in the northwest part of Carmarthen Bay are weak, barely reaching a knot at springs.

Description

Saundersfoot is a small seaside town on the northwest side of Carmarthen Bay. The coastline to the north and east is renowned for its wide sandy beaches and the whole area is popular with holidaymakers during the season. From a yachtsman's point of view, Saundersfoot's enclosed harbour is a safe haven once you are inside, although it is usually chock-a-block with local boats some moorings are available to visitors both in the harbour and outer wet moorings. It is recommended you book in advance, ☏ 01834 812094. The bottom dries out to firm sand and visitors usually lie alongside one of the quays. Saundersfoot Sailing Club has a pleasant clubhouse on the west side of the harbour.

The town centre is near the harbour with good shopping, although it's best to get

Saundersfoot harbour dries at low water

there early in the morning before most of the tourists are up and about. There is fresh water, a boatyard and chandlery on the quay. Fuel is not available alongside, but there's a garage in town. The station is on the same branch as Tenby, connecting with Carmarthen and thence east or west via the main coast line.

Outer approaches

As for Tenby, except that you have to work north into Carmarthen Bay for another two miles. Between Tenby and Saundersfoot, clear Monkstone Point by at least a quarter of a mile since underwater rocks extend southeast for a cable from the Monkstone itself. Coming from the east, say from Ferryside, the coastline is straightforward once you have cleared Carmarthen Bar.

Entry

Enter or leave Saundersfoot within two hours of HW. Approach the southeast breakwater head from due east. When about 250m from the breakwater, curve northwest towards a position 100m NNE of the entrance. Turn in towards the harbour when the entrance is fully open. Watch out for local fishing boats coming out and leave the north breakwater head close to starboard on entry.

Entry at night

Straightforward once you have passed Monkstone Point, which is unlit. Coming from Tenby Roads, take back-bearings on the northeast sector of Caldey Island light Fl(3) WR.20s, until you have identified Saundersfoot breakwater light Fl.R.5s and this bears less than about 300°. Then head northwest until the breakwater light bears due west about half a mile distant and proceed as above. There is a yellow marker to show the end of the sewer outfall. Port and starboard hand buoys at the harbour entrance indicate the deepest water of the channel.

Berths and anchorages

Saundersfoot Harbour Berth alongside the southwest quay wall (2 berths) or the north wall immediately to starboard on entry (1 berth west of the steps). These berths are clearly marked 'Visitor'. If in doubt ask the Harbourmaster, whose office is on the northwest quay, or info@saundersfootharbour.co.uk. There are sometimes one or two drying moorings available in the middle of the harbour. Three seasonal pontoons are installed outside the harbour but they are quite a long way out.

Outer anchorage

In Saundersfoot Bay, half a mile southeast of the harbour entrance at springs and about three cables offshore. At neaps, you can sound further inshore from the spring position. The holding is good in fine sand and the anchorage is sheltered from NNE through west to SSW. A riding light should be shown at night.

NORTH COAST

CARMARTHEN BAY

THE TOWY ESTUARY

Summary

The Towy and Taf Rivers share a common shallow estuary in the northeast corner of Carmarthen Bay. The mouth is two miles wide, between Ginst Point and Tywyn Point, and the approaches are strewn with extensive drying sandbanks and a bar. The tide flows strongly through these mostly unmarked dangers and the estuary is hostile in onshore winds. A glance at the chart would persuade most strangers not to enter, except with local knowledge or a local pilot. Yet it would be a pity to miss this wild, attractive stretch of water if conditions happened to be favourable. With careful pilotage, given light to moderate offshore winds and sufficient rise of tide, the estuary can be entered safely by boats of moderate draught that can take the ground.

The drying anchorages off Ferryside, a little way up the Towy, and at Laugharne up the Taf, are well worth the effort of navigation required to reach them. There are hospitable clubs on each side of the Towy River – the River Towy Yacht Club on the east shore at Ferryside and the Towy Boat Club further upstream on the west shore at Pilglas.

Tides HW Ferryside is at HW Milford Haven −0005, or HW Dover −0505. Heights above chart datum at Ferryside: 6.7m MHWS, 0.1m MLWS, 4.5m MHWN, 0.8m MLWN.

Port Control There is no port authority for the Towy Estuary. Members of local boat clubs may survey the Bar periodically and where possible mark the most dangerous features during the season.

Tidal streams and currents Streams can be strong, both in the rivers and in the outer estuary. A spring flood may exceed five knots locally, especially across sandbanks and in the channel off Ferryside. Although neap tides make for more moderate rates, it is nonetheless preferable to plan a first visit near springs when there will be plenty of water over the shoals at HW. In any case strangers should not attempt to enter the Towy estuary until an hour before HW Ferryside, by which time the streams will have moderated.

Description

The Towy and Taf Rivers join and meet the sea in the northeast corner of Carmarthen Bay, about seven miles northwest of the entrance to Burry Inlet. Either side of the mouth, dunes and burrows present a rather featureless and austere coastline to strangers and much of this low-lying land is used as firing ranges by the Ministry of Defence.

Like Burry Inlet, the outer Towy estuary is wide and shallow with extensive sandbanks, making pilotage tricky except near high water and entry inadvisable in onshore winds. The sandbanks are continually shifting and the channel isn't really marked, but despite that don't write off the estuary as a port of call. Both the Towy and the Taf are most attractive once you get in, and well worth visiting if conditions permit. Gentle offshore winds and a moderate spring tide will allow strangers to enter safely. Follow the directions carefully and aim to cross Carmarthen Bar about an hour before local HW.

A couple of miles into the Towy on the east bank, the sleepy waterside village of Ferryside looks across the river towards the imposing ruins of Llansteffan Castle. The River Towy Yacht Club is on the foreshore next to Ferryside station and a number of local boats are moored north of the landing stage, drying out about two hours each side of LW. The village has basic shopping, but the nearest chandler and boatyard is at Burry Port.

Opposite Ferryside is Llansteffan village, just upstream from the castle. The river is shallower on this side, although you can sound in towards the beach and take the ground. A mile above Ferryside and Llansteffan, past the Towy Boat Club and its moorings, the river begins to narrow and shoal. Shallow draught boats can navigate as far as Carmarthen near HW, but masted boats can only reach the railway bridge half a mile below the town.

NORTH COAST

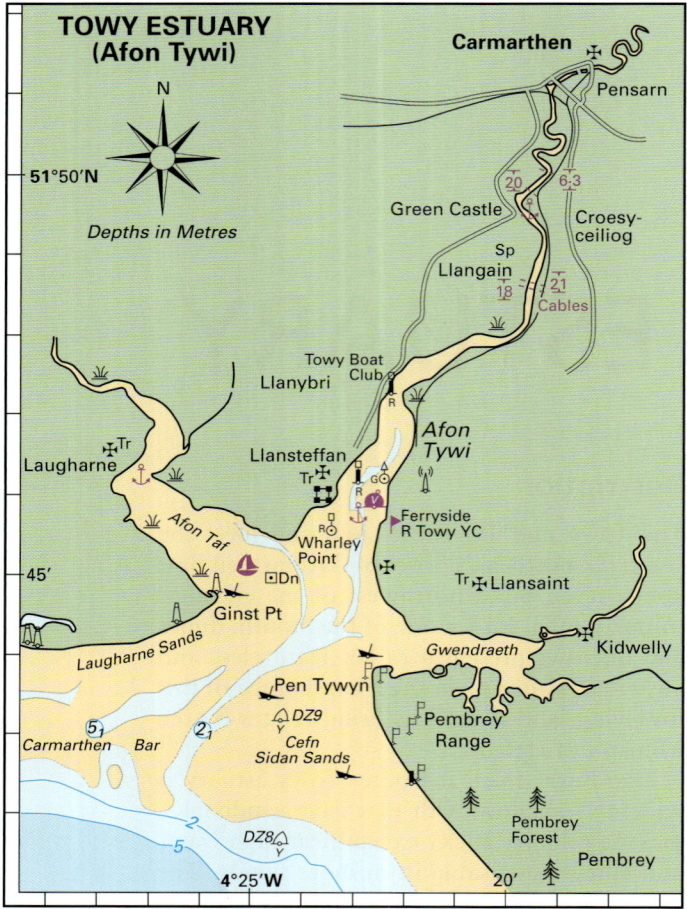

Various high-tension electricity cables cross the river, with a least height of about 15m. It's best not to anchor in the upper reaches without local knowledge.

The Taf River is shallower than the Towy and joins the estuary just north of Ginst Point. The attractive village of Laugharne, where Dylan Thomas spent his last years, is two miles northwest of Ginst Point. Here is another impressive ruined castle and shoal-draught boats can dry out on the sand opposite Thomas's boathouse. The Taf is navigable on the tide by small craft almost as far as St Clears, six miles above the entrance.

Outer approaches

The mouth of the Towy lies between two low sandy promontories – Ginst Point on the west side and Tywyn Point on the east – but first you must reach a safe approach position just outside Carmarthen Bar. The Carmarthen Bay Navigation Committee has been disbanded and there is no navigation authority for the Towy estuary. Local boat owners are happy to help visitors. The broad guidelines below should get you in safely in quiet weather near high water.

Arriving from the west up the Bristol Channel, you enter Carmarthen Bay either seaward of Caldey Island or by the inshore passage via Caldey Sound. Using the seaward route, the mouth of the Towy, just outside Carmarthen Bar, lies just under nine miles at about 061° from Spaniel E cardinal buoy. If you use the inner route, the mouth of the Towy is 8.4 miles at 069° from Woolhouse S cardinal buoy or 9.4 miles at 079° from Tenby breakwater.

Coming from the east round the Gower Peninsula, the mouth of the Towy, just outside Carmarthen Bar, is 9.3 miles at about 336° from just off Worms Head, or 11.2 miles at 349° from the West Helwick W cardinal buoy. From Burry Inlet, the Carmarthen Bar approach position lies just over seven miles at about 320° from the South Channel entrance off Burry Holms.

Although Carmarthen Bay is largely clear of navigational dangers, numerous yellow danger zone buoys mark areas used by the Army and RAF for artillery testing. A safety craft patrols the bay when firing is in progress and yachts may sometimes be asked to avoid particular zones. Permission is needed to cross Pendine Range on the approach to the Towy estuary and intending visitors should contact the Range Controller ☏ 01994 452240, VHF 16 or 73. There is usually no firing at weekends or holiday periods.

Entry

Carmarthen Bar and the sand banks around it shift regularly and for that reason waypoints for entry have been removed from these directions. Precise instructions for crossing the bar and entering the estuary become out of date very quickly so local advice is recommended if you would like the challenge of exploring the Towy Estuary. The best source of the latest information of movements of the Bar is the Towy Boat Club Facebook page, www.facebook.com/thetowyboatclub, or the River Towy Yacht Club, also on Facebook.

You should only consider entry into the rivers in quiet conditions, especially with no significant wind from south or west. Note that an extensive stony bank runs well out from the east shore to the south and southwest of St Ishmael's Church. In season, the end of this bank is often marked by a small S cardinal buoy.

Once across the bar you then make good more or less due north true, keeping the ruins of Llansteffan Castle very fine on the port bow and leaving a red post beacon to port. From here head NNE towards the River Towy Yacht Club landing stage and round up just beyond the landing in midstream, west of the local moorings.

To enter the River Taf, leave the danger zone pontoon off Ginst Point about three cables to port and then steer towards the highest part of Wharley Point. When close under the point, alter to the WNW for Laugharne village, keeping roughly 200m off the north shore and fetching up about a quarter of a mile east of Laugharne Quay.

Entry at night

On no account should strangers enter the Towy estuary at night, even in calm conditions. There are no navigation lights and there is no reliable way of locating the channel.

Berths and anchorages

Off Ferryside Anchor in midstream, a little way north of the River Towy Yacht Club landing stage and just west of the local moored boats. This should put you over a firm drying sandbank and away from the fast-flowing deeper water near the Ferryside shore. Good shelter from all quarters, but choppy in strong southerlies near HW. You can land at the club stage.

Off Green Castle in Black Pool About 4½ miles above Ferryside is Black Pool, a narrow stretch of river opposite Green Castle. Shoal-draught boats with local knowledge can anchor here in perfect shelter, having come up from Ferryside near HW. Visitors should first check with the yacht club or with the Towy Boat Club as to the current depths and state of the bottom.

Off Laugharne Anchor about a quarter of a mile due east of Laugharne village over firm sand. Good shelter from all quarters and you can land on the beach near Laugharne Quay.

The shifting sands of the Towy estuary *Crown Copyright*

BURRY PORT

Summary

Burry Inlet is a wide, shallow estuary between the Gower Peninsula and the Dyfed coast, opening into the east side of Carmarthen Bay. The inlet faces west and is peppered with shifting sandbanks. Strangers should only attempt to enter in quiet weather near HW. Burry Port, on the north shore of the estuary, has developed into a sizeable marina, mostly for small local yachts and fishing boats. Access to the marina is via a sill gate and locals come and go for about 2 hours each side of high water, though a bit longer at springs.

A huge build-up of sand and silt over many years have reduced depths in the marina basin to about 0.5m so, at the time of writing, visiting Burry Port is only suitable for bilge keel boats. The new operators of the marina, The Marine Group, have developed a new dredging machine and there is an ongoing dredging programme. It is strongly recommended that anyone considering visiting Burry Port should contact the harbour master in advance to check the suitability of their boat. Passage above Burry Port is not recommended. The old docks at Llanelli, three miles further up, are no longer accessible.

Tides HW Burry Port is at HW Milford Haven –0005, or HW Dover –0455. Heights above chart datum: 7.8m MHWS, 0.9m MLWS, 5.8m MHWN, 3.0m MLWN.

Port Control Carmarthenshire County Council. Harbourmaster ☎ 01554 777744.

Burry Port Marina, Carmarthenshire SA16 0ER ☎ 01554 835691, 07817 395710 info@themarinagroup.co.uk

Tidal streams and currents Streams in the estuary can be strong, reaching 4 knots at springs off Burry Port and over sandbanks. Off Burry Port the flood flows ENE until half an hour before local HW. There is then a short stand until about half an hour after HW, when the ebb begins to run WSW. Since depths in the approaches can vary as the sands shift, and because the streams often set across the channel, strangers should only approach or leave Burry Port during the last hour of the flood.

Description

Burry Inlet, which separates the Gower Peninsula from the Dyfed coast, is the broad, shallow estuary of the Loughor River, whose sandbanks and shoals are continually shifting. The tide runs strongly through these dangers and the estuary is often written off by yachtsmen as being bleak and inhospitable. Yet the area has a rather haunting atmosphere and is worth a visit if weather and tides permit. The Gower itself has rugged cliffs, striking headlands and wide, surf-washed bays of fine sand. Its low north shore is a wild region of drying flats, where horses graze the salt marshes and locals still gather cockles using donkey carts.

Burry Port lies nearly five miles northeast of Burry Holms, a conspicuous islet off Limekiln Point at the northwest corner of the Gower. Burry Port harbour was built nearly two hundred years ago to export coal, iron and copper from the nearby valleys and was once a haven for small coasters. The harbour had fallen into decline until it received a major boost in 2002 as part of significant investment in Llanelli's Millennium Coastal Park. Burry Port now has a sizeable marina basin, accessed by a sill gate through which locals who know these tricky waters come and go for about 2½ hours each side of high tide. Local charter fishing is being encouraged and the harbour has an agreeable mix of working and pleasure boats. The minimum depth in the marina is currently about 0.5m and there is an active dredging programme. At the time of writing the marina is really only suitable for bilge keel boats or others that can easily take the ground.

Burry Port is a very unassuming but friendly place and you can still feel some vibes of history from when cargoes of coal and metal ore were shipped out from here, first in the days of sail and later by small steam coasters. On the harbour's west quay are Burry Port Yacht Club and Burry Port Marine Services, which has

BURRY PORT

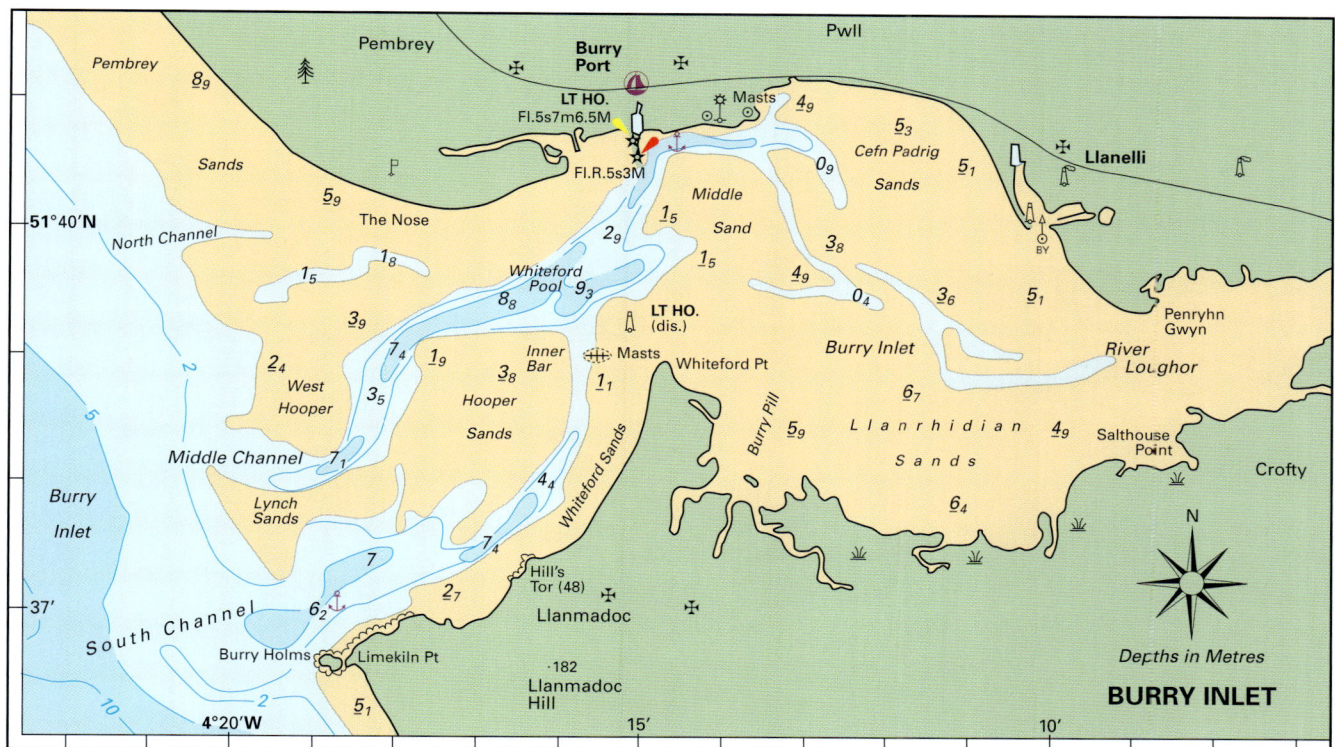

chandlery and can carry out most repairs. They can also arrange to deliver diesel or petrol. The club members welcome visitors. The town is only a short walk from the harbour and has reasonable shopping. The nearby station has connections west to Milford Haven and east via Swansea. Burry Port has plenty of pubs and the Cornish Arms, near the harbour on Gors Road, does good bar meals. The Hope and Anchor is also a convivial place, behind the harbour near the station.

Outer approaches

Burry Inlet opens into the southeast part of Carmarthen Bay, where the sandy bottom shelves gradually from seaward towards the mouth of the estuary. The passage across the bay from Saundersfoot or Tenby is straightforward and it's roughly 14 miles ESE from Tenby harbour to the entrance of the Burry Inlet South Channel and an approach waypoint just northwest of the conspicuous

The marina at Burry Port *The Marine Group*

Bristol Channel and Severn Cruising Guide • 31

NORTH COAST

Whiteford Point lighthouse on the north edge of the Gower peninsula *Crown Copyright*

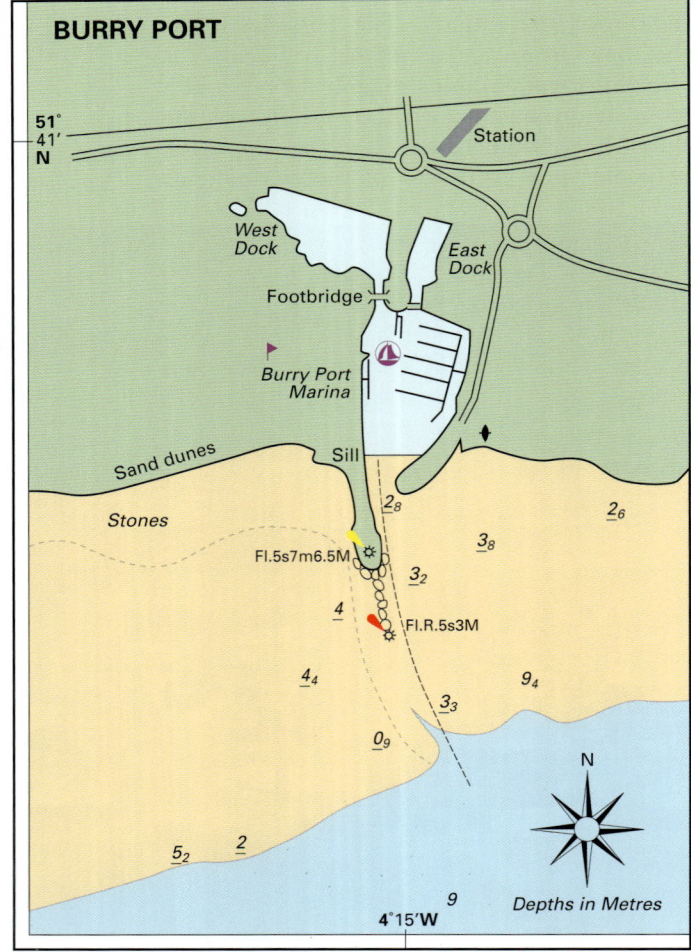

islet of Burry Holms. From Ferryside to the South Channel entrance is 12½ miles and from Swansea entrance you can reckon about 20 miles via the Helwick Channel.

In quiet weather there's a temporary anchorage, known as The Kitchen, close north of Worms Head. This spot is fairly sheltered from due south or from easterlies and the bottom is mostly sand. The Kitchen is useful if you are early on the tide for Burry Inlet, but stay clear of the gap between Worm's Head and Rhossili Point – the tide runs strongly through these narrows near half-tide.

Entry

To enter Burry Inlet, aim to arrive at an outer approach position northwest of Burry Holms about an hour before HW. At the time of writing it was best to use the South Channel just north of Burry Holms islet and Limekiln Point. The sand shifts and charts should be treated with some scepticism. Be careful to avoid the Lynch Bank, West Hooper Bank and the Hooper Bank, there is shallow water across much of the entrance to the north shore by the Nose. Coming from the west don't be tempted to cut the corner, even following a local, as it can be very shallow.

32 • Bristol Channel and Severn Cruising Guide

Looking towards Burry Port entrance

As you get near Burry Port harbour, you'll see the buoys marking the final approach channel. Identify Burry Port west breakwater (Fl.5s 6.5M), which has a low white lighthouse with a red roof, but don't confuse this with the old Pembrey harbour breakwater, half a mile further west. The approach channel is marked by two red and three green buoys, these are lit at night. After severe weather these buoys can sometimes move or be lost and the depth in the channel can vary and be less than that over the sill. When approaching in daylight the disused Whiteford Point lighthouse is a good marker. On the north-west tip of the Gower this is thought to be the last cast iron lighthouse in Britain.

Burry Inlet is definitely a stretch of water for quiet settled weather, preferably light easterlies or northeasterlies. The mouth of the estuary is unpleasant in moderate westerlies or southwesterlies, and evil in fresh winds from these directions, when heavy seas break across the entrance. If bound seawards from Burry Port, leave about three quarters of an hour before local HW. The channel is tortuous above Burry Port, and dangerous in places where the strong tide could carry you over hidden obstructions.

Entry by night

Do not attempt to navigate Burry Inlet at night.

Berths and anchorages

Burry Port Marina The sheltered marina is now run by The Marine Group which is helping to develop facilities in conjunction with Carmarthenshire County Council. The basin is entered via a sill gate which stays open for 2½ hours each side of high water. The gate has three vertical lights, any red lights mean the gate is closed, two greens over a white mean the gate is open. Depth over the sill is 2.5m but it's worth checking with the harbour office. Boats leaving the marina should give way. Once inside there is currently a minimum depth of about 0.5m and the pontoons are snug and well protected. A new lifeboat house has been opened and the marina will be redeveloping the old lifeboat house with modern facilities for yachtsmen, showers, laundry, rubbish disposal etc. and a new harbour office.

Anchorage off Burry Port You can anchor off the harbour entrance in quiet weather, about 1½ cables ESE of the west breakwater head in 8–9m. You'll find moderate holding on a sandy bottom, strong currents and fair shelter from WNW through north to northeast.

Lynch Pool There's a fair weather anchorage in Lynch Pool, over a sandy bottom close north of Limekiln Point in depths between half a metre and 3m LAT. This spot is open to the west, but reasonably sheltered in winds from between east and south.

THE GOWER PENINSULA

From the land, the Gower Peninsula is an attractive, unspoilt holiday area that encompasses a variety of wild coastal scenery. The low tidal flats of the north shore contrast markedly with the dramatic cliffs and wide bays of the west and south. Yet from seaward the Gower can seem somewhat hostile from the yachtsman's point of view. There are one or two quiet weather anchorages suitable for lunch and a swim, or for awaiting a fair tide, but the peninsula is generally rather exposed and it is usually wise to admire the many vistas while passing by as quickly as possible.

It's about 26 miles from Burry Port around the Gower to Swansea entrance, taking the best part of a tide under sail. There's a complication though, in that the east-going stream starts running off Worm's Head soon after local LW, whereas you have to leave Burry Port near HW. If weather permits, you can wait for the new flood at the Worm's Head anchorage, because it's rarely worth pushing a foul tide south of the Gower. Coming from Tenby or Saundersfoot bound eastwards for Swansea, leave about two hours after HW and allow for the weaker cross-tide of the ebb across Carmarthen Bay.

In moderate weather it's usually quicker to take the Helwick Channel inside Helwick Sands. This long, narrow shoal stretches due west for over six miles from just off Port Eynon Point. The West Helwick W cardinal buoy guards the W end of the sands while Helwick Pass, the cut between Port Eynon and the east end of the shoal, is marked by an E cardinal buoy. Helwick Pass can be rough in fresh westerlies, or in any wind against the tide, the seas generally being steepest near low water.

Deep-draft yachts should only use Helwick Pass above half-tide. With less than 1.5m draft you can, in reasonable weather, aim to pass Worm's Head about an hour before local low water and so stem the last of the ebb down towards Port Eynon Point. Helwick Pass will then be taken near low water and you'll arrive off Oxwich Point at slack when the overfalls are quiet. Be sure to avoid the wreck, with only 2.4m over it, about half a mile southeast of Port Eynon Point. In any fresh wind over tide conditions, clear Oxwich Point by two miles to miss the worst of the race.

There are pleasant daytime anchorages at Port Eynon and Oxwich Bay, whose beaches

The striking south coast of the Gower
Crown Copyright

34 • Bristol Channel and Severn Cruising Guide

THE GOWER PENINSULA

are popular with holidaymakers. You'll find reasonable shelter in light to moderate winds from west through north to northeast. Interestingly, a sizeable fishing fleet used to operate out of Port Eynon in the days of sail, and there was also a considerable limestone trade with Devon. There is no port now, but the Ship Inn in Port Eynon village still feels like a sailors' haunt. Just round the Pwlldu headland you can tuck into the little bay which may be quieter as it is a longer walk for land-based visitors.

Just over six miles ENE from Oxwich Point is Mumbles Head, with its famous lighthouse on the offlying rocks and the well-known pier and lifeboat slip round the corner to the north. Coming from the west, avoid Mixon Shoal (dries 0.7m), a small bank half a mile SSW of Mumbles lighthouse. A red can buoy with bell is moored close south of this danger and should normally be left a good two cables to landward. Above half-tide in quiet weather, yachts of moderate draught can cut inside Mixon by keeping about 400m off the Coastguard station and a similar distance off the lighthouse, on the direct line between Oxwich Point and the SW Inner Green Grounds (known locally as the Swigg) S cardinal buoy.

Once past the Mixon buoy Swansea Bay opens up, with Swansea harbour entrance just over three miles to the NNE and the industrial complex of Port Talbot conspicuous to the east. Keep at least a quarter of a mile east of Mumbles lighthouse to avoid the Cherry Stones race.

The distinctive Worms Head on the Gower

There's a useful anchorage in Mumbles Bay, about three quarters of a mile north of the lighthouse at springs but closer inshore at neaps. You'll find reasonable shelter here from north through west to southwest, with good holding in stiff mud. Local moorings are laid here during the season, and both the Mumbles and Bristol Channel yacht clubs have their premises ashore.

The Gower is especially inhospitable at night, with only Mumbles Head lighthouse Fl(4)20s15M, the Mixon red buoy Fl(2) R.5s and two fixed red vertical lights on the end of Mumbles pier to help you round the corner towards Swansea. The East Helwick E cardinal buoy is lit, but Helwick Pass is not recommended at night. The best policy is to stay well offshore at night, outside Helwick Sand, until Swansea Bay opens up and you can begin to identify the harbour approach lights.

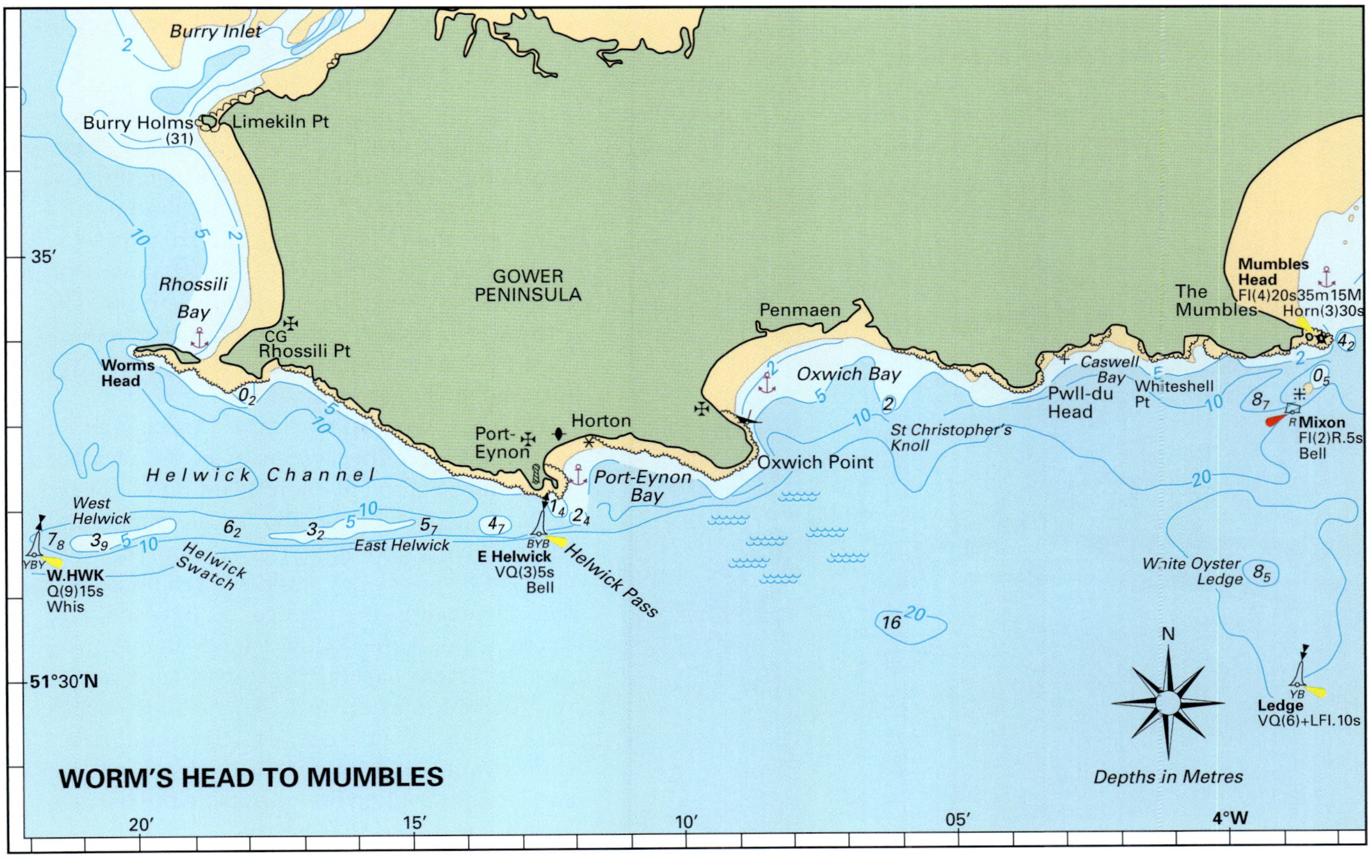

WORM'S HEAD TO MUMBLES

SWANSEA

Summary

The lively city of Swansea is situated near the mouth of the River Tawe at the head of Swansea Bay. Swansea Yacht Haven, an attractive marina with excellent facilities, is on the west bank of the river, half a mile in from the harbour pier heads. Access to the marina is through the Tawe barrage lock and then the marina lock, from 0700–2200 in season and at any tide except low springs. The Tawe approaches are well buoyed and entry is possible in practically all weather conditions.

Tides HW Swansea is at about the same time as HW Milford Haven, or at HW Dover –0450. Heights above chart datum: 9.6m MHWS, 1.0m MLWS, 7.3m MHWN, 3.2m MLWN.

Port Control Swansea Dock Authority. VHF working 14, with 24 hr listening watch on 14 and 16. For marina call *Swansea Yacht Haven* on 37 (M1).

Tidal streams and currents A mile or two south of Mumbles Head the east-going stream starts at about LW Swansea and the west-going stream at HW Swansea, with a maximum rate of about 2½ knots at springs. A stronger local stream runs close past Mumbles pier, reaching 3½ knots on a spring ebb. Further offshore, south of Scarweather and Nash Sands, rates are even stronger up to 5 knots at springs on both flood and ebb. Unpredictable eddies occur near the shoals, and there are heavy overfalls off the west tail of Nash Sand on a weather-going tide.

Description

Swansea, or 'Abertawe' in Welsh, is a large provincial city which has grown up at the head of Swansea Bay where the River Tawe ends its journey through a long valley of mining villages. The Gower Peninsula forms the west shore of the bay, ending in Mumbles Head with its distinctive pier and lifeboat slip. On the east side of Swansea Bay, the straight coastline between Porthcawl and Neath starts off in the south as sand-dunes and burrows, giving way at Port Talbot to a rather dour esplanade of smelting works, steel-rolling mills and factory chimneys.

The entrance to Swansea harbour is actually the mouth of the Tawe, where two long breakwaters reach out into deep water across the broad mudflats that fringe the bay. A barrage protects the river from flooding and you enter the river through the barrage lock, which operates from 0700–2200 in season and at almost any tide except low springs. The entrance lock and swing-bridge for Swansea Yacht Haven are on the west side of the river just above the barrage lock.

Swansea is straightforward of access and a good port of refuge. Even in heavy weather from the south or southwest it's always possible to negotiate the breakwaters and reach shelter, although the sea can be very steep in Swansea Bay under these conditions. The channel is maintained at half a metre depth as far as the commercial dock entrance, just inside the harbour to starboard. Contact the harbourmaster for up to date depth information. Watch out for ferries and other ships coming in or out of the docks. There are two orange holding buoys outside the barrage lock if you arrive after hours.

The pedestrian bridge across Swansea marina
Swansea Marina

SWANSEA

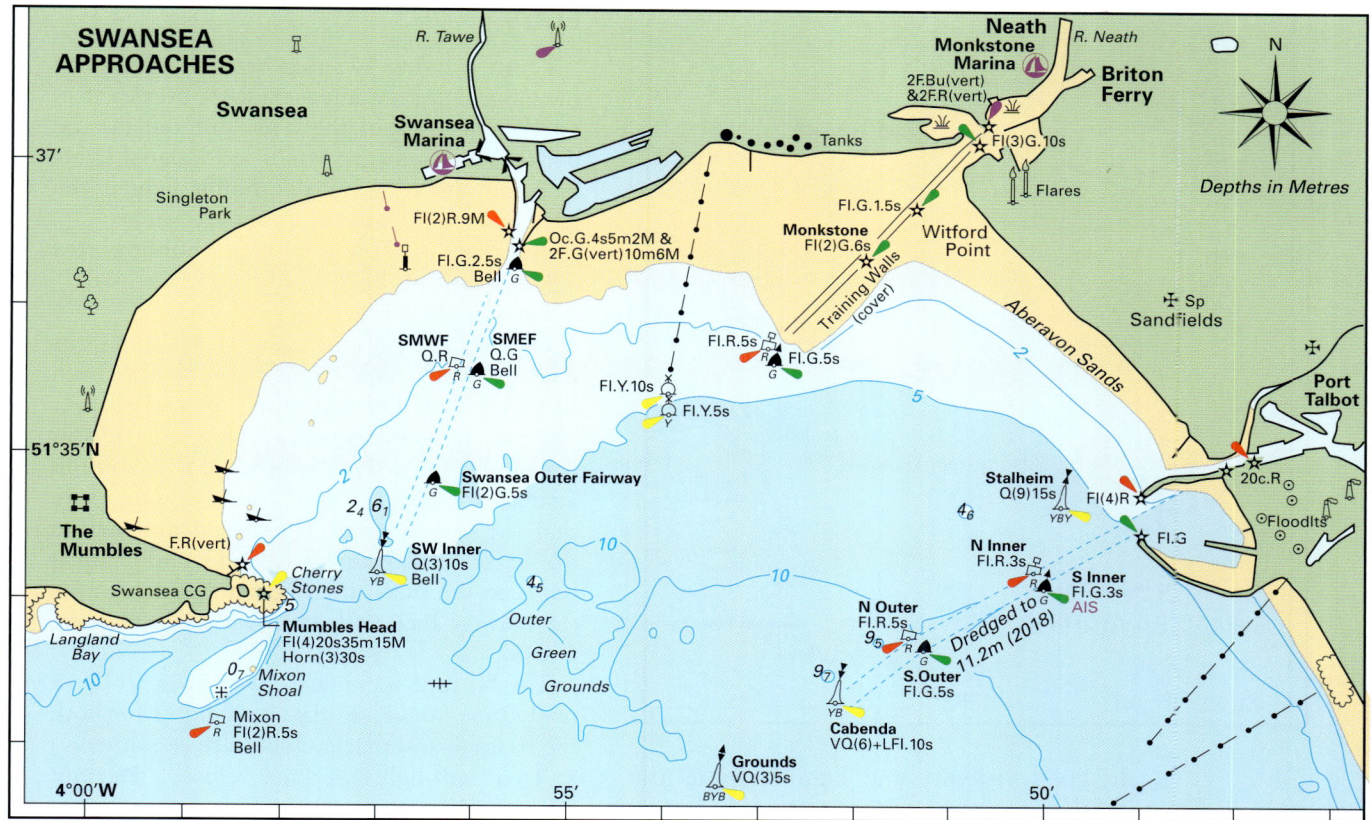

Since Swansea's maritime quarter was first developed, the marina waterfronts have matured into a pleasant setting for boat owners. The marina has excellent facilities, a beach just opposite and an attractive mix of new and old brick buildings around the basins. There are plenty of pubs, cafés and restaurants and Hanson At The Chelsea is good for seafood. Swansea is well placed between Milford Haven and Cardiff. Local boats often cruise across to Ilfracombe or Watchet at weekends.

Outer approaches

The coastal approaches to Swansea from the west are covered in the previous chapter on the Gower Peninsula. Once past the Mixon red buoy and clear to the east of Mumbles Head, make for the 'Swigg' (SW Inner Green Grounds) S cardinal buoy that lies just under a mile east of Mumbles lighthouse. From the Swigg make good 020° towards the harbour pier heads, following the red and green buoys of the dredged channel. The first green buoy, Swansea Fairway Green Grounds, is only eight cables NNE of the Swigg.

Approaching Swansea from the southeast involves keeping clear of Nash Sand and Scarweather Sands, and giving a good berth to the overfalls off Nash Point and in the region of the West Nash and Middle Nash buoys. If you are coming along the coast from Barry, the simplest tactic is to stay 1–1½ miles off Nash Point and then continue just north of west until you are about two miles south of West Nash W cardinal buoy. Then make good to the northwest, leaving the West Scar W cardinal buoy close to starboard. On this leg beware of being set towards the Scarweather Sands if the tide is flooding. Swansea pier heads lie eight miles due north true from the West Scar buoy.

In quiet weather, good visibility and if the tide permits, you can save some distance by cutting inside either Nash Sand or Scarweather Sands or both. By passing close under Nash Point you can take the Nash Passage between the headland and the East Nash E cardinal buoy. This pass is less than a quarter of a mile wide and is best entered above half-tide, quite feasible if you leave Barry just before local HW with a view to carrying the full six hours of the Channel ebb westwards.

To enter the Nash Passage, make good three-quarters of a mile at 325° from the East Nash E cardinal buoy. Then make good about 300° so as to leave Tusker Rock red can buoy a cable to starboard and Porthcawl Point just under a mile to starboard. Now follow the coast a mile offshore, entering Swansea Bay by the back door by passing a cable east of Kenfig E cardinal buoy. Once you are safely clear to the north of Kenfig Patches, make good about 311° for the 7½ miles or so to the Swansea Outer fairway green buoy off Swansea entrance.

NORTH COAST

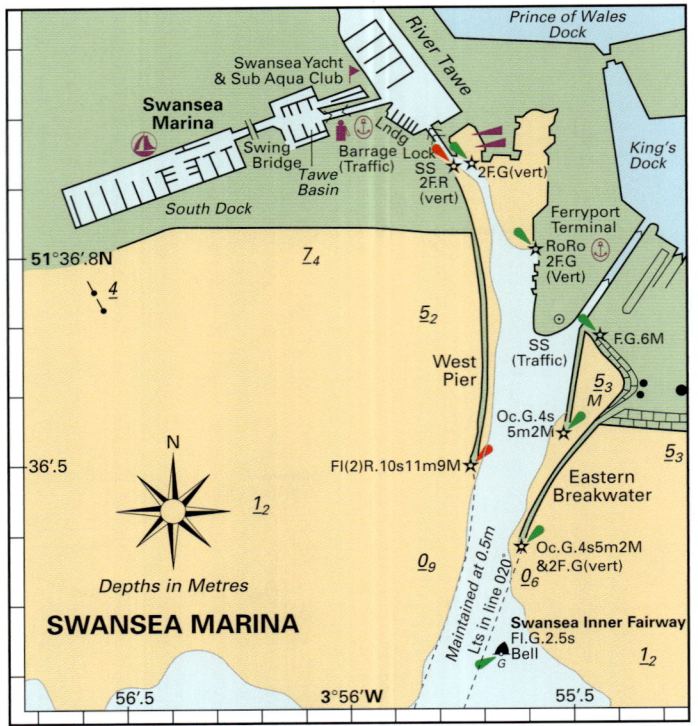

Entry

All craft entering Swansea harbour must obey the signal lights mounted inside the breakwaters on the east side of the river, just outside the docks. From seaward you'll see 9 signal lights in 3 columns of 3 and the **middle** light in the left-hand (west) column applies to yachts:

- Red light – Wait out in the holding area southwest of the West Pier
- Green light – Enter

Having said all this, there are occasions when the yacht signal light seems to have been forgotten and left on 'stop'! If you suspect this may have happened, call *Swansea Docks Radio* on VHF 14 or else proceed **with caution** against the signal until you are quite sure that the way is clear. The speed limit within the harbour is 5 knots. Keep in mid-channel between the piers, then bear to port towards the barrage lock and stay west of the holding buoys.

The barrage lockmaster works on VHF 18 (call *Tawe Lock*) and the signal lights for both the barrage and marina locks are as follows:

- Two red lights – Lock closed. Do not proceed
- One red light – Wait
- One green light – Enter lock with caution

The marina basin in Swansea

In good visibility and lightish winds this coastal shortcut is straightforward, but in brisk weather or poor visibility it's safest to use the big-ship route outside all the dangers.

SWANSEA

- Red and green lights together – Free flow operating. Proceed with caution.

For the marina lock, call *Swansea Marina* on VHF 80.

Entry at night

Approaching from the west, the Mumbles light Fl(4)20s is a key mark for providing clearing lines off the Gower coast. When coming up-Channel, a sound plan is to keep a couple of miles south of the West Helwick W cardinal buoy and then track just north of east towards the Ledge S cardinal buoy, about four miles south of the Mumbles. This line keeps you nicely outside Helwick Sands and clear of the Oxwich Point overfalls, although you can begin to borrow inshore once Mumbles light bears less than 045°.

The Swigg S cardinal buoy bears 015° from the Ledge buoy, distant 4.3 miles, and you usually need to allow for a good cross-tide. Check the set and drift carefully as you approach the Mumbles and keep Oystermouth Castle (floodlit at night) open of Mumbles pier head lights 2F.R(vert) to clear the Cherry Stones race. The harbour leading lights in line at 020° mark the east edge of the dredged channel and are obscured when bearing less than 020°. The front lights are two fixed vertical greens and the rear light is a single fixed green, all with a 6-mile range. The green starboard hand channel buoys are lit.

Approaching from the southeast, strangers should stay outside Nash and Scarweather Sands and make for the West Scar W cardinal buoy. From here you can track due north towards Swansea harbour entrance, leaving Mumbles Head just over 1½ miles to the west. Allow for the last of the west-going ebb if you have carried the tide down from Barry. The Nash Passage is navigable at night with GPS, quiet weather and good visibility. The trick is to make use of the northwest sectors of Nash Point lighthouse Fl(2)WR.15s, having first

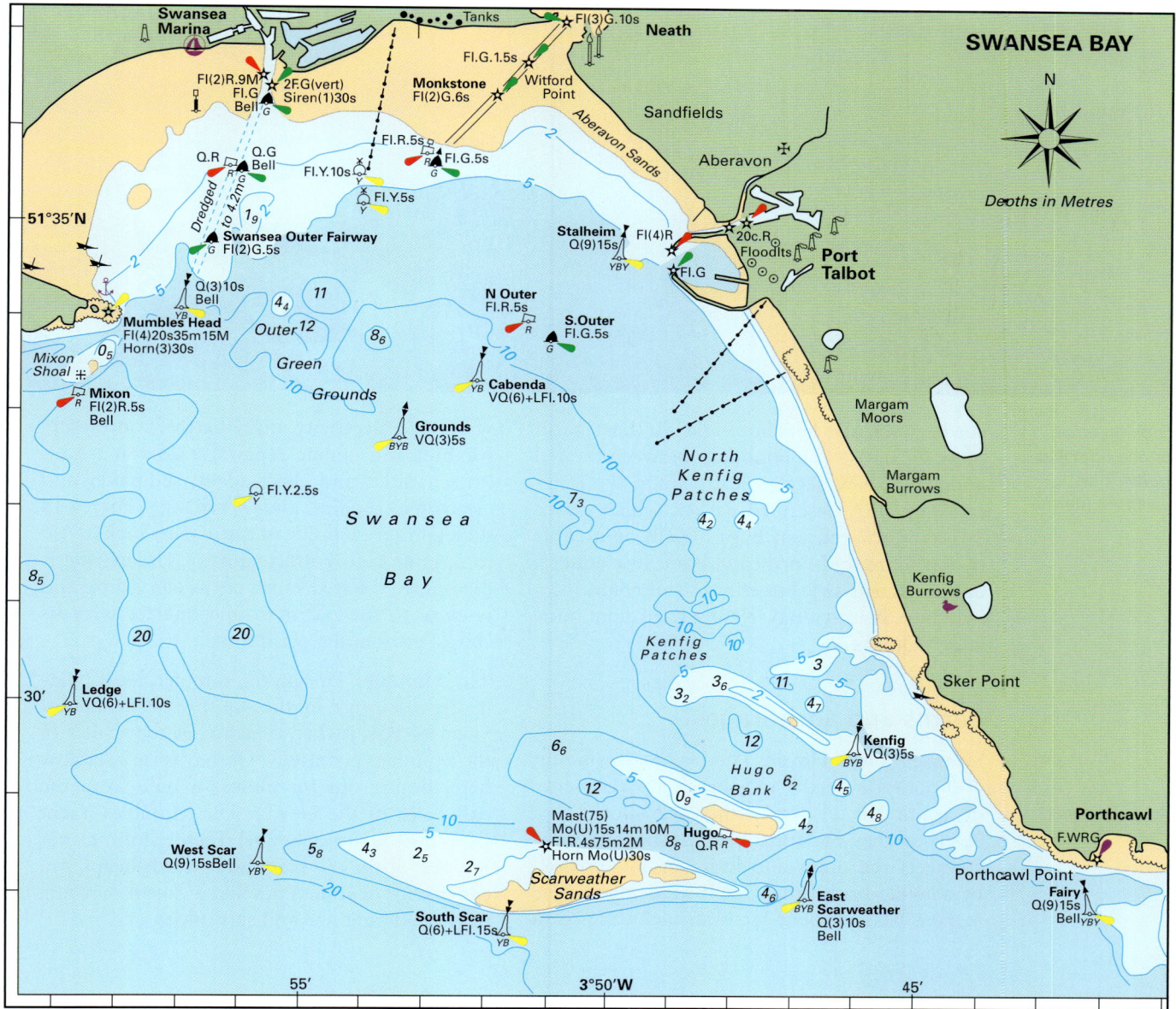

Bristol Channel and Severn Cruising Guide

NORTH COAST

Looking down on the lightship *Helwick* in Swansea Marina

cut between the headland and the East Nash buoy Q(3)10s. The boundary between the red and white NW sectors leads along the inner track of 300° described earlier, which leaves Tusker Rock red can buoy Fl(2)R.5s a cable to starboard and Porthcawl Point just under a mile to starboard. For the coastal route from here into Swansea Bay, Kenfig E cardinal buoy is lit VQ(3)5s.

Berths and anchorages

Swansea Yacht Haven The marina has about 400 pontoon berths and there's always plenty of room for visitors, who are allocated a berth as they lock through. A short channel connects the outer and inner basins, crossed by a swing-bridge that opens on demand. The marina has excellent facilities including fresh water and electricity at the berths, contractors for hull and engine repairs, a 25-ton travel-lift, chandler and chart agent, sailmaker and electronic repairs and servicing. There's a diesel pump each side of the marina lock (0700 to 30mins before office closes). The marina is pleasantly situated south of the city centre and is close to the old maritime quarter with its shops, pubs and restaurants.

The Mumbles During the summer, local boats lie to moorings in the south-west corner of Swansea Bay, tucked close under the shelter of the Mumbles peninsula. The bay is very shallow here, drying out for almost a mile from the east coast of the Gower. The Mumbles Yacht Club and Bristol Channel Yacht Club are not far west of the old pier and towards neaps you can anchor or sometimes find a vacant mooring near the drying line and stay afloat.

Dylan Thomas at Swansea and Laugharne

If you are moored in Swansea marina for a few days what better way to get to know the city than through the eyes of arguably its most famous son, Dylan Thomas. The bronze statue by John Doubleday is on the north side of the marina close to the National Waterfront Museum and the Dylan Thomas Theatre. Across the footbridge to the south is a statue of Captain Cat, one of the characters from *Under Milk Wood*. The Dylan Thomas trail is a level half-hour stroll around the main sights of the city he loved.

Born in Swansea in October 1914, Thomas had his first poem printed in his school magazine. After leaving school at 16 he became a reporter for the South Wales Daily Post, but only worked there until the end of 1932 when he left to write full time. Almost two thirds of Dylan Thomas' poems were written before he was 20.

In 1936 he met Caitlin Macnamara in London and apparently proposed to her straightaway. They met again later that year at Laugharne and were married in 1937. When the Second World War came and Thomas went to Carmarthen to join up, he failed his medical and started writing scripts for Government propaganda films. Throughout the war Thomas and his wife travelled frequently between London and South Wales. He always felt at home in smoky London pubs with fellow writers.

After the war Dylan Thomas wanted to return to Laugharne with his growing family and in 1949 they moved into the Boat House, down on the riverside. Shallow-draught cruising boats can get up the Taf River to this sleepy village, which lies two miles upstream from the mouth of the Towy estuary. Laugharne became the Thomas family home and Dylan spent his last years here. The Boat House is now a much visited memorial to the life and works of Dylan Thomas. During the early 1950s Thomas undertook three ambitious lecture tours in America and on the last of these trips, in November 1953, he was taken ill and died in hospital in New York.

Possibly his most famous and evocative piece is *Under Milk Wood*, a play for voices, which he wrote for the BBC. The plan was for Dylan Thomas to record the script himself on his return from the States but it wasn't to be. In the event the play was published in 1954 with the memorable first recording of Richard Burton playing First Voice.

The Dylan Thomas statue by the Pump House, Swansea
Swansea Council / Dylan Thomas Centre

The Boathouse at Laugharne where Dylan Thomas lived and worked
Crown Copyright

BRITON FERRY

Summary

Briton Ferry and the industrial Port of Neath lie at the mouth of the Neath River, which flows into Swansea Bay three miles ENE of Swansea entrance. The approaches are shallow and the river dries to thick mud, but entry is possible above half-tide. A 1½ mile buoyed channel follows a training wall marked by beacons. Strangers should only enter in daylight and moderate offshore weather. Inside the river on the west bank, Monkstone Cruising and Sailing Club have their own dredged yacht basin, just below the road bridge. The basin is sheltered and visitors are welcome.

Tides As for Swansea, i.e. at HW Milford Haven or HW Dover −0450. Heights above chart datum: 9.6m MHWS, 1.0m MLWS, 7.3m MHWN, 3.2m MLWN.

Port Control Neath Harbour Commissioners, Briton Ferry ℡ 01639 633486. No VHF listening watch.

Tidal streams and currents The streams in Swansea Bay are weak, but rates are faster in the offing. Refer to the Swansea chapter for details. In the Neath River a spring ebb can reach three knots and a spring flood two knots, the rate and height being partly affected by the volume of fresh water coming down from inland.

Description

The Neath River wends its way seawards from the Fawr Forest through another South Wales mining valley, the Vale of Neath. Past Briton Ferry and the Port of Neath, the river emerges into Swansea Bay about three miles ENE of Swansea harbour entrance. The Neath estuary is shallow, drying at low tide to a thick, unsavoury looking mud. The surrounding area is mostly industrial, with a scrap metal works sprawling on the east bank and Port Talbot not far away. Noise from the works' power hammers and the nearby M4 tends to work against a peaceful riverside atmosphere.

But over on the west bank, just below the road bridge, the friendly Monkstone Cruising and Sailing Club thrives amidst all this bustle. They have a well-established clubhouse and their own yacht basin, which was first excavated by the members themselves back in 1984 and now provides a sheltered haven with a least depth of about a metre retained by a sill gate.

The river is entered across mudflats by way of a 1½ mile buoyed channel, only accessible above half-tide. The channel is kept reasonably clear by a training wall on its southeast side. Entry is fairly straightforward, the outer buoys lying about three miles N by E from Swansea Grounds E cardinal buoy and a similar distance 057° from the Swigg S cardinal buoy. The Neath River is not a safe port of refuge – yachts should make for Swansea in heavy weather – but there is good shelter inside the yacht basin. The small town of Briton Ferry is 15mins walk across the road bridge, but the Ferryboat Inn is handy on the west bank.

Outer approaches

As for Swansea, the outer entrance buoys for the River Neath entrance channel lie three miles at 057° from Swigg S cardinal buoy, 7.6 miles at 013° from West Scar W cardinal buoy and 6.6 miles at 324° from the north end of the passage inside Kenfig Patches. Several cooling towers and chimneys are conspicuous at Port Talbot and at the chemical works on the east side of the Neath estuary.

Entry

The entrance channel into the River Neath lies between a 1¾ mile training wall to starboard, marked by three well-spaced green posts, and a slag training bank to port, whose inner end is marked by three red posts. The outer end of this channel is marked by a red and a green buoy that form an entrance gateway.

From the outer buoys you follow the channel northeastwards, turning slightly to starboard when you reach the inner end of the training wall. Leave to starboard the rough slag breakwater that extends from the south pier head of the disused Briton Ferry dock and follow the line of the east shore as the channel curves northwards. You'll see the road bridge

BRITON FERRY

ahead and the club premises and basin on the west bank. The marina is entered through a sill gate fitted with a tide gauge and semaphore arm on the left hand entrance tower, that shows whether the gate is open or closed, when the arm is completely down the gate is open. Edge into the basin and ask one of the members about a berth. The channel entrance carries about 23ft of water at MHWS and 12ft at MHWN. Fresh onshore winds from south and southwest can make entry difficult.

Entry at night

It is not recommended that strangers enter the Neath River at night, although the posts marking the entrance channel are lit as far as the inner end of the training wall.

Approaching Monkstone marina near Briton Ferry on the River Neath
Dean Williams

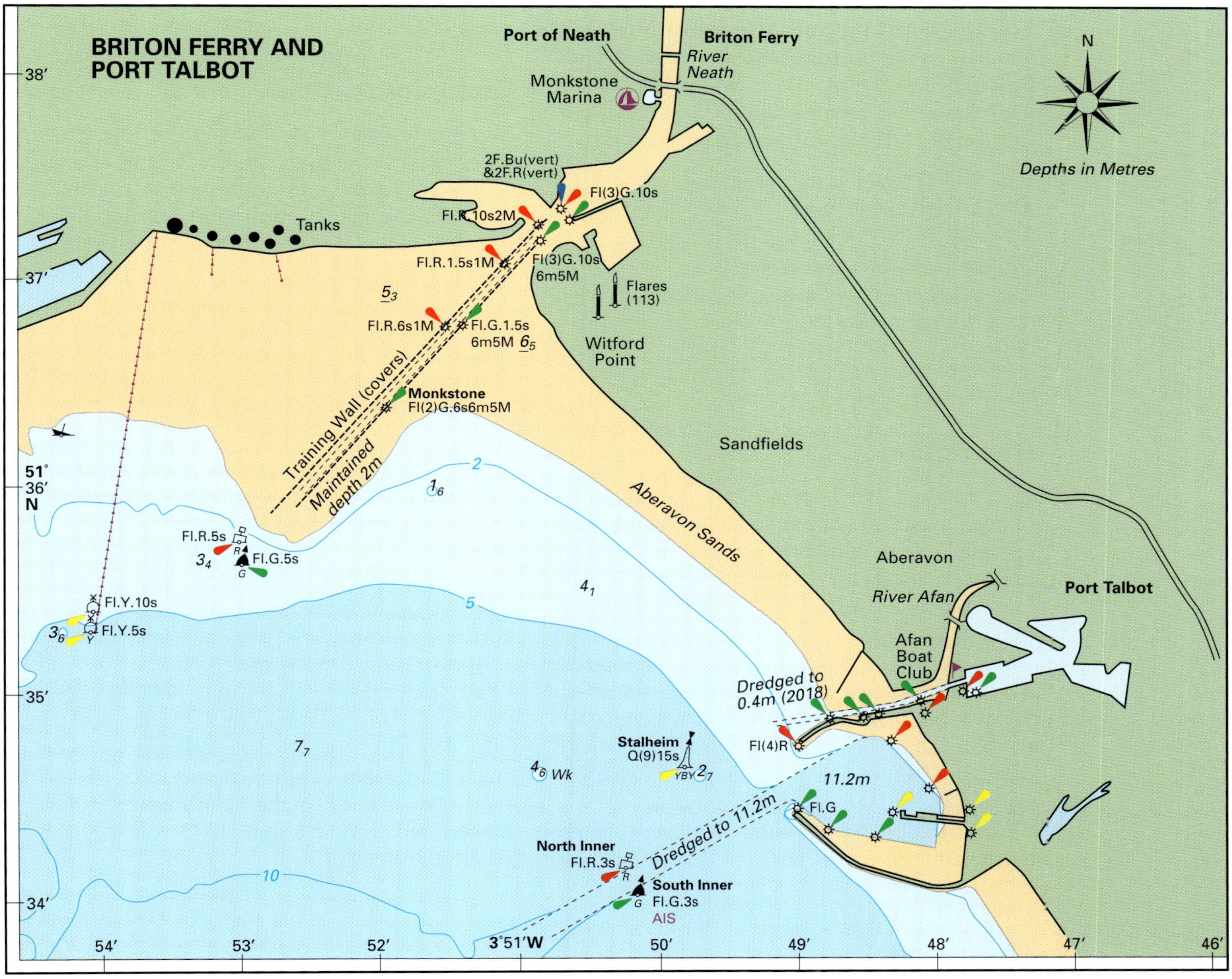

PORT TALBOT

Summary

Port Talbot is 2½ miles southeast of the entrance to the Neath River, on the northeast side of Swansea Bay. Its large tidal harbour serves the huge iron ore terminal that is so prominent on this stretch of coast. The harbour is sheltered by two massive breakwaters and is prohibited to yachts, but close north of this complex is the narrow estuary of the River Afan. The river doesn't quite dry, but is shallow at low springs and the bar at the entrance often breaks. You can normally enter two hours after low water in quiet weather, but the Afan should be avoided in fresh onshore winds. Afan Boat Club have their premises on the east bank and can usually arrange a mooring for visitors.

Tides HW Port Talbot is at HW Milford Haven –0005, or HW Dover –0455. Heights above chart datum: 9.6m MHWS, 1.0m MLWS, 7.3m MHWN, 3.3m MLWN.

Port Control None for the River Afan.

Tidal streams and currents Rates in the northeast corner of Swansea Bay are weak. In the River Afan itself, a spring ebb can reach 3 knots and the flood 1½ knots. Five miles south of Port Talbot entrance, spring streams up to 4 knots run near Kenfig Patches and Hugo Bank.

Description

The iron ore terminal at Port Talbot is an imposing sight from seaward. Steel mills and cooling towers dominate the skyline and the harbour's south breakwater is almost a mile long. Yachts are not allowed into this complex but can use the narrow estuary of the River Afan, close to the north. Entry to the Afan is straightforward from a pilotage point of view, but sufficient rise of tide is needed over the bar and in the immediate approaches you must avoid a wreck with 0.1m over it, which is marked by Stalheim W cardinal buoy.

You can only get less than about half a mile up the Afan River, as far as a weir just below the road bridge. Afan Boat Club is a tiny oasis of boating enthusiasm next to a vast industrial sprawl and its members have some moorings below the bridge where you can stay afloat near neaps. The clubhouse and landing slip are on the east bank, just above the disused entrance lock for the old Port Talbot docks. There are shops about 15mins walk from the slip. The River Afan is not an attractive port of call, but is fascinating to visit when cruising because the club's very existence seems so unlikely in the light of all that stands around it.

Outer approaches

More or less as for Swansea and Briton Ferry, except that the entrance to the River Afan lies just over three miles northeast of Swansea Grounds E cardinal buoy. Approaching from the SSE along the coast from the direction of Porthcawl, pass a mile off Sker Point and a couple of cables east of Kenfig E cardinal buoy. Then make good about 330° for six miles along the coast, aiming to pass about three quarters of a mile off the Port Talbot main breakwater. Having crossed the buoyed entrance channel for Port Talbot harbour near the North Inner red buoy, head north for half a mile to leave Stalheim W cardinal buoy (marking a wreck with 0.1m over it) about a quarter of a mile to starboard. Then turn in eastwards, keeping north of the Stalheim buoy and steering to pass north of the Port Talbot north breakwater.

Approaching from the direction of the Mumbles, make good 4½ miles at 080° from the Swigg buoy, or not quite six miles at 072° from just south of Mixon red buoy, to reach much the same approach position. From Swansea entrance or the Neath outer buoys, simply make good about 107° towards the mouth of the Afan.

Entry

You enter the Afan River at about 082°, leaving to starboard the large north breakwater for the main Port Talbot tidal harbour sometimes called the Lee Breakwater. A much smaller breakwater on the north side of the Afan entrance is left a short cable to port. The channel follows close alongside the starboard-hand breakwater and then turns north opposite the lock gates for the old Port Talbot dock. The Afan Boat Club is just north of this lock on the east side of the river.

Do not approach the Afan any earlier than two hours after low water otherwise depths will be skimpy. In moderate onshore winds the bar will break until well after half-flood. Don't enter the river in fresh onshore winds without local knowledge. If in doubt, the nearer high water you come in, the better.

Entry at night

This is reasonably straightforward in quiet weather. The Port Talbot main breakwater heads are lit, Stalheim W cardinal buoy is lit and there are lights along the Port Talbot 'Lee Breakwater' that you leave to starboard when entering the Afan.

Berths and anchorages

It's usually best to obtain the use of one of the Afan Boat Club moorings. Otherwise anchor in the river clear of the moorings, opposite the disused entrance to the old docks.

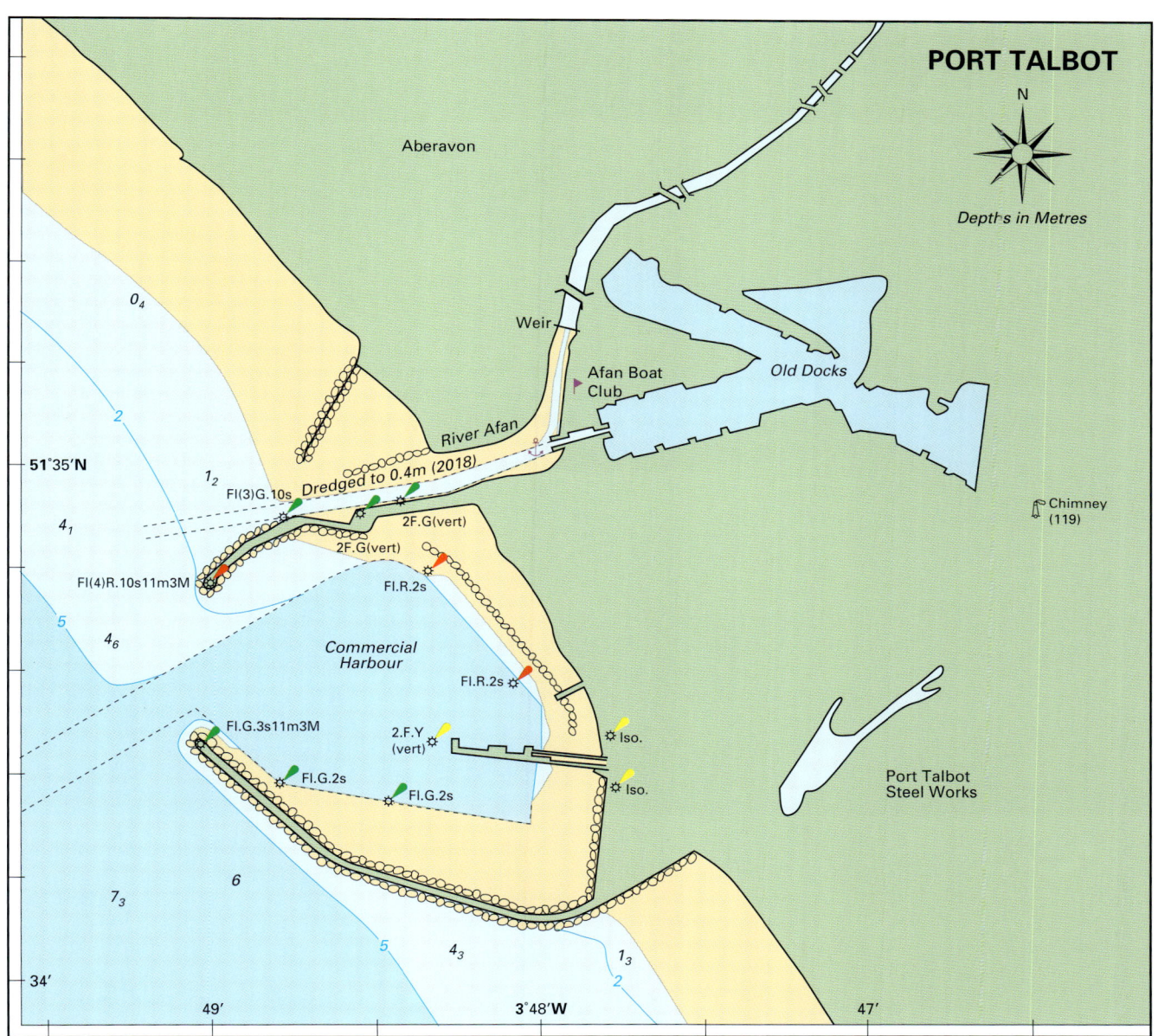

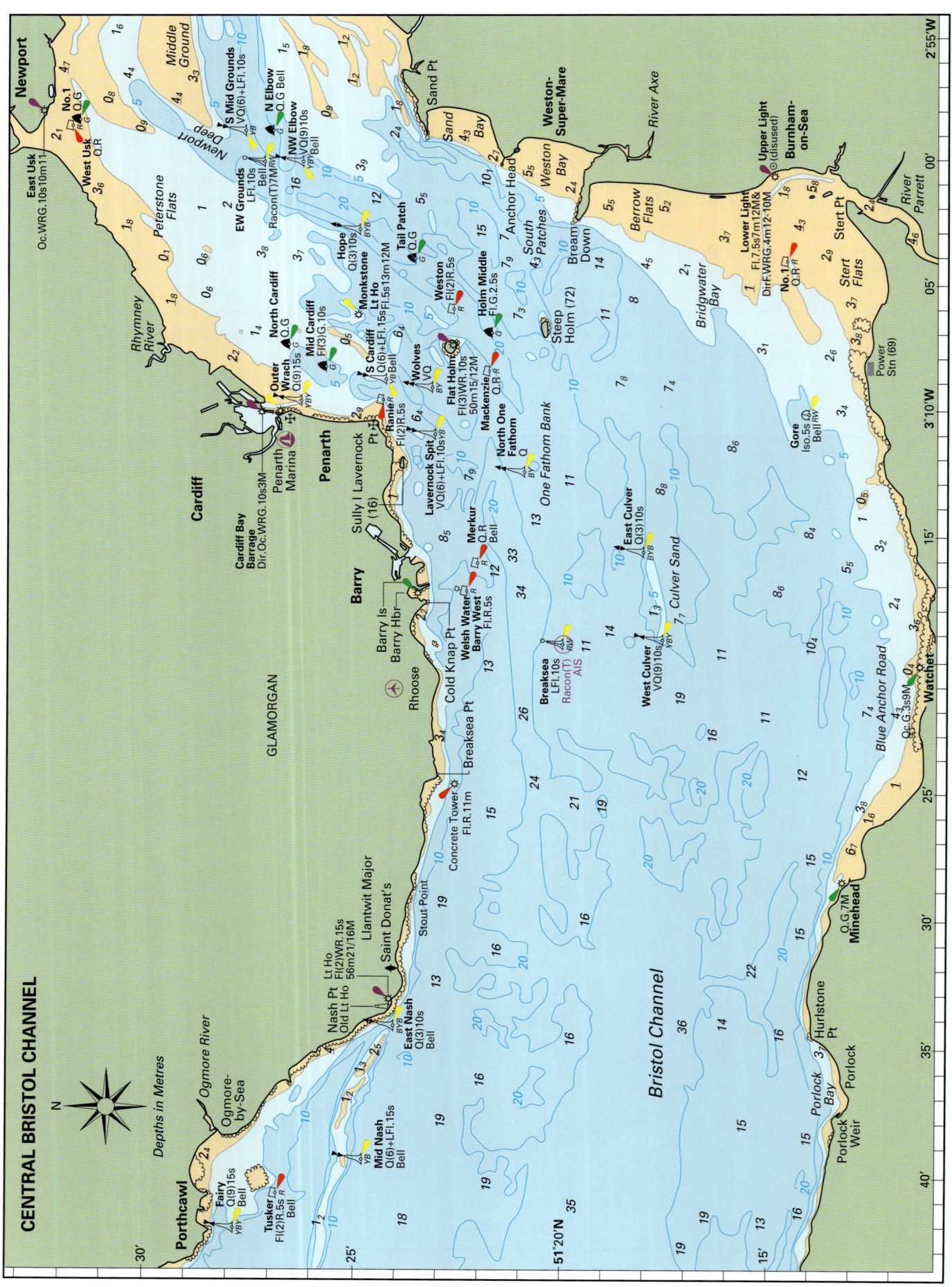

PORTHCAWL

Summary

Porthcawl is a traditional South Wales seaside resort about 12 miles southeast of Swansea entrance. The picturesque harbour area, enclosed by stone piers, has seen considerable developments in the last few years. A lock gate at the entrance has turned the formerly drying harbour into a pleasant marina with 70 berths for both leisure and commercial vessels. It is well protected from the north and west but winds from between east and south send in a nasty surge. The approach is from the southwest, between Porthcawl Point and Fairy Rock W cardinal buoy, before rounding the west breakwater and turning northwest towards the entrance. Seaward of the breakwater, the Bristol Channel tide flows strongly along the coast, reaching six knots at springs.

Tides HW Porthcawl is at HW Milford Haven, or HW Dover –0500. Heights above chart datum are 9.9m MHWS, 1.0m MLWS, 7.5m MHWN, 3.3m MLWN.

Port Control Bridgend County Borough Council. Harbourmaster VHF 80 or ☏ 01656 782756. Porthcawl Marina ☏ 01656 815715, it is essential to contact the marina in advance of visiting. Porthcawl Harbour Boat Club ☏ 01656 782342.

Tidal streams and currents The streams are strong seaward of Porthcawl's west breakwater, setting along the coast roughly WNW on the ebb and ESE on the flood. Spring rates sometimes reach six knots and the approaches can be rough in a weather-going tide. There is often turbulence off the breakwater, especially during the ebb, and heavy overfalls may occur up to 1½ miles west of Porthcawl Point. Avoid being set towards Tusker Rock, an extensive drying reef 1¼ miles southeast of Porthcawl entrance.

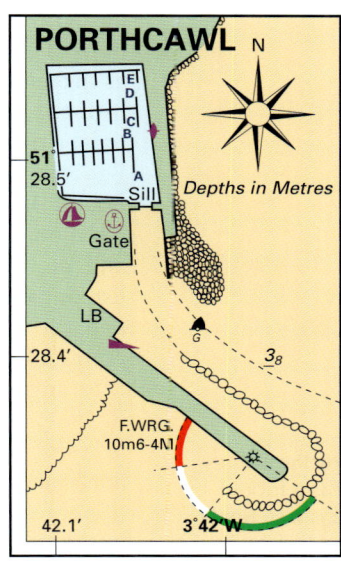

Description

In the middle part of the last century Porthcawl was a busy little coal port, although how even

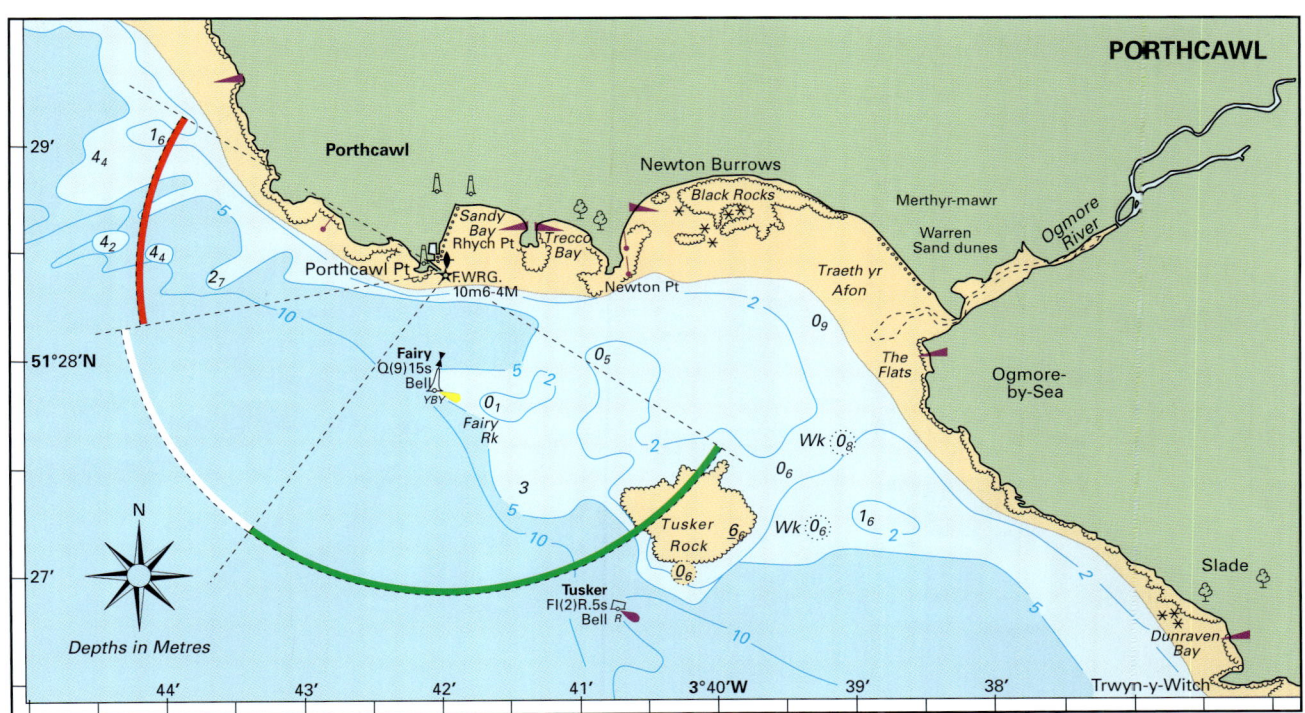

Bristol Channel and Severn Cruising Guide • 47

NORTH COAST

the handiest barges managed to work into the entrance under sail is a mystery to me. Under pressure of competition from Barry and Port Talbot, Porthcawl docks ceased trading in 1906 and the present small harbour, once the outer basin, is all that remains of a much larger complex. The inner basin was filled in after the Second World War to make a car park. No longer a port as such, Porthcawl remains a busy holiday resort and retains its rather traditional style. It's an amiable seaside town where visitors still relax in deckchairs on the beach, buy ice creams, candy floss and proper sticks of rock.

The harbour is near the town centre, which has a good selection of shops, restaurants and pubs. The old Jennings building, built in 1832 as the terminus of a horse-drawn tramway that brought iron and coal to the harbour, has been redeveloped and now houses the Harbour Bar and Kitchen, Coffi Co and Double Zero Pizzas on the ground floor with work/living units on the upper floors. The Custom House and the Old Pilot Lookout Tower, both also listed, have been restored to their former glory and the tower is now appropriately used by National Coastwatch.

Strangers should only make for Porthcawl in quiet weather, since the approaches soon become rough in a weather-going tide. The harbour has a narrow dog-leg entrance and offers good shelter in northerlies and westerlies, but even moderate winds from between east and south will send in an unpleasant swell.

The Salt Water Inn, The Square is popular with visitors and locals alike as is the Lorelei Hotel just off the Esplanade. If you fancy stretching your legs the Jolly Sailor pub in Newton village is worth the walk and you could always get a taxi back.

Outer approaches

Allow for the strong tidal streams when approaching Porthcawl. The entrance lies not quite four miles east of Scarweather Sands and only 1¼ miles northwest of Tusker Rock, a notorious and extensive reef that dries to 4.4m. Tusker Rock uncovers as Porthcawl harbour approaches dry.

Coming from Swansea Bay, the most direct route lies between Sker Point and Kenfig Patches E cardinal buoy, thence keeping a good mile off the coast to avoid the worst overfalls off Hutchwns Point and Porthcawl Point. When Porthcawl west breakwater head is bearing about 075°, steer so as to leave Fairy W cardinal buoy a quarter of a mile to the south and approach Porthcawl. If the overfalls are quiet you can keep closer inshore round Hutchwns Point and follow the coast round eastwards towards Porthcawl.

Coming from the east in moderate weather you may, in quiet weather or if wind and tide are together, approach Porthcawl by cutting inside Nash Sand (see the Swansea chapter for details of the Nash Passage). Stay south of Tusker Rock red can buoy and leave Fairy W

Porthcawl now has a locked basin so boats no longer dry out

PORTHCAWL

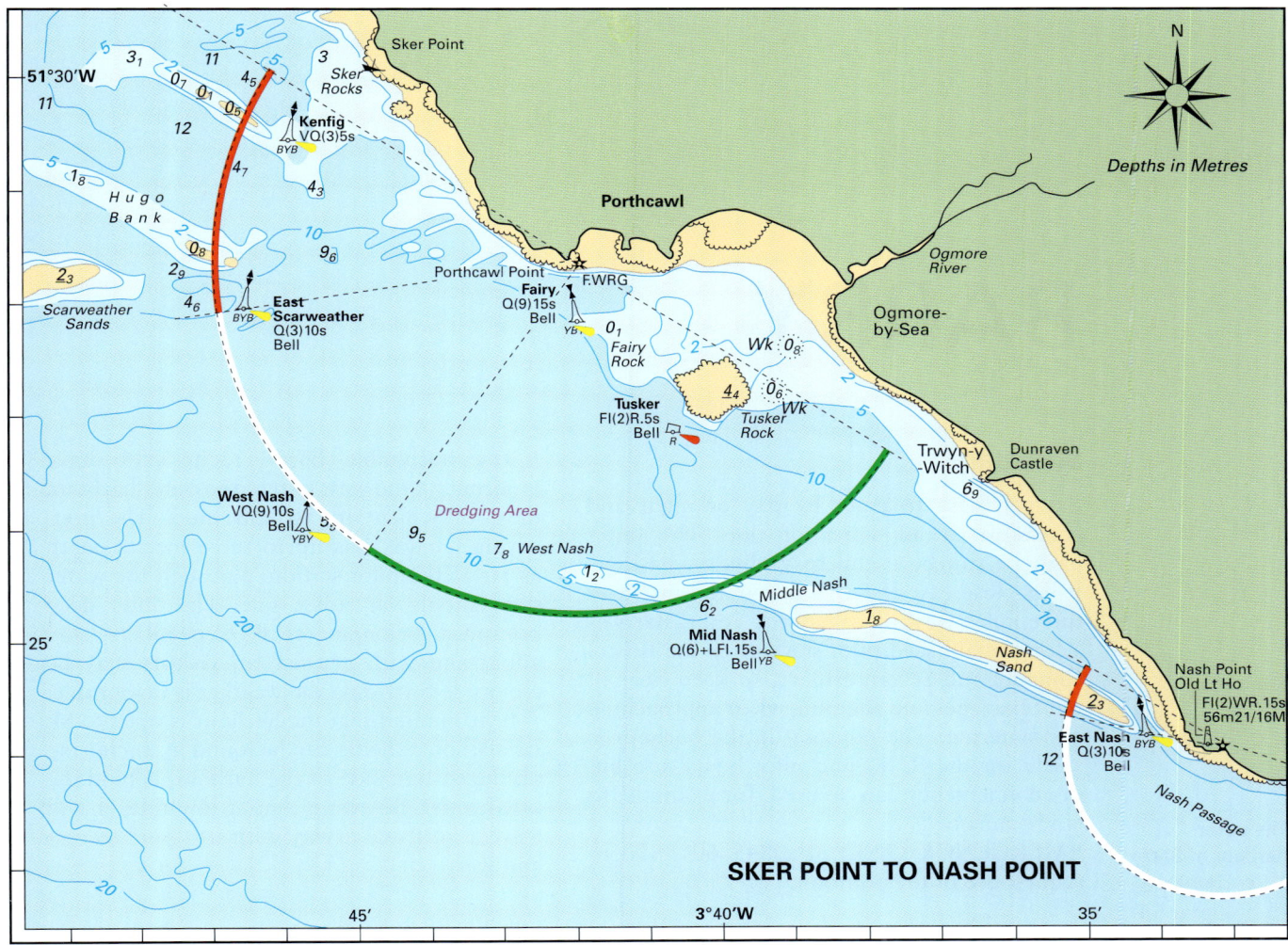

SKER POINT TO NASH POINT

cardinal to the east. Coming from seaward, or from the east if conditions are unsuitable for the Nash Passage, leave West Nash W cardinal buoy a good three quarters of a mile to the east and southeast to avoid the worst overfalls off the end of Nash Sand. Then make good to the ENE for Porthcawl.

Above half-tide, in quiet weather only, the locals cut straight across the West Nash bank west of Mid Nash S cardinal buoy. This can save you up to seven miles when coming from the east, but take the deep-water passage round the West Nash buoy if in doubt about conditions.

Entry

You approach Porthcawl from the southwest, leaving Fairy W cardinal buoy about a quarter of a mile to starboard. There are drying rocky ledges close west of the west breakwater, so only head up for it when the lighthouse bears west of north, distant two cables. Leave the breakwater head close to port, following its line hard along to the northwest for a short way and then turning north off the wide landing slip to leave the beacon at the end of the old collapsed east breakwater to starboard.

The marina is accessible 3 hours each side of HW and there is about 2m depth in the central part of the harbour.

Entry at night

Not recommended for strangers, because of the strong tides off the entrance and the various dangers in the approaches. However, entry is possible using the sector light exhibited from the west breakwater head F.WRG, which leads in between 036–082°. When you are a mile from the entrance stay on the green (east) limit of the white sector, which leaves Fairy W cardinal buoy Q(9)15s about two cables to starboard and clears the rocky ledges to the west of Porthcawl west breakwater.

Berths and anchorages

If you are too early on the tide to enter the harbour there's a temporary anchorage about three cables SSE of Porthcawl west breakwater, but the holding is poor and the current strong. It is best to book a berth in the marina before setting off and then call the harbour master as you are approaching the entrance.

Bristol Channel and Severn Cruising Guide • 49

BARRY

Summary

Barry is easy to enter by day or night and accessible at all states of tide. The outer harbour can be useful to yachts on passage. It lies close east of Barry Island and just over three miles west of Lavernock Point. Barry is a long established pilot station for the Bristol Channel and Severn estuary, so keep clear of pilot launches and shipping when approaching and entering. The pontoon in the harbour is solely for the RNLI and pilot boats' use but in an emergency can be used, for example, to land someone.
EMERGENCY ONLY ☏ 0845 6018870 to request use of the pontoon.

The hospitable Barry Yacht Club have moorings in the west part of the outer harbour, most of which dry to soft mud. The non-drying fairway has up to three metres depth as far as the pilot station, although the water soon shoals on either side. The outer deep moorings, belonging to BYC members, stay afloat and with permission, visitors may lie alongside providing the weather is favourable.

Bear in mind that the harbour is open to SE winds; some shelter can be found by anchoring on the eastern side of the harbour, behind the breakwater. Be aware that at low tides it will leave a narrow fairway with soft mud to east and west.

The outer harbour at Barry
Karen Donkin

Tides HW Barry is at HW Avonmouth −0020 or HW Dover −0435. Heights above chart datum: 11.4m MHWS, 0.9m MLWS, 8.7m MHWN, 3.7m MLWN.

Tidal streams and currents Streams in the offing are strong, particularly west of Barry between Nash and Rhoose Points – spring rates here reach five knots and more or less follow the line of the coast. There's a constant west-going set across the harbour entrance.

Description

Barry began life as a coal port, but the docks later handled a great variety of cargo. The town is less busy than formerly and is some way from the outer harbour, but the closer High Street offers many independent shops and you can find trendy bars and restaurants at the interesting 'Goods Sheds' which are close to Asda, a 15 minute walk from the yacht club.

Barry Yacht Club have their waterside premises next to the old lifeboat slip in the west corner of the outer harbour. There is usually spare space in the harbour, and club members are always ready to help visiting yachts, whether it's to use a vacant mooring or tie up carefully to a moored boat. If you're able to get ashore, the YC's slipway is accessible HW±3. BYC's Compass Bar is open on Thursdays 1930-close; Friday 1830-close; Saturday 1300-1800; Sunday 1200-1900 (closing time at weekends will be later during summer months). Food is available on Friday evenings, and for the best Sunday lunch, from The Lighthouse Catering (☏ 07563 502661 to pre-order), breakfast is available from 1000-1200 on Saturdays (no booking required).

Barry is the headquarters of the Bristol Channel Pilots and Barry Roads is a focus for shipping movements, so keep this in mind when approaching and entering the harbour.

Barry Island, now a peninsula, lies close west of the harbour and was once the haunt of pirates and smugglers. Barry Old Harbour, just west of Barry Harbour is steadily silting up and rarely used.

Outer approaches

Coming along the coast from the west, keep at least six cables off Breaksea Point, well outside the Breaksea power station intake tower Fl.R. Give a similar berth to Rhoose Point and the rocky shallows in the bay just beyond. You'll probably notice traffic in and out of Cardiff Airport, which lies a little way back from the cliffs just west of Rhoose Point, and this stretch of coast also has several prominent tall chimneys. A red can buoy, 'Welsh Water Barry West' Fl.R.5s, lies nine cables off Friars Point, although yachts need not pass outside it.

Knap Point and Friars Point are fairly steep-to and between them is the shallow

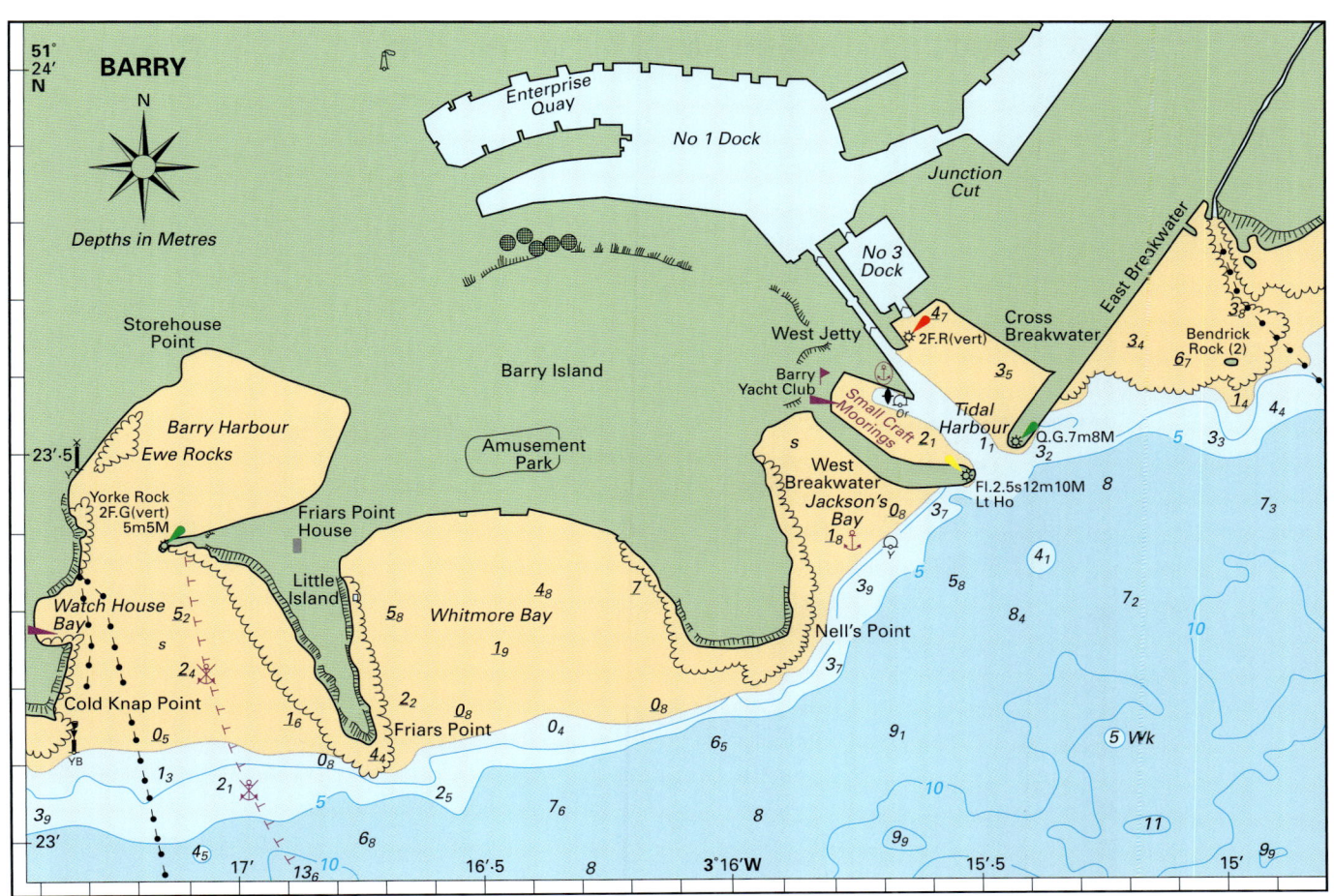

NORTH COAST

Moorings off the Barry Yacht Club
Karen Donkin

entrance to Barry Old Harbour. You then pass Whitmore Bay and the striking seaward-facing red brick houses, some sporting the iconic turrets reminiscent of older houses on Barry Island, on Nell's Point, the southeast corner of Barry Island. Barry harbour breakwaters will now be seen just beyond Nell's Point to the northeast. When making this coastal passage from the west, remember that all headlands between Porthcawl and Barry have strong tidal streams flowing round them. Coming from the east along the coast, say from Penarth, keep

Looking out to the breakwaters at Barry
Karen Donkin

BARRY

outside the Ranie buoy Fl(2)R.5s, half a mile ESE of Lavernock Point. In fresh wind over tide conditions, work offshore to the SSW so as to clear the broken water over Lavernock Spit, the shallow spur extending well over a mile SSW of Lavernock Point whose seaward end is marked by Lavernock Spit S cardinal buoy. If coasting close inshore in quiet weather do not cut inside Sully Island, which lies a mile or so WSW of Lavernock Point and is joined to the mainland by a half-tide causeway. When approaching Barry from the east, stay well seaward of Bendrick Rock, which is 400m ENE of the harbour entrance and never covers.

Approaching Barry directly from the south, there are no navigational dangers for yachts once Culver Sand has been safely cleared. This long narrow bank lies about six miles south of Barry harbour and is nearly two miles from end to end. Culver Sand has depths down to 1.3m and is guarded at its east and west extremities by cardinal buoys. The Breaksea Light, just over 4 miles from Barry entrance is now a safe water mark (LF.10sW) where larger vessels board and land their pilots

Entry

Straightforward, between the east and west breakwaters in a northwesterly direction, but note that the tidal set across the entrance is invariably west-going during both ebb and flood. Once inside the pier heads you'll see the end of the long pier lying in a NW direction

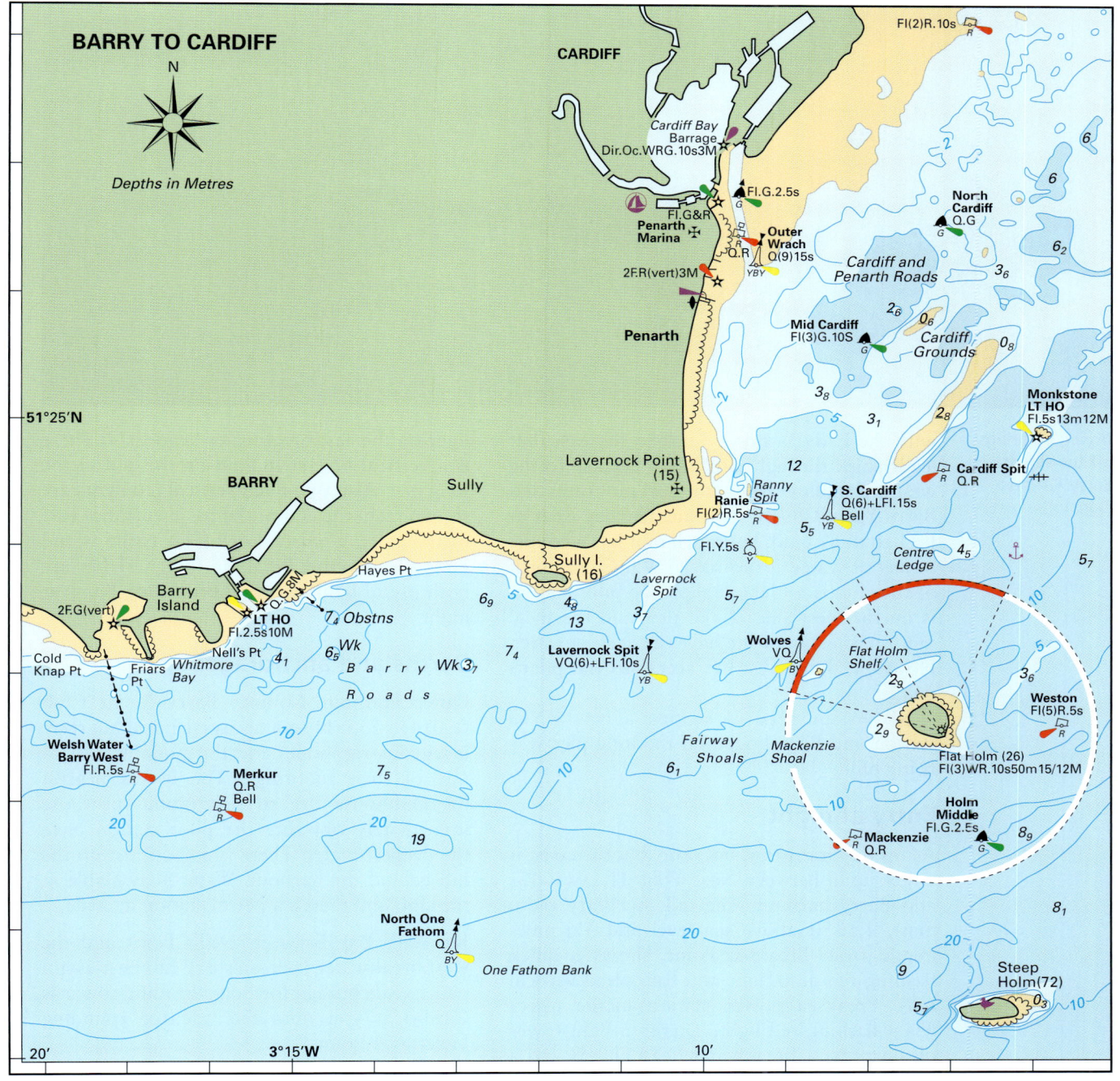

Bristol Channel and Severn Cruising Guide

NORTH COAST

Drying moorings off the slip at Barry *Karen Donkin*

with the Lady Windsor Lock to the east that leads ships through into Barry Docks. To the west is a shallow bay with local moorings and Barry Yacht Club at its head. The bay dries at LAT to thick mud, but much of it has a couple of feet of water at ordinary LWS. Close north of the club is a lifeboat slip. The pilot station is on the west side of the pier and the local moorings just opposite have the deepest water. However, don't obstruct access to the pilot's quay.

NB At the time of writing a new RNLI station and Pilot Lodge on the long pier was being built.

Entry at night

As for daytime entry, but note that the coast is largely unlit between Nash Point Fl(2)WR.15s and Barry harbour. The tall St Hilary radio mast, 1,135ft above sea level and 4½ miles inland from Breaksea Point, shows a quick flashing red aero light and four fixed vertical reds. Breaksea power station intake tower has a flashing red light. There's a light-tower on Barry west breakwater head Fl.2.5s and a light on the east breakwater head Q.G. There is a vertical blue strip light on the end of the long pier. Also two fixed vertical red lights are shown from the end of the basin entrance east of the Lady Windsor Lock. Flat Holm island Fl(3)WR.10s and Breaksea light LFl.10s are both useful lights when approaching Barry at night.

Berths and anchorages

Outer Harbour Contact Barry Yacht Club ☏ 01446 735511 (not always manned but there is an answerphone) for the possible use of one of their moorings. The berths nearest the clubhouse dry to soft mud, but those immediately opposite the pilot station have the deepest water. There is a shop just up the hill behind the harbour. Water is available at the club and there's a petrol station at Asda.

Jackson's Bay Between Nell's Point and the west breakwater Jackson's Bay can be a useful passage anchorage for boats heading towards Cardiff if you miss the tide for rounding Lavernock Point.

National Coastwatch Institution

There are times when it's good to know someone is watching you and, thanks to the National Coastwatch Institution (NCI), that is the case for fishermen, yachtsmen, coast path walkers, windsurfers, swimmers and lots of other people around the coast of England and Wales. From Fleetwood in Lancashire to Filey in Yorkshire, there are 59 stations and nearly 2700 volunteers keeping a watching and listening brief from towers, huts, Martello towers, portacabins and all manner of buildings along the coast.

The NCI came into being in 1994 after a reorganisation of the Coast Guard service ended the physical manning of look-out stations. One tragedy that spurred people to action was when two Cornish fishermen lost their lives within sight of the old Bass Point look-out. With the help of the Sea Safety Group a meeting was held with local people and a voluntary organisation was created which is now NCI. It is a charity run by volunteers and funded entirely by donation, it receives no government support. The Bass Point lookout is leased from the National Trust at a peppercorn rent and became the first NCI station, opening in November 1994.

On a visit to Porthcawl I chatted to a lady in uniform who was sitting by a well-stocked second-hand book stall just below the NCI look-out. Although not on watch duty that day she was busy trying to raise funds as it costs £10,000 or more a year to run each station. The Porthcawl watch post is in a refurbished Victorian look-out tower on the esplanade next to the lifeboat station. The recent improvements to make the harbour a locked basin for yachts has increased the activity afloat and the lovely beaches are a draw for swimmers, jet-skis, kayaks, windsurfers and all types of water sports.

Lying between Cardiff and Swansea close to the notorious Scarweather Sands, Tusker Rock and Nash Sands, Porthcawl is one of the NCIs busiest stations, in 2021 it was involved in 67 incidents. Up in the lookout there is a massive pair of binoculars trained on the Bristol Channel from Swansea about ten miles to the west to Nash Point in the east and across to Minehead in Somerset and Ilfracombe on the north Devon coast. There are no NCI stations along the coast of Somerset and north Devon and this is a busy stretch of water with commercial shipping going up to Avonmouth, Sharpness, Newport, Cardiff and Barry.

In the 'office' there are also four screens linked to CCTV cameras, these monitor the beaches and areas not visible by line of sight from the tower. Many of the volunteers have past experience at sea or with marine services but each one has to complete a training programme before they start to do watches. There is AIS and radar as well to help identify the position of vessels, tracking them is an essential part of the job, as is being able to accurately decipher messages relayed over VHF.

NCI stations are linked electronically to the nearest Coast Guard station, for Porthcawl this is Milford Haven, and any potential incident is reported as the watch-keepers are not authorised to call out the lifeboat themselves. The many rescues are a coordinated effort between NCI, the RNLI, the Coast Guard and Search and Rescue. Fortunately the majority of incidents have happy endings but it is reassuring to know that these dedicated people are keeping *eyes along the coast*.

Stations are manned through the hours of daylight with two staff on duty so it is important there are enough volunteers at each station. Porthcawl has nearly 40 people on their books at the moment but with two people at a time doing four hour watches it is a huge commitment. The NCI does an amazing job helping to 'assist in the protection and preservation of life' around our coasts so it is really important that we all support it in any way we can. Their website, **www.nci.org.uk**, tells the full story and you can volunteer or donate to help continue this impressive organisation.

The busy Coastwatch tower at Porthcawl

CARDIFF BAY

Summary

Converted from Penarth's historic docks in the late 1970s, Penarth Marina lies within the 500-acre lake created by the Cardiff Bay Barrage, whose three sea locks allow 24-hour access. Outbound barrage locks normally work on the hour and half-hour and inbound locks at quarter past and quarter to the hour. Listen on 18 for barrage locking instructions and follow the signal lights carefully. The Penarth Marina has excellent facilities and a calm residential atmosphere. Cardiff Bay Yacht Club has pontoons just on the north shore at the turn into the River Ely and they welcome visitors. Further up the river on the starboard hand is Cardiff Marina. There are also short stay visitors' pontoons in the northeast corner of Cardiff Bay.

Tides HW Penarth is at HW Avonmouth –0015, or HW Dover –0430. Heights above chart datum outside Penarth Lock: 12.2m MHWS, 0.9m MLWS, 9.4m MHWN, 3.6m MLWN. The outer lock sill is 3.5m above chart datum.

Port Control First call *Barrage Control* on VHF 18 or ☏ 02920 700234. Once through the barrage lock call *Penarth Marina* on VHF 80 or ☏ 02920 705021; Cardiff Marina ☏ 02920 396078 or Cardiff Bay Yacht Club ☏ 02920 666627, VHF 37.

Tidal streams and currents Streams in the Cardiff Barrage approaches are moderate, reaching two knots at springs in Cardiff Roads near the buoyed entrance channel. Further out, near Monkstone lighthouse, rates reach four knots at springs. Off Lavernock Point the streams can run up to five knots for the middle two hours of the ebb.

Racing to catch the lock at Cardiff Bay

NORTH COAST

The short stay moorings in Cardiff

Description

The huge and highly successful Cardiff Bay Barrage project, completed in April 2000, involved building a 1.1km dam between Penarth and Cardiff docks, shutting out the powerful Bristol Channel tides and creating a 500-acre freshwater lake in place of the gloomy drying mud. This sheltered expanse has helped regenerate thousands of acres of industrial wasteland and Cardiff's smart new eight-mile waterfront is now fringed with prestigious commercial headquarters, leisure complexes and government buildings, including the Welsh National Assembly.

The barrage itself has three large locks, each 40m long by 10.5m wide, and fish pass safely through specially designed sluices. The barrage has completely changed the atmosphere of Cardiff Bay, making it an attractive cruising destination and improving the whole feel of the area. The new retained depths also allow boats to venture safely up the River Ely, which is a freshwater nature reserve.

Penarth occupies a pleasant position on the south side of Cardiff Bay and its attractive seafront faces up the Severn estuary, sheltered from the prevailing westerlies. Penarth is a traditional Welsh seaside town that still has signs of its Victorian and Edwardian heydays. Its famous pier opened in 1895 to encourage paddle-steamers across the Bristol Channel. Old photographs of Penarth show these flamboyant vessels backing and filling off the pier, packed with day-trippers from Bristol and Weston-super-Mare. The tradition continues as the elegant 1940s motor vessel *Balmoral* runs Channel cruises from Penarth Pier. The beach and pier are popular during the season, but the tourism is never frantic. Penarth Yacht Club have their elegant premises at the south end of the Esplanade, and ships pass close by on their way to and from Cardiff Docks.

Penarth Marina has matured over the years and its waterside houses and apartments give the place a restful, residential atmosphere. The facilities are excellent and there's plenty of room for visitors. You can eat well at La Marina on the first floor of the Custom House, while on the ground floor is the popular Spanish style brasserie El Puerto.

As you turn into the River Ely the Cardiff Bay Yacht Club has pontoons on the starboard hand and visitors can moor on the wave-breaker pontoon at the eastern end. Slightly further upstream you arrive at Cardiff Marina, part of the Marine Group, in the International Boat Village. As well as all the normal facilities you would expect they can sort out most boating problems with engineers, mechanics, sailmakers etc available through the service centre. A pedestrian and cyclists bridge, Pont y Werin, with 4.5m clearance crosses the river about halfway through the marina so this has to be opened for masted yachts to access the upper part. Contact Barrage Control on VHF 18 to ask for the bridge to be lifted.

Outer approaches

The approaches to Cardiff Bay are fairly straightforward, Cardiff Grounds bank being the main danger in the offing. Coming from the south or west, clear Lavernock Point by three-quarters of a mile and pass midway between Ranie red can buoy and South Cardiff S cardinal bell buoy. Then make good about 352° for two miles for the Wrach approach channel to Cardiff Bay, steering to leave Penarth Pier a good two cables to port and the Outer Wrach W cardinal buoy close to starboard.

Coming from further up the Severn estuary via Bristol Deep, stay well south of Monkstone lighthouse and continue WSW for 1¾ miles to leave Cardiff Spit red buoy a couple of cables to the north and South Cardiff S cardinal buoy close to the north. Then make good about 345° for two miles for the Outer Wrach W cardinal buoy. Approaching Penarth from the northeast, say from Newport or the River Rhymney, most boats would pass between Cardiff Grounds and Cardiff Flats, entering Cardiff and Penarth Roads near the North Cardiff green buoy and then making directly for the Outer Wrach W cardinal buoy.

Strong winds from the east can make it choppy approaching the barrage, although Cardiff Grounds and Cardiff Flats serve as partial breakwaters from that quarter. In heavy easterly weather try to arrive off the barrage soon after half-flood, when you'll have plenty of water in the approach channel but there will not be enough depth over the outer banks to erode their protection.

The inner basin at Penarth Marina

Entry

From the Outer Wrach W cardinal buoy, follow the dredged Wrach channel just west of north for a short half mile, leaving Penarth Head red can buoy close to port. About 300m beyond this buoy you turn off to port along a shallow channel towards the barrage locks, leaving to port two red buoys and to starboard first the red-green-red Barrage buoy and then No. 3 green buoy. Passing between two overlapping breakwaters, you'll see the three large barrage locks straight ahead.

The dredged Wrach shipping channel carries plenty of depth for yachts at any tide, while the smaller spur off to the barrage locks will be deep enough for most boats except at dead low springs. If in doubt about depths in the barrage lock channel, call Barrage Control on VHF 18.

Barrage Traffic Signals

Traffic lights are located on each of the three barrage locks and their signals should be carefully followed:
- Three vertical flashing reds – Emergency. Stop and contact *Barrage Control*
- Three vertical reds – Do not enter lock
- Three vertical greens – Enter lock
- Green, white, green – Enter lock on instruction from *Barrage Control*

Once clear of the barrage locks, turn immediately to port for the marina entrance and call *Penarth Marina* on VHF 80. The water level in the marina is normally held at the same level as Cardiff Bay so you should be able to enter or leave the marina on 'free flow' and avoid locking. Normally vessels will be able to proceed straight through the lock into the marina basin, but watch out for a slight flow within the marina lock area. If, however, the water level within the bay has dropped significantly, you may have to lock into the marina conventionally.

Marina Traffic Signals

- Two red lights – Danger, keep clear of lock.
- Single red light – Lock in use, keep clear.
- Green light – Enter lock on instruction from marina staff.

Entry at night

Monkstone lighthouse Fl.5s is a key mark when approaching from the east and Flat Holm island Fl(3)WR.10s when approaching from the south and west. The red sectors of Flat Holm shine over Cardiff Grounds to the north and over Wolves Rock (dries 2m) to the northwest and the various shoals off Lavernock Point. Wolves Rock is also guarded by a N cardinal buoy VQ.

All the buoys mentioned under 'outer approaches' are lit. Off Lavernock Point, which is unlit, it's important to pass between Ranie red buoy Fl(2)R.5s and South Cardiff S cardinal Q(6)&LFl.15s. Then make directly for the Outer Wrach W cardinal Q(9)15s, picking up the Wrach channel sector light whose white sector leads in between 347–350°. The Wrach channel and barrage channel buoys are all lit and show the way in.

Berths and anchorages

Penarth Marina Penarth Marina is now part of the Boatfolk group, there is plenty of space in two large basins linked by a short channel crossed by a swing-bridge. Facilities are excellent and comprehensive. Diesel and petrol at the fuel berth next to the travel-hoist ramp in the inner basin. It's not far to walk into Penarth town, which has plenty of good shops, pubs and bistros.

River Ely Just north of Penarth Marina, the River Ely joins the southwest corner of Cardiff Bay opposite the barrage locks. Once a drying muddy estuary, the Ely now has plenty of water at all tides. Visitors can arrange to moor

Locking out of Cardiff Bay

CARDIFF BAY

alongside pontoons either at Cardiff Bay Yacht Club ☎ 02920 666627 near the river mouth on the north bank, or at Cardiff Marina ☎ 02920 396078, a quarter of a mile upstream on the same side. At Cardiff Bay Yacht Club, visitors berth on the seaward side of 'A' pontoon, the first pontoon you reach coming into the river.

Cardiff Bay Just below the road bridge across the River Taff the Cardiff Yacht Club has its club ☎ 02920 463697.

Cardiff short-stay berths Cardiff Harbour Authority provides day visitor pontoon berths in the northeast part of Cardiff Bay, near the attractive city waterfront. These pontoons are opposite the Roald Dahl Plass near the Oval Basin, and also directly in front of the conspicuous red brick Pier Head building. There's no need to book a short stay berth because the system works just like a car park. You obtain a 'pay and display' ticket on the pontoons, up to a maximum 24 hours, and the access number for the gate is printed on the ticket.

For environmental reasons there are aeration pipes on the seabed within the barrage so anchoring is not permitted anywhere in Cardiff Bay.

Top left: There's always lots of activity in Cardiff Bay

Top right: One of the three locks in the Cardiff Barrage

Bottom left: Ivor Novello was born in Cardiff

Bottom right: The lower basin at Penarth Marina

Flat Holm and Steep Holm

As their names suggest these two small islands between Cardiff and Weston-super-Mare in the narrowing upper reaches of the Bristol Channel are indeed one flat and one steep. Geologically they are carboniferous limestone and probably the extremities of the Mendip Hills. They are now both nature reserves but each has an intriguing and colourful history. Occupation of the islands can be traced back to Stone Age times and, as with Lundy, the Vikings used the islands when they came on raiding forays up the Bristol Channel. During the Middle Ages there were monastic settlements on them and in the 6th century each island had its resident saint, St Cadoc on Flat Holm and St Gildas on Steep Holm.

Inevitably the islands were used for smuggling and piracy over the years. It is said that in the 18th century the Revenue men knew what was going on but had no boat to reach the islands and confiscate the contraband. A cave on the east cliff of Flat Holm was supposed to be a store for tea and brandy.

The Vikings were not the only people to recognise the strategic location of the Holms and in Victorian times they were fortified, part of Palmerston's coastal defence which ran from Brean in Somerset to Lavernock Point in Glamorgan. Four batteries were built on Flat Holm and six on Steep Holm and although they were dismantled in the late 1800s they were refortified during the Second World war and can still be seen today.

Flat Holm it almost circular and extends to about 35ha (85ac) with a highest point of 32m (105ft). It is part of the City and County of Cardiff which runs the Flat Holm Project. The first lighthouse here was manned from December 1737, 25 tons of coal a month was needed to keep the light going. Trinity House took the light over in 1819, raising the height by 5ft in 1825 to create the current prominent structure. A larger light was installed in 1867 which was converted to electricity in 1969 and now runs on solar power.

Other buildings on the island include the old farmhouse, which was turned into a hotel at the turn of the 20th century but was not a success. It has now been made into accommodation for visitors to the island. There is also a pub on Flat Holm, the Gull and Leek. Rare plants growing on the island include the wild peony, wild leeks, rock lavender and dove's-foot crane's-bill. Many sea birds breed here and there is a large population of slow worms.

Steep Holm is part of Somerset and from the air looks a bit like a mouse without a tail. It is just under 20ha (nearly 50ac) but increases by about a quarter at low water springs. The island rises to 78m (256ft) but has no lighthouse. Since 1976 it has been owned and run by the Kenneth Allsop Memorial Trust as a nature reserve.

Evidence has been found of Roman occupation with coins, pottery and what might have been a watch tower. In the 12th and 13th centuries rabbits were bred on the island for both meat and fur, to trim noblemen's clothing. In the 1700s Steep Holm was an important fishing community, supplying the Bristol fish market with about half a ton of fish a day.

Derelict houses on Steepholm *Mark Harris*

For several centuries title to the island was hotly disputed by various strains of the de Beauchamp family and the Seymours, who were also relatives. Steep Holm now seems to be in good hands and the mission statement of the Trust is: 'To protect, preserve and enhance for the benefit of the public the landscape, antiquities, flora, fauna, natural beauty and scientific interest of the island of Steep Holm in the County of North Somerset and to advance the education of the public in the natural sciences.' As well as being a nature reserve and bird sanctuary Steep Holm is a SSSI and home to rare plants, including the wild peony as on Flat Holm.

Getting there

Although it is possible to anchor off either of the islands it is not to be recommended and boats certainly shouldn't be left unattended. To really enjoy the away-from-it-all and otherness it is best to arrive by RIB from Cardiff or Weston-super-Mare. For details of timetables and prices checkout **www.bayislandvoyages.co.uk**, ☎ 07393 470476.

Flatholm with its lighthouse *Mark Harris*

Off Penarth town In settled westerly weather you can anchor off Penarth itself, about a quarter of a mile southeast of the Penarth Yacht Club landing slip, in about two metres least depth over mud and sand. Make sure you are well inside the shipping fairway and show a riding light at night. This anchorage is well sheltered from the west and northwest and can be convenient if you are bound up the estuary and want to leave Penarth just before low water.

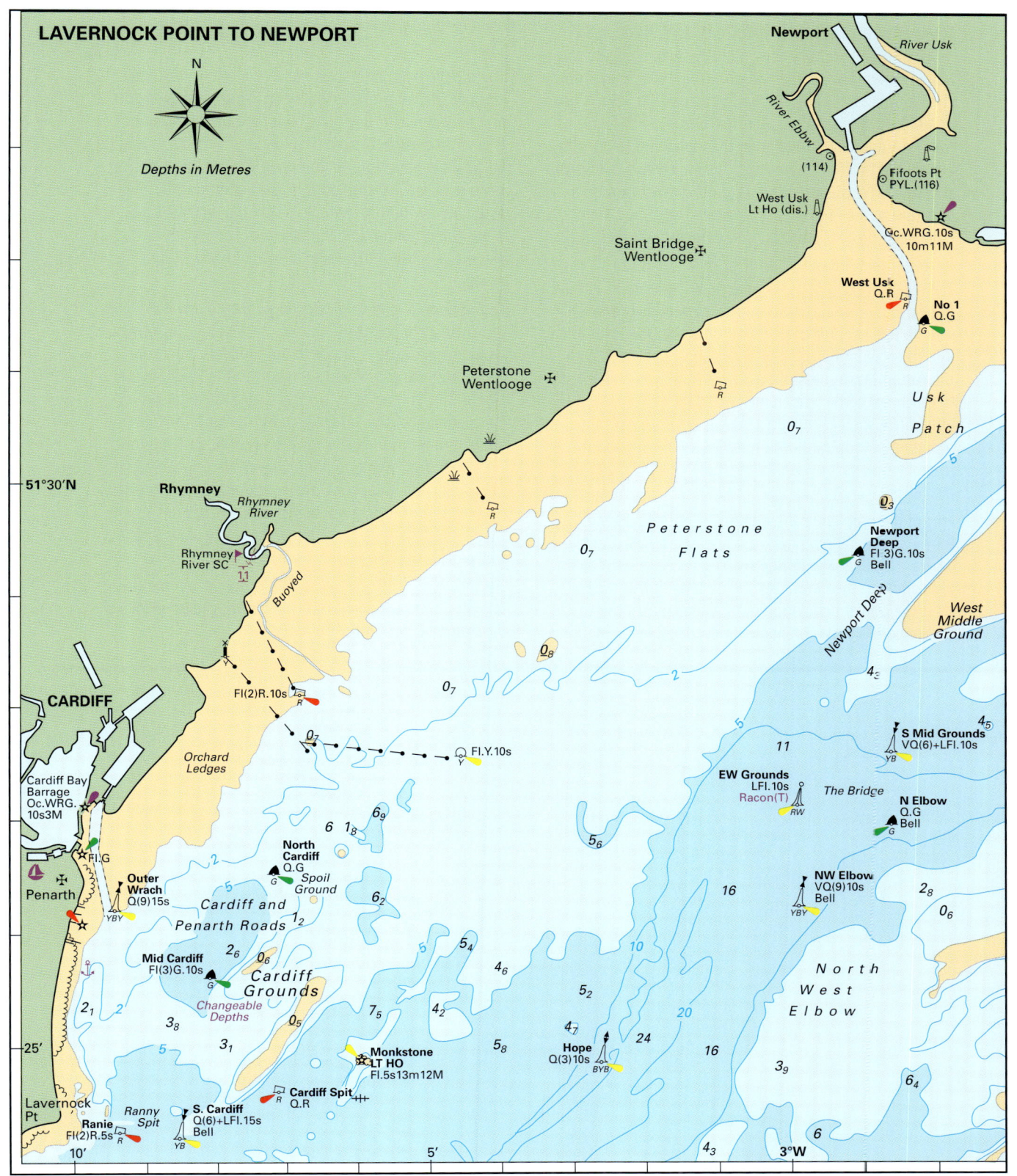

Bristol Channel and Severn Cruising Guide

Harnessing the tides

One headline runs 'Tidal energy from the estuary could generate seven percent of the UK's energy needs'. So the possibility of a barrage across the Bristol Channel is on the radar again.

Proposals to harness the energy of the enormous tidal range in the Bristol Channel, globally second only to the Bay of Fundy, have come and gone for a very long time. The first plan for a physical barrier across the Severn was in 1849. At that time the objective was more for ease of transport and flood prevention than anything to do with energy but by 1925 there was a scheme that would have seen 800 MW of electricity being generated through a structure at the English Stones. Since the 1930s there have been probably eight or ten different schemes put forward.

The most recent proposals were finally shelved in 2013, principally on environmental impact grounds but there was no real support for the plan from the UK Government and three separate committees of MPs rejected it. With the current awareness of climate change and policies to reach net zero carbon emissions the demand for alternative sources of electricity has encouraged a grouping of local authorities, the Western Gateway, to formulate plans for yet another study into the feasibility of a scheme.

Part of the problem is the number of possible locations for a barrage, ranging from the English Stones, roughly where the old Seven Bridge crosses, to as far west as Ilfracombe to the Gower. As the barrage moves further west the power generation potential increases but so do the possible environmental impact problems. The most frequently promoted location seems to be from Brean Down, on the Somerset coast, to Lavernock Point which would effectively enclose Flat Holm and Steep Holm. Suggestions range from fixed barrages across the estuary to tidal 'fences' or lagoons in selected areas of the Channel.

There have been proposals put forward to create tidal lagoons in Swansea Bay, between Cardiff and Newport and in Bridgwater Bay but at the time of writing none of them had been approved. The long term effect on wildlife, particularly fish migration and populations, have not yet been exhaustively studied so there are many unknowns associated with this technology. On the positive side it has the potential to generate reliable supplies of electricity without the uncertainties of wind or solar power.

Environmental and wildlife groups, particularly the RSPB, are strongly opposed to most of these plans, any of which would cause huge changes to the mudflats, intertidal zones and fish movement to and from the River Severn. About 75,000 migratory birds are said to winter on the wetlands of the Severn estuary, nearly 17,000ha of which is a Ramsar site so the area is of huge importance both nationally and internationally. Quite unimaginable quantities of mud and silt move around the river on every tide, bringing food for numerous different species so any man-made structure that affects the tide will also impact this precious habitat.

Balancing all the competing demands is an enormously complex and sensitive problem which has to be resolved very carefully for future generations.

RHYMNEY RIVER

Summary

The Rhymney River is a narrow, winding tidal pill about three miles northeast of Cardiff Bay. The approaches dry for a mile offshore at LAT and strangers should only enter near high water. There is a small but active local club a little way up the river – Rhymney River Motor Boat, Sail and Angling Club. The immediate surroundings can seem rather bleak, close to the Cardiff Docks link road with a steel works not far away. But the river flows through wild marshland and has a curiously restful atmosphere. In quiet weather it makes an interesting call for small, shoal-draft boats and visitors are always made welcome.

Tides HW in the Rhymney River is at HW Avonmouth –0015, or HW Dover –0430. Approximate heights above datum: 12.1m MHWS, 0.6m MLWS, 9.2m MHWN, 3.3m MLWN.

Port Control None. The local moorings are administered by the Rhymney River Motor Boat, Sail and Angling Club. Members are sometimes listening on VHF 16 within a couple of hours of high water.

Tidal streams and currents The streams in the immediate approaches can reach 2–3 knots at springs, flowing more or less along the line of the coast and thus directly across the entrance channel.

Description

The Rhymney River is an unusual little backwater a few miles up the Severn estuary from Cardiff and Penarth. Its narrow mouth faces southeast and may be approached by pioneering mariners near high water by way of a sinuous channel across broad, off-lying mudflats. This channel is kept buoyed by the members of the Rhymney River Motor Boat, Sail and Angling Club, whose small clubhouse stands on the west bank of the river about half a mile up from the entrance. The members' boats are generally under 25ft and of shallow draught, and these should also be the main qualifications for any visiting craft.

Although the nearby steel works lend a rather gloomy aspect to the Rhymney, the river flows through wild, marshy scrubland and the club moorings represent a pocket haven of peace and quiet amidst the industrial outskirts of Cardiff. The river actually flows quite a long way to reach the Bristol Channel and forms

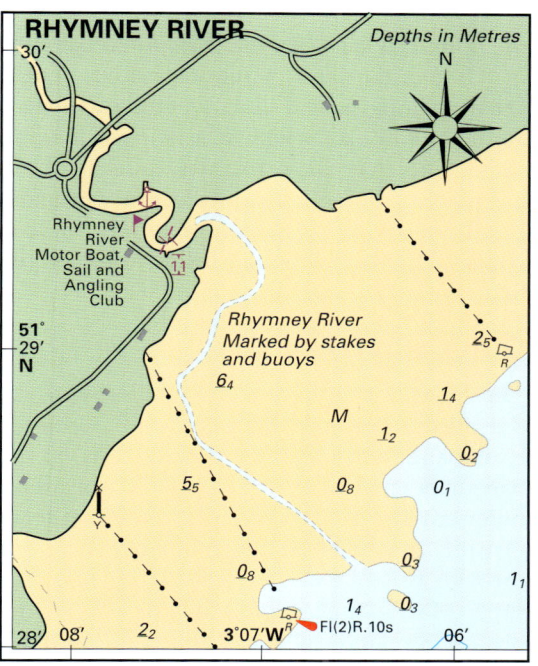

High and dry
Stuart Robertson

Bristol Channel and Severn Cruising Guide • 65

NORTH COAST

It's a long way down at low water Stuart Robertson

the boundary between the traditional counties of Glamorgan and Monmouthshire. There are no shops nearby, but water is available at the clubhouse, which has its own landing stage. The river dries to thick mud at about half-ebb. Although it's unwise to approach the Rhymney in fresh onshore winds, there is good shelter once you are inside and past the first bend.

Outer approaches

The North Cardiff green conical buoy marks the north extremity of the Cardiff Grounds banks and, lying about 1¾ miles SSW of the Rhymney channel entrance, serves as a useful outer fairway buoy if you are coming up from Cardiff. If you are coming down the Severn through Bristol Deep or across from Weston-super-Mare, make instead for a yellow obstruction buoy which lies about 1.4 miles at 120° from the Rhymney channel entrance.

The tide is critical when entering the Rhymney and strangers shouldn't arrive off the outer buoys until an hour before high water. Therefore it's unusual for boats to approach the river directly from the east via Bristol Deep, as the flood will have been running strongly up-Channel for nearly five hours. Conversely, if you lock out of Cardiff Bay about 1½ hours before high water, you'll be well placed to take the last of the flood up towards the Rhymney. Don't try to enter the river in fresh winds from between east and south.

Entry

To reach the outer buoys of the Rhymney channel entrance, make good 1.8 miles at 015° from North Cardiff green buoy, or 1.4 miles at 300° from the yellow obstruction buoy out in the offing. The obstruction, a pipeline, is no hazard for small boats near high water. A useful landmark ashore is a conspicuous pumping station some way down-Channel of the river entrance. The top of this building is mostly glass and often looks like a white band from seaward.

Tracking towards WGS84 waypoint 51°28´.256N 03°06´.483W, you'll soon pick up the first of the Rhymney club buoys, a small green can left close to starboard. About three cables to port you'll see a larger red can buoy marking the end of a sewer outfall. This buoy has nothing directly to do with the Rhymney entrance channel, although it's a useful guide in the approach (there are a number of similar sewer buoys along this stretch of coast and you should not pass to landward of them). Continue to the northwest past two more green cans, the second of which is paired with a red-and-white post. Now turn northeast to follow the line of the shore, passing between two pairs of green-and-white and red-and-white posts, known locally as the No. 4 gates.

Now turn almost due east for a short way, leaving No. 5 red can buoy to port and another green-and-white post to starboard. The channel finally swings to the NNW and you now steer straight for the entrance. Aim to leave a 'Dayglo' red triangular beacon on the east bank to starboard, before turning hard-a-port into the river.

On this last leg before reaching the mouth, avoid being set up-Channel to the northeast. On this side of the entrance the bottom is foul with dangerous metal stakes. Once inside the river keep to the middle, following to starboard round the first bend and fetching up in the reach opposite the clubhouse.

Entry at night

On no account should strangers attempt to enter the Rhymney River at night. Although the North Cardiff buoy is lit Q.G, as is the yellow obstruction buoy Fl.Y.10s, the club buoys and post are all unlit and it's virtually impossible to pick up the entrance channel.

Berths and anchorages

You can anchor anywhere in the river providing you keep clear of local moorings, but the best stretch is just opposite the clubhouse. Because the river is narrow it's best either to anchor fore-and-aft, or to run out a kedge to make a standing moor. The Rhymney dries out to thick mud soon after half-ebb.

NEWPORT AND THE RIVER USK

Summary

The River Usk flows into the Severn estuary almost nine miles northeast of Cardiff Bay and a similar distance WNW of Portishead Marina. The mouth faces south and is fringed with drying mudflats, but a buoyed fairway leads as far as Newport Docks and there's plenty of water in the entrance above half-tide. Keep clear of ships using the fairway. Yachts aren't allowed into the docks, but Newport and Uskmouth Sailing Club have their premises further upriver on the south bank, just over half a mile up from the dock entrance and two miles in from the outer buoys. The area is heavily industrial and the Usk dries most of its width to dubious looking mud, but a narrow channel in midstream affords a reasonable anchorage off the club at all but very low spring tides.

Tides HW Newport is at HW Avonmouth −0015, or HW Dover −0430. Heights above chart datum: 12.1m MHWS, 0.2m MLWS, 9.0m MHWN, 2.9m MLWN.

Port Control Newport Docks are run by Associated British Ports, but yachts in the river are not subject to port control.

Tidal streams and currents Spring streams offshore can reach 4–5 knots in Bristol Deep and 3–4 knots in Newport Deep, giving a tricky cross-set if you approach the Usk near half-tide. The streams in the river itself can also reach 4–5 knots at springs, particularly on the ebb. It's generally preferable to enter the Usk a little before HW slack.

Description

The Usk is a long river, starting its seaward journey in wild, mountainous country on the western edge of the Brecon Beacons. Unfortunately for coastal boat owners, the last few miles through industrial Newport are the least attractive. At low tide near the town bridges, all that remains of the Usk is a narrow, murky stream winding between factories and steep banks of mud. It's difficult to believe that, far upstream, fine salmon lurk in clear pools.

However, further down near the mouth of the Usk the river feels more open and rural, despite the great brick building and prominent chimney of Uskmouth power station on the south shore. Just upstream from the power station, at the mouth of a drying creek known as St Julian's Pill, the hospitable Newport and Uskmouth Sailing Club have their premises, built by the members years ago and gradually improved and developed into a well organised and landscaped site with a sizeable boat park. The club has lines of drying moorings in the river and a pontoon juts out downstream from the clubhouse. Visitors can lie alongside this pontoon, which starts to dry soon after half-ebb. There's another pontoon in St Julian's Pill, opposite a row of moored yachts. Fin-keeled boats can moor safely alongside the Pill pontoon, settling into deep soft mud as the tide falls, but be careful of the overhead power cables nearby.

Club members have built their own slipway and can launch and recover boats using a mini travel-lift, a Wise 'boat-handler' trailer towed by a tractor. Although on a grey day at low water the surroundings look unpromising as a cruising base, in sunny weather with the tide up this stretch of the Usk feels spacious and attractive, despite the rather austere views across to the docks just opposite. Visitors calling here will find good shelter, secure holding and a warm welcome at the club, which has a comfortable well-stocked bar. Shops aren't easily accessible and the club lies within a fenced complex owned by Uskmouth power station, so you need to be self-sufficient in stores. However, visitors can come and go through the main power station entrance, which is always manned by a security guard. It's about a mile walk down West Nash Road to Nash village, where the Waterloo Inn in St Mary's Road keeps some fine beers and does excellent bar meals. If you take a taxi into Newport itself, the Monusk Tapas and Wine Bar on Millennium Walk, ☏ 07496 725246, has a great riverside setting and contemporary food.

NORTH COAST

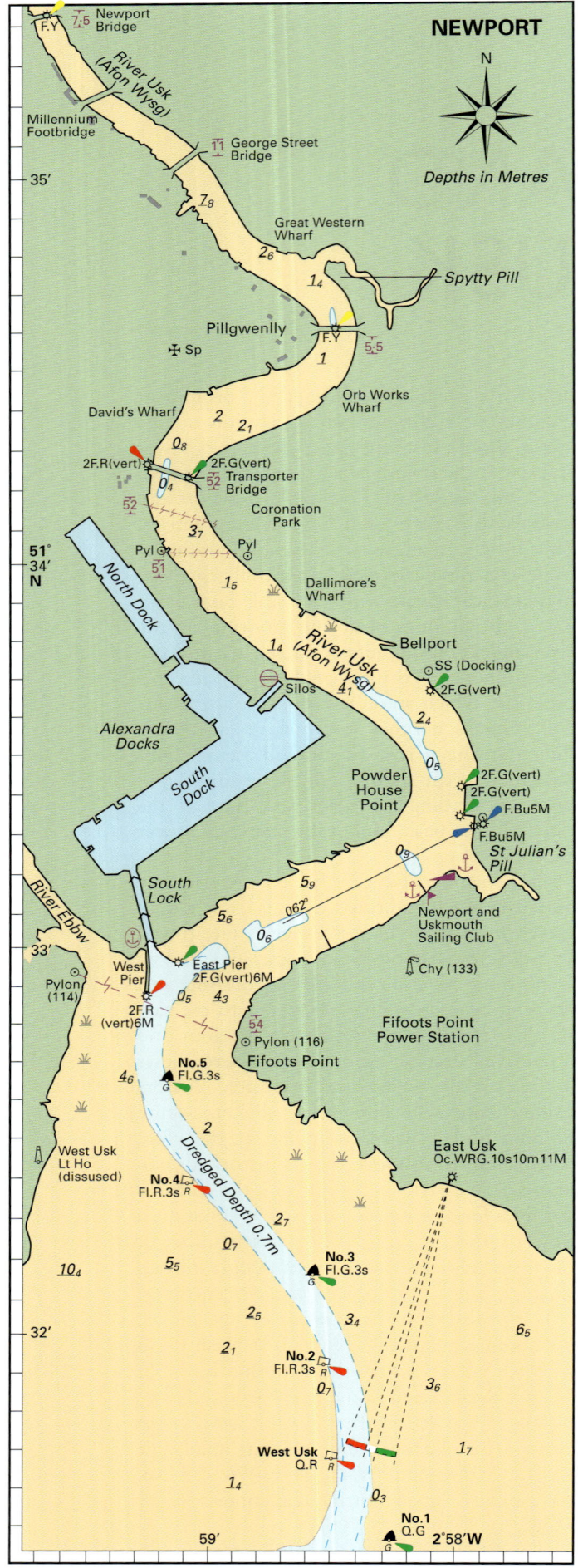

Outer approaches

The Usk entrance is fringed with mud. In the offing, to the south and east, are the extensive drying sandbanks known as the Usk Patch, Welsh Hook, Middle Grounds and Welsh Grounds. The first three are mostly covered above half-tide, but parts of the Welsh Grounds dry to over 5m. Local boats sail over these banks when the tide serves, especially when bound to and from the east, but strangers should stick to the channels except in quiet weather near high water.

Five miles south of the mouth of the Usk, the main Severn channel divides near the English and Welsh Grounds fairway buoy. Bristol Deep leads upstream towards Avonmouth and Newport Deep turns northeast towards the Welsh shore. Newport Deep green conical buoy, guarding the southwest extremity of the Usk Patch bank, serves as the outer mark for approaching the Usk. Below half-tide, while the Middle and Welsh Grounds are uncovered, the powerful streams in Bristol Deep follow the line of the deepest water. Above half-tide the streams cross the banks, running broadly northeast or southwest in the general direction of the Severn estuary, setting across the buoyed channel in places.

If approaching Newport from down-Channel, aim to make a position half a mile west of the English and Welsh Grounds fairway buoy about 1½ hours before HW Newport. From here make good 013° for 2.3 miles to leave Newport Deep green conical buoy half a mile to starboard, and then make good 023° for a similar distance to the first pair of Newport entrance buoys, the No. 1 green conical and West Usk red can.

Coming from Penarth, lock out through the barrage at about half-flood and, staying inside Cardiff Grounds bank, leave the North Cardiff green buoy a cable to starboard. Then follow the line of the shore, tracking about 050° for 5¼ miles to leave Newport Deep green buoy three quarters of a mile to starboard before continuing northeast for 2¼ miles for the Usk outer buoys. Coming down-Channel from Portishead, lock out of the marina about two hours before local high water and push the last of the flood to arrive off Newport at, or soon after, high water there.

Entry

Entry to the Usk is straightforward above half-tide, once the West Usk and No. 1 buoys have been located. Follow the buoyed fairway as far as the dock entrance and then turn to starboard upriver, keeping very slightly south of midstream. At MLWS there's a least depth of about 0.3m in the channel, so a good hour's rise of tide is necessary even for shallow draft boats. The tidal stream is a more critical factor than the depth and entry near high water should ensure relatively still conditions for manoeuvring and anchoring. Fetch up opposite the Newport and Uskmouth Sailing Club, just beyond the power station and about 10m outside the local moorings.

Entry at night

Approach as by day, using the English and Welsh Grounds fairway buoy LFl.10s and Newport Deep green buoy Fl(3)G.10s. Coming up-Channel leave both these lights half a mile to starboard. Coming down-Channel via Bristol Deep, pass the fairway buoy half a mile to the north before turning northwards for Newport Deep. The East Usk light Fl(2)WRG on the east side of the river mouth is the key mark in the entrance, its white sector leading west of Newport Deep buoy and nicely up to the No. 1 green buoy Q.G and the West Usk red Q.R. From here follow the lit buoys to the dock pier head 2F.R(vert) and then pick up a pair of leading lights situated on the east shore of the river, just upstream from the sailing club beyond St Julian's Pill. These are fixed green lights, to be kept in line bearing 062°. Think about anchoring after half a mile on this line.

Departure from Newport

If you are bound down the Bristol Channel from Newport, leave the River Usk about two hours *before* local HW so as to take full advantage of the next period of west-going tide. If you are bound up-Channel towards Portishead Marina or the Upper Severn, leave the Usk as soon as you safely can after local low water.

Berths and anchorages

River Usk Anchor in the river opposite the club and about 10m outside the local moorings. It's best to moor to two anchors

Newport and Usk Sailing Club moorings on the River Usk
Jim Orr

NORTH COAST

laid in line with the tide, and a riding light is necessary at night. Sometimes you can use one of the moorings for a short stay, but enquire at the clubhouse first. Don't moor alongside the club pontoon, except briefly near high tide to take on fresh water.

St Julian's Pill Just beyond the club, on the south side of the river, is a narrow creek called St Julian's Pill where you can anchor out of the tide and settle into soft mud near low water.

The sheltered club moorings in St Julian's Pill
McMoss

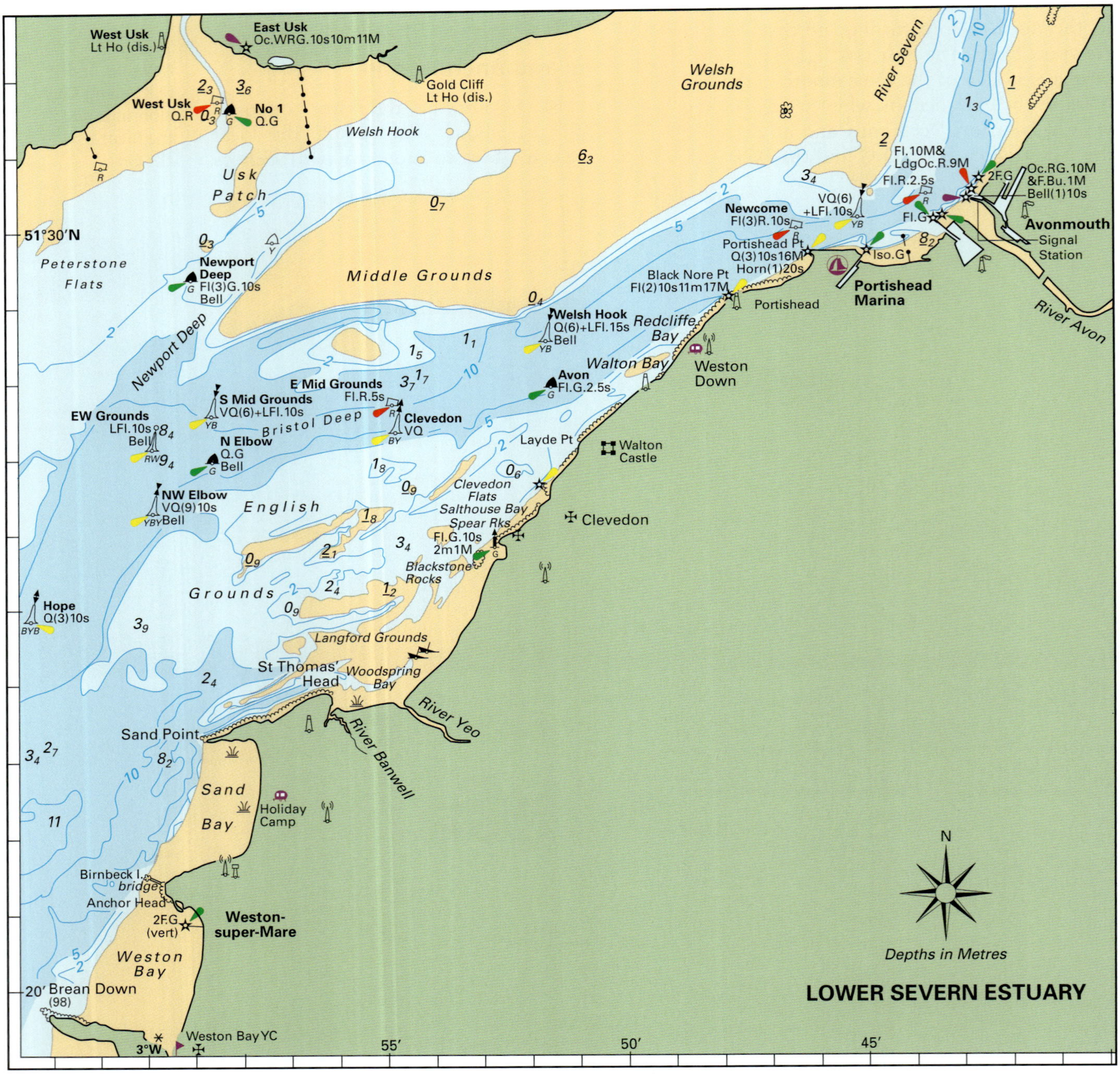

LOWER SEVERN ESTUARY

Depths in Metres

70 • Bristol Channel and Severn Cruising Guide

Newport transporter bridge

If you are cruising the Bristol Channel and venture up to the friendly Newport and Uskmouth Sailing Club be sure to explore a bit further up the River Usk where you will see the Newport transporter bridge. This amazing structure was opened in 1906 and is one of only two such bridges in the UK, the other is at Middlesborough crossing the River Tees. Fewer than twenty similar structures were built in the world and of those only six are still working. The gondola, which is suspended under the main gantry, can carry six cars and 120 passengers.

Designed by Ferdinand Arodin, a French engineer, and Robert Haynes, the Newport Borough Engineer, the bridge has clearance of 54m at high water with a span just short of 200m. This was to allow easy passage for masted ships to reach the docks in Newport but within a few years most ships were no longer powered by sail and so it now seems rather over specified but looks dramatic and elegant. The design was originally developed because the banks of the Usk are very low at the crossing point and a traditional bridge would have needed a very long approach ramp. A ferry would also have been impractical because the river dries out to mud soon after half-ebb and a tunnel would have been technically difficult and very expensive. Access was needed for workers who lived in Newport to reach their work at the steel works which were expanding on the east bank of the river.

The bridge is now a Grade 1 listed structure and major repair and refurbishment works were carried out from 2020. These works include a new visitor centre on the west side of the river which tells the story of the bridge's construction and history, and also describes other

The gondola on the Newport transporter bridge

transporter bridges around the world. Parts of the structure show the decorative ironwork used when the bridge was first built and more recent less aesthetic replacements are being returned to their former glory. The gondola is moved by hauling cables driven by twin 35hp electric motors from a winding house on the east end of the bridge. This very special bridge is worth crossing if you have never used it before.

The writer Leslie Thomas, who was born and grew up in Newport, describes the city's transporter bridge in a nostalgic way in his autobiography *In my wildest dreams*: 'The River Usk still sidles like a muddy snake below the old girders of the Transporter Bridge which was to me as a child one of the wonders of the world'. Today it can still be classed as one of those wonders.

The transporter bridge spans the River Usk

ST PIERRE PILL

Summary

St Pierre Pill is a narrow drying inlet on the north shore of the Severn estuary, almost midway between the two Severn bridges. Its entrance through marshy saltings is just over half a mile north by east of Charston Rock lighthouse. Although open to the south, St Pierre is partly protected from that direction by the natural breakwaters of Charston Rock and Charston Sands. Even in a strong southerly on a high spring tide, the inlet is perfectly safe if a little choppy. An unusual and interesting hideaway, St Pierre Pill provides a sheltered bolthole for moderate draught boats that, for example, may be bound upstream towards Sharpness but find they are too late on the tide. Several local boats are moored in the Pill all year round, mostly belonging to members of the friendly Chepstow and District Yacht Club.

Tides HW St Pierre Pill is at HW Avonmouth +0010, or HW Dover –0405. Approximate heights above chart datum: 13.2m MHWS, 0.8m MLWS, 9.9m MHWN, 3.2m MLWN.

Port Control None. The local moorings are administered by the Chepstow and District Yacht Club, whose members are very welcoming to visitors. Their handbook can be downloaded from the club website.

Tidal streams and currents In this part of the Severn estuary streams can be fierce, sometimes reaching eight knots at springs in the Shoots, 1½–2 miles south by west of St Pierre Pill. Opposite the mouth of the Pill and near the old Severn Bridge, spring rates in the estuary can reach 5–6 knots.

Description

St Pierre Pill, a small drying inlet on the north shore of the Severn estuary, is in peaceful rural surroundings more or less between the two Severn bridges. Charston Rock and Charston Sands lie not far south of the Pill, providing a natural breakwater which usually leaves a relatively quiet area of water off its mouth. St Pierre is the base for members of the Chepstow and District Yacht Club, who maintain moorings there during the season.

St Pierre is a useful little haven in that rather forbidding stretch of the Severn between Avonmouth and Sharpness. It's worth considering if you are bound upstream for Sharpness and find yourself late on the tide, or if you are coming downstream and suspect, at the old Severn Bridge, that conditions in the Shoots are likely to be nastier than you had bargained for. There's not much room in the Pill for visitors, but you can usually squeeze in somewhere. Ideally, anchor fore-and-aft to prevent swinging in the narrow channel, or you may be able to use one of the local moorings. Entry to the Pill is possible for two hours either side of high water and the inlet dries to soft mud soon after half-ebb.

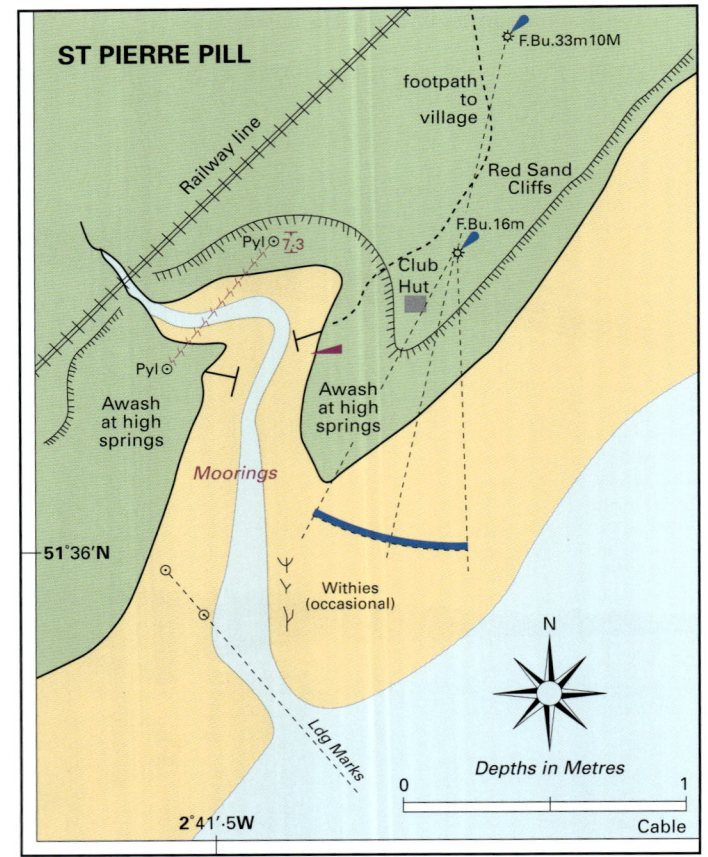

ST PIERRE PILL

St Pierre Pill at half tide
Reuben Howes

The club hut stands on the east arm of the Pill, above the low red cliffs that are prominent from the estuary. A narrow drying spit marked by withies extends well SSW from these cliffs. There are pontoon landing stages off either shore of the inlet and the head of the Pill is crossed by a railway bridge on the picturesque line between Newport and Chepstow. Nearest shops are at Mathern village about a mile inland, where The Millers Arms serves hearty meals every day (their Sunday roasts are well worth trying) and the Bass and Theakstons are well kept. You can get fuel at a garage about half a mile beyond the shops. The garage also has a basic but useful shop open every day between 7am and 9pm. The garden centre just opposite has a small restaurant which is convivial for lunch.

Water and electricity can be made available at St Pierre Pill in exchange for a small donation to the club, by contacting a member using one of the phone numbers posted at the club hut.

An evening high water
Reuben Howes

Bristol Channel and Severn Cruising Guide • 73

NORTH COAST

Top: Chepstow and District Yacht Club moorings in St Pierre Pill *Reuben Howes*

Bottom: The Club's leaning posts next to the slip *Reuben Howes*

Outer approaches

Coming up-Channel, follow the directions in the Upper Severn chapter, leaving Avonmouth 1½ hours before high water there. Having passed under the new Severn Bridge and left Old Man's Head W-cardinal beacon two cables to starboard, make good just east of north true to leave Charston lighthouse about 300m to starboard. Then steer north to pass between the lighthouse and Black Rock Point, but when midway between Charston lighthouse and the Welsh coast, head NNE and follow the shore towards the mouth of St Pierre Pill. Make for an approach position with the club hut bearing just east of north true, a quarter of a mile off.

Coming down-Channel, pass under the old Severn Bridge and leave Chapel Rock lighthouse a quarter of a mile to starboard. Then make good about 263° for just over a mile towards St Pierre, closing the shore well before reaching the mouth so as to tuck inside Charston Sands. When about two cables from the low red cliffs, follow the line of the shore south-west until the club hut bears just east of north true, a quarter of a mile off.

Note A sometimes alarming local phenomenon is that the tidal turbulence in the vicinity of the Shoots channel and Charston lighthouse is likely to cause false echo-sounder readings.

Entry

Only approach St Pierre Pill within two hours of high water. From the approach position, look for the leading marks (reflective triangles) that take you into the mouth of the Pill heading about north-west, before you turn to starboard towards the local moorings at just east of north. This inner line leaves the shallow spit (sometimes marked by withies) to starboard. It's important not to cut any corners as you approach and enter the Pill, or you'll find yourself stuck in sticky mud. On the inner line you'll be steering as if to pass between two pontoon landing stages up ahead, one jutting out from each shore. Leave the moored boats close to port. Sound carefully as you come into the inlet and fetch up wherever you can find room.

Entry at night

Not advisable except in an emergency, although locals can edge into the Pill using the arcs of visibility of Redcliffe leading lights.

Berths and anchorages

In the Pill Anchor fore-and-aft if possible to avoid swinging, or sometimes you can use a vacant mooring having asked one of the locals first. Temporary berthing is allowed alongside the club pontoons – bilge-keelers can use either pontoon, but fin-keelers are advised to use the west pontoon, on the port hand as you come in. The Pill dries out to soft mud soon after half-ebb.

Mathern Oaze Near neaps and in settled weather you can anchor in the main Severn estuary north-east of St Pierre, off the stretch of shore between St Pierre Pill and the mouth of the Wye known as Mathern Oaze. Edge as close in as the tide will allow. The bottom is mud and the streams are relatively quiet in here, especially at neaps.

THE RIVER WYE AND CHEPSTOW

A mooring under the cliffs at Chepstow

In the Middle Ages the Wye was a busy trading river and by the turn of the 17th and 18th centuries quite large boats were using it as far as Hereford. The river joins the Severn estuary just west of Beachley Point and the old Severn Bridge crosses its mouth. Two miles upstream at Chepstow the quays would have been active with barges for hundreds of years but only small boats moor there now and the steeply sloping banks are muddy. Although mostly drying, the Wye has one or two pools where keelboats can stay afloat at low water. Perhaps the most convenient for yachts on passage is just above the M48 Severn Bridge. Moor bows to two anchors laid in line with the tide, opposite a red beacon on the west bank. While not exactly picturesque this spot makes a bolthole if you miss the Severn tide, whether you are bound upstream for Sharpness or downstream for the Shoots.

The Chepstow Boat Club has a pontoon between the A48 bridge and the old Chepstow bridge, just opposite the 18th century Boat Inn. The pontoon is accessible for about two hours either side of HW Chepstow and there is also a deep-water visitor's mooring but it is recommended that you contact the moorings officer on ☏ 07968 111843 if you intend to visit Chepstow. The Club website **www.chepstowboatclub.co.uk** has navigation information for passage making as well as some fascinating historic maps of the River Wye.

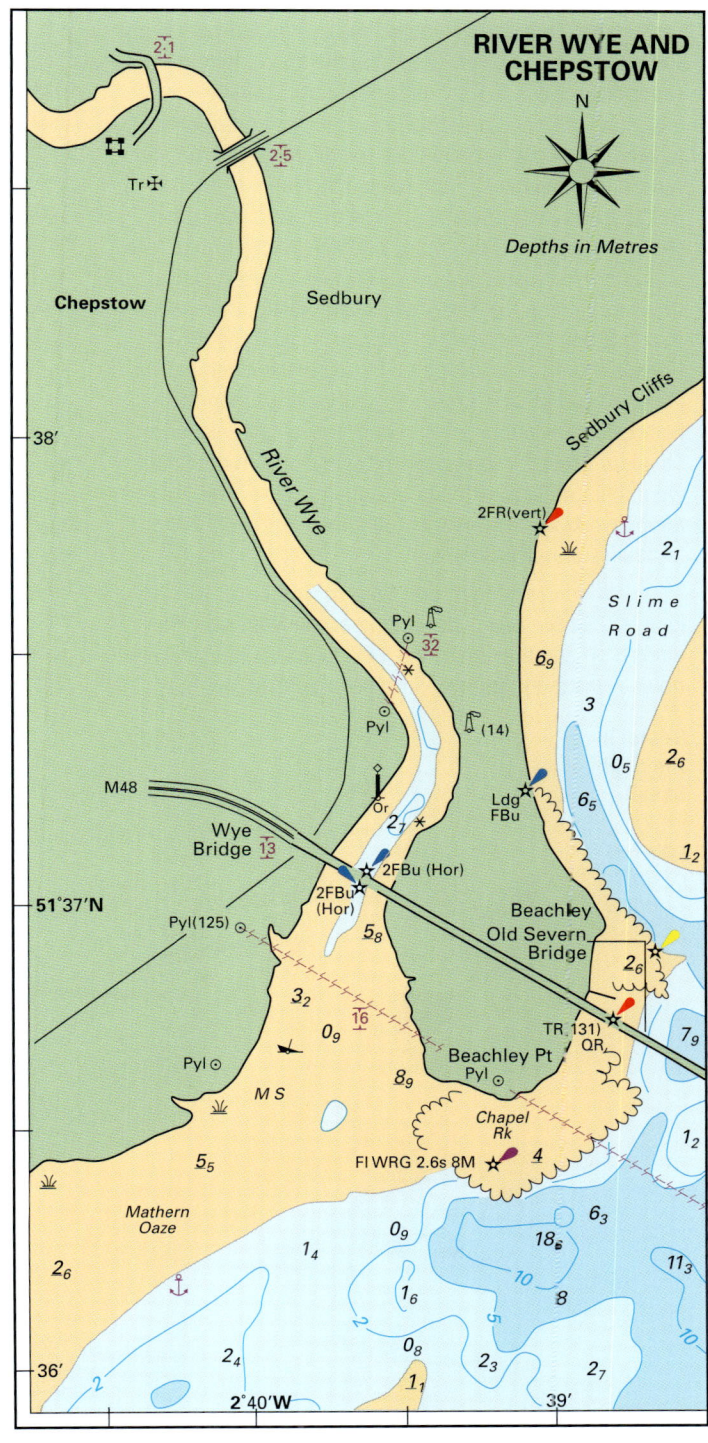

Traditional boats of the River Severn

The River Severn rises in the heart of Wales and flows 220 miles from Plynlimon past Shrewsbury, Stourport, Worcester, Tewkesbury and Gloucester. The river is tidal from Maisemore, just north of Gloucester, but the estuary is said to start at the second Severn crossing.

From about the 15th century, the traditional working craft of the River Severn and its connecting waterways was the *trow* – pronounced to rhyme with crow. These distinctive and highly practical boats were open cargo carriers, taking between 40 and 80 tons, increasing to over 100 tons in the 19th century. Cargoes in the hold were retained within vertical canvas side-cloths held up by rails.

Early trows were double-ended, beamy and flat-bottomed so that they could safely ground in the tricky shifting sands of the Severn. They had square sails to take advantage of more or less following winds and always worked the strong estuary tides to advantage. On narrow canals and rivers, they were hauled by teams of men. As the trows developed most were built with transom sterns and by the 1800s many had been converted to fore and aft rig, with several built as ketches. As well as river trows trading on the River Severn and inland, there were also coasting trows transporting coal around the Bristol Channel from the Welsh ports. These vessels often had either a fixed or lifting keel and sailed better than their flat-bottomed counterparts, particularly when unladen. To adapt trows for sea-going the side cloths in the hold were replaced with wooden boxing up to the level of the bulwarks and the cargo would then be covered with tarpaulins or hatch-boards.

Trows varied in size from 64ft long by 14ft beam to 72ft long by 19ft 6in beam, depending on the waterway they worked on and the size of the locks. Some of the smaller trows worked up the River Severn as far as Shrewsbury and right up the shallow River Wye to Hereford. Trows were built in yards all around the area from Brimscombe on the Thames and Severn Canal, to Lydney, Hereford, Bristol and Cardiff. Although most trows were wooden, ten iron trows were built at Stourport towards the end of the 19th century.

The Severn Trow *Spry*

The National Register of Historic Vessels has the following notes about *Spry*, the last surviving Severn trow ... 'built in 1893 by William Hurd of Chepstow using pitch pine above the waterline and elm below, on double sawn-oak frames. She was originally rigged as a cutter with a jib, staysail, topsail and gaff mainsail and this rig has now been restored.

'*Spry* worked as a dumb barge until 1950 and languished as a hulk at Worcester for the next 25 years, occasionally being used as a Boy Scout hut. Rescued jointly by the Severn Trow Preservation Society, the Upper Severn Navigational Trust and the Ironbridge Gorge Museum, she has been fully restored to seagoing condition. You can see her in a dry-dock at Madeley, Telford, as an exhibit in the Ironbridge Gorge Museum ... '

Further down the Bristol Channel flatners are distinctive types of fairly small, simple, easily constructed boats that were used historically along the north coast of Somerset for a variety of commercial purposes. Ranging from about 16ft to 23ft in length, flatners were double-ended craft with flat bottoms and virtually flat sides, cheap and easy to build, and capacious for their length. Their fascinating story is well told in the Watchet Boat Museum (**www.wbm.org.uk**) and encompasses many different watermen's trades around the shallow channels of the Somerset Levels as well as along the coast and up the dramatically tidal estuaries.

Bristol in the days of sail
Image courtesy of Bristol Culture/ M Shed

Withy Boats and Turf Boats were specific kinds of flatners used to carry peat and cut withies along the drainage canals of the Levels. Some of these boats were clinker built, but most were crudely constructed from rough elm boards. Their flat bottoms and rugged build made it relatively easy to pull these boats up onto the marshy banks to cross between different ditches.

River flatners of around 20ft had gently curved bottoms that made it easy to launch them down the sloping muddy banks of Somerset's rivers, including the Axe and the Parrett. On the Parrett in particular these boats were rowed upstream on the early flood tide and salmon were caught using large dip nets. Modern versions of these boats have been built with flat plywood sides sheathed in GRP.

Seagoing versions of the flatners were fitted with a dagger-board, rudder and short mast, then rigged with a simple spritsail and tiny jib to make them handy for fishing in more open waters such as Bridgwater Bay and the coastal reaches off Weston-super-Mare.

The particular boats used in Watchet, known locally as 'Flatties', had a double-planked bottom to take the wear when they were launched down the rocky foreshores that lie off and either side of Watchet harbour.

Top: A Somerset flatner
Watchet Boat Museum

Middle: Flatner sailing off Burnham-on-Sea *Watchet Boat Museum*

Bottom: Bristol pilots in Crockerne Pill
Image courtesy of Bristol Culture/M Shed

LYDNEY

Summary

Lydney Dock is on the north bank of the River Severn, about eight miles above the old Severn Bridge opposite Berkeley Power Station. Once used by barges and small coasters, then later by yachts, this historic old coal port for the Forest of Dean became virtually derelict until a restoration project gave the harbour a new lease of life. Years of accumulated silt were removed from the dock and new lock-gates installed. Once again, yachts and motor boats may now enter this attractive wet basin on what is a charming rural stretch of the Severn estuary. Lydney Yacht Club have their premises on the north side of the entrance lock and always give a warm welcome to visitors. See page 85 for Lydney plan.

Tides HW Lydney is at HW Avonmouth +0035, or HW Dover −0340. Approximate heights above chart datum: 9.3m MHWS, 0.6m MLWS, 5.6m MHWN, 0.5m MLWN. LW height in these upper reaches of the Severn is affected by fresh water flow and may be raised by up to a metre after heavy rains.

Port Control Contact the Harbour Master on ☏ 07768 861282 or call *Lydney Dock* on VHF 37 (M1) at tide times. Boats approaching Lydney should keep radios on as all movements are controlled by the Harbour Master by VHF or mobile phone.

Tidal streams and currents The river ebb starts running soon after local high water and the flood soon after local low water. The strongest streams are in mid-river and on the Berkeley side, reaching five knots on a spring ebb. Rates are less fierce close off Lydney lock, especially on the flood.

The upper basin at Lydney

LYDNEY

Description

Lydney Dock, once a small but active coaster port serving the Forest of Dean, gradually fell into disuse despite several attempts over the years to revive it for pleasure boating. Through all this, Lydney Yacht Club has been based in the dock, with an active programme of winter meetings and summer sailing events. The members have always offered a warm welcome to any visiting boats and have their clubhouse in an old shipwright's house on the north side of the entrance lock.

Lydney has been a port since Roman times when iron ore was shipped out from mines in the Forest of Dean. In 1810 the Severn and Wye Railway and Canal Company started to build the present docks and by 1821 the present outer harbour was completed. From that time Lydney was a busy railway port for over 100 years, handling over 300,000 tons of coal a year at its peak. Trade continued into the 1960s when rail access to the harbour ceased. Until the mid-1970s timber came up to a local mill by barge from Avonmouth. During the mid-1980s, when marina housing developments were popular, the dock was sold for development but nothing came of this proposal. The lock-gates ceased to operate in the late 1990s and visiting boats could no longer enter.

The Environment Agency has managed the docks since 1996 and two years later the Lydney Docks Partnership was formed to put a sympathetic and sustainable development plan in place. In 2003 the Heritage Lottery Fund gave a substantial grant towards renovation of the docks and work began in the summer of 2003, since then tons of accumulated silt have been removed from the harbour basin and new lock-gates fitted to complete an extensive flood defence scheme. In July 2005, during Lydney Yacht Club's annual regatta, the docks were reopened to boats.

In 2020 Lydney harbour was awarded over £2m funding from the Coastal Community Fund and substantial redevelopment works have started in the harbour. The aim is to protect the character and historical significance of the area, linking the restored dock with Lydney town through walking and cycle routes. A café has recently opened along with an information hub and an art trail is being constructed which links into Lydney's industrial heritage.

For the present, Lydney Dock is a restful port of call in a rural part of the Severn estuary, far from the madding crowd. Lydney Yacht Club have their premises and bar on the east side of the outer harbour, and members are always very hospitable to visitors. Outside the lock, north of the entrance pier head, there are some

Dried out on the slip at Lydney Yacht Club

NORTH COAST

The leafy basin above the lock at Lydney Docks

drying berths along the river foreshore. Lydney is straightforward to approach, once you have made the tricky passage up the Severn estuary from Avonmouth. Before visiting Lydney it's a good idea to contact the yacht club ☏ 01594 842573. There are no shops or other facilities near the dock and Lydney town is 1½ miles inland.

Outer approaches

Coming up-Channel, follow the directions in the Upper Severn chapter. When abreast Berkeley Power Station turn to the northwest, stemming the flood, and crab in a northerly direction over Saniger sands towards Lydney pier. If you are carried upstream past the pier, edge close to the west shore where the relatively slack water will enable you to motor back towards the lock.

Entry

The dock entrance is just west of the pier. Watch out for cross-set as you approach, even on the last of the flood. The outer entrance is 10m wide, with depths over the sill of 3.5m at high water neaps. The outer basin is 82m long and 22m wide. The lock is 27m long and 6.5m wide with 4m over the inner sill. The inner basin is 231m long and 32m wide with depths of 3m.

Lydney Dock can be entered 7-days a week. Boats should give the Harbourmaster six hours' notice before arrival or sailing on tides predicted to be 8.4m or over at Sharpness. On tides predicted to be less than 8.4m, you should give 24 hours' notice. Contact the Harbourmaster ☏ 07768 861282, or call *Lydney Dock* on VHF 37 (M1) during tide time.

Boats arriving should aim to be off Lydney no more than 20mins before high water, while boats leaving should be ready to enter the lock an hour before high water. Skippers should take care not to arrive off Lydney too early as grounding in the area is dangerous.

Entry at night

Yachts can enter Lydney at night, although in practice few visitors will probably be navigating the Upper Severn in the dark. The outer harbour pier head shows two fixed red vertical lights and at the root of the pier head a flashing amber light indicates when you can proceed and enter the lock.

Berths and anchorages

In the Dock Moor alongside the quays in the dock itself, opposite Lydney Yacht Club or pick up a mooring in the inner basin.

Estuary moorings and anchorages The nearest safe anchorage is just over five miles downstream on the west side, close inshore in a crook in the river opposite a white house three cables north of the Inward Rocks leading lights. You can also anchor in Slime Road just above the old Severn Bridge, tucking close inshore towards Slimeroad Pill.

SARA saves the day

The Severn Area Rescue Association, known as SARA, is an entirely voluntary multi-disciplinary search and rescue organisation covering the upper Severn Estuary, lower River Usk, the middle reaches of the River Severn and the surrounding areas. SARA provides lifeboat cover for the tidal rivers and inland waters, mud rescue on rivers and lakes in their area. As a Mountain Rescue Team they provide technical rope rescue for the cliffs of the River Wye valley, and missing person search and rescue in Gloucestershire, Herefordshire, Worcestershire, and the West Midlands.

When Peter was compiling the first edition of this book, several of the SARA volunteers took him around the Severn estuary to some of the corners that cruising boats could never reach, and especially to some of the reefs and shoals of the Shoots channel to which no conscientious yachtsman should ever have ventured so close!

SARA is the largest independent lifeboat service in the UK, second only to the RNLI, with five operational lifeboats declared to HM Coastguard and over 150 volunteer members. It has grown steadily over the years and currently operates from eight stations – at Beachley near the original Severn Bridge, Newport (South Wales), Sharpness old lock, Cirencester, Tewkesbury, Upton-upon-Severn and Kidderminster. SARA provide a rescue service for these areas and may be called out by the Coastguard, Police, Fire and Rescue services and Ambulance Services. During severe flooding and other events in recent years SARA operates away from their home area around the Severn to provide rescue services. SARA is not part of the Royal National Lifeboat Institution but the two organisations work closely together.

SARA was founded in 1973 and celebrates its 50th anniversary in 2023. Its first base was at Tutshill, near the present Beachley station. The organization became a registered charity in 1976 and a Charitable Incorporated Organisation in 2022.

On average, SARA is called out twice a week and some of the land searches continue for a number of days. In 2021, despite the pandemic, SARA was called out 113 times (55 land searches, 38 lifeboat calls, 22 inland water incidents, 4 rope rescues, and 3 casualty evacuations). Cal outs range from fishing boats with engine problems in the fast flowing river to missing person searches to rescuing dogs stranded on beaches by the incoming tide.

As a completely voluntary organisation financial support is vital. It costs over £130,000 a year to keep the service going so if you can help in any way check out the website **www.sara-rescue.org.uk**.

Members of the SARA Sharpness team *SARA*

THE RIVER SEVERN FROM AVONMOUTH TO SHARPNESS

Past the Hen and Chickens the Slime Road Sands will rapidly dry

The 17-mile passage up to Sharpness from either Portishead Marina or the mouth of the Avon requires careful pilotage and sound seamanship. Undoubtedly fascinating in fine weather, this potentially treacherous stretch of water is not to be trifled with on account of the powerful tides, numerous shoals and the shallowness of the upper reaches. The channel is fairly well marked, but there are several tricky turns where the navigator has to keep his wits about him, especially in poor visibility. Although the passage can be taken at night using the various sets of leading lights, strangers should stick to clear daylight and quiet weather.

The tide and passage timing are the key factors for safe navigation. The rise and fall at Avonmouth can exceed 13m at springs, and although neap rates in the river are around 2–3 knots, spring rates can touch 8–10 knots in places. It is important not to start out too early from Portishead Marina or Avonmouth or you can find yourself running out of water with the fast-flowing flood pushing you onward. Conversely, if you attempt the passage too late the ebb will have set in before you reach Sharpness. It's a good idea to inform Sharpness Radio in advance of your trip, giving date and time of departure, destination, ETA and particulars of your boat (VHF 16/13). Confirm your departure with *Bristol VTS* (16/12).

Yachts should aim to arrive off Sharpness about half an hour before high water there, i.e. just before HW Avonmouth. If you can motor at five or six knots the trip should take barely two hours in a good run of tide, so be leaving Portishead Marina or the River Avon entrance about two hours before high water there. Faster boats must leave correspondingly later and slower boats a little earlier. Watch out for commercial shipping entering or leaving Avonmouth.

THE RIVER SEVERN FROM AVONMOUTH TO SHARPNESS

From a departure position two cables northwest of Avonmouth pier heads, make good 013° for four miles along the Redcliffe leading line to leave the Lower Shoots W cardinal beacon a cable to starboard and pass under the Prince of Wales bridge midway between the central towers. Reasonable visibility is particularly important on this first stretch since the marks are well spaced and the flood sets strongly across your track to the northeast. Although yachts should always give way to ships using the buoyed channel, there's much to be said for holding well up-tide to the west side of the fairway, rather than risk slipping towards the dangers on the east side. From a mile before the bridge to half a mile after it, you pass through The Shoots, a narrow channel between the rocky English Stones shoal to the east and various smaller drying patches to the west. Because of these constrictions, The Shoots has the fastest streams and potentially turbulent water in the passage up to Sharpness.

As you pass under the bridge, alter to port to make good due north true for half a mile, leaving Old Man's Head W cardinal buoy two cables to starboard and a red beacon about 250m to port. On this leg remember that the tide will be setting strongly northeast across your course. A cable or so past the red beacon, alter to starboard to make good 054° towards the middle of the old Severn Bridge, leaving Charston Rock lighthouse two cables to port as you pass it. Now the stream will be more or less behind you and at this point yachts with VHF should establish contact with Sharpness Radio on 13.

As you get nearer the bridge, steer to leave Chapel Rock lighthouse, on an islet just beyond the entrance to the River Wye, about a quarter of a mile or slightly further to port, so that you are positioned well in midstream. Once abreast Chapel Rock make for the quick flashing blue light under the centre span of the bridge. The current is often turbulent around

The old lock house and disused entrance at Sharpness

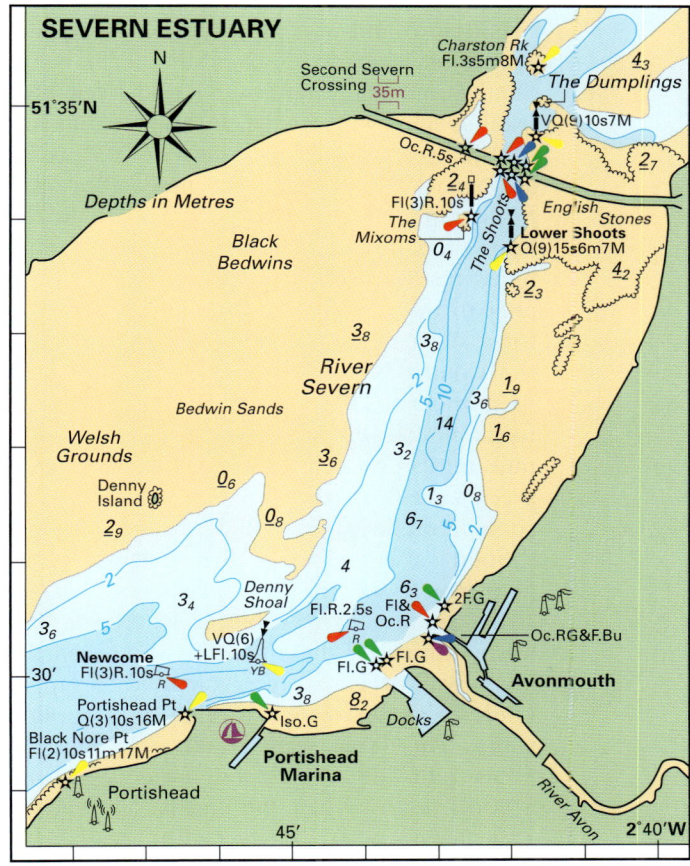

Bristol Channel and Severn Cruising Guide • 83

UPPER SEVERN

the bridge as it surges through the narrows over an uneven bottom, so plenty of power and some attentive steering are usually needed. Once under the bridge come round steadily and boldly to port to leave Lyde Rock beacon about 100 metres to the southwest, heading northwest and then north so as to tuck close under Beachley Point into Slime Road. Your plotter should show the extent of this turn.

Follow round past the prominent red cliffs at Sedbury keeping 1½–2 cables off the bank. Slime Road white day marks and fixed blue leading lights will now be close astern and you should keep them in line astern at 204° as far as Inward Rocks Point, 2½ miles above the bridge. Once you have passed Inward Rocks Point, the Inward Rocks fixed blue leading lights come into line astern and you should alter to the ENE and make good about 070° for a short mile along this stern transit until the Counts N cardinal light-float is a cable to starboard. Then transfer to the Sheperdine fixed blue leading lights ahead for another mile until, just before you reach the Ledges green light-float, the two Narlwood beacons come into line astern at 225°.

Soon after passing the Counts light-float you'll see the two Narlwood beacon structures about two cables to starboard. The northernmost of these beacons stands on the north wall of a tidal reservoir used to supply Oldbury nuclear power station with cooling water. This large walled lake is submerged above half-tide and should always be given a good berth. When the Narlwood beacons come into line astern at 225°, follow this aft transit northeast to leave Hills Flats green buoy a cable to starboard.

After passing Hills Flats, come to starboard a little so as to make good about 062° for a short mile, turning just before you reach it to leave Hayward Rock N cardinal beacon 100m to starboard and picking up the fixed blue Conigre leading lights. Follow this transit for just over half a mile at 078° until you are about 250m from the east shore and then come back to the northeast so as to leave Berkeley Bull Rock light structure not quite 100m to starboard, keeping Fishing House white and orange beacons in line astern at 218°. Note that coasters sometimes pass to the east of Bull Rock light structure when bound downriver against the last of the flood.

Keep about 300m off the bank as you pass the narrow entrance to Berkeley Pill and the shallow bight of Panthurst Pill. You'll see Sharpness pier heads up ahead, jutting out from the east shore, about a mile upstream from Berkeley Pill. On the bank just beyond Panthurst Pill is a fixed blue light, known locally as the 'swinging light'. At this point it's usually a good plan to round up into the tide and then drop astern towards the pier heads, keeping control by running slow ahead. Ships may be locking out as you arrive, so call *Sharpness Radio* on VHF 13 for instructions.

Sharpness locks are worked for about an hour and a half before local HW, and after HW only as commercial traffic dictates. Having locked in yachts should pass through the docks, negotiate the two swing bridges (call VHF 74) and then turn hard-a-port into a cut where Sharpness Marine have their pleasant bankside berths. This quiet backwater was the original lock basin between the tidal Severn and the Gloucester and Sharpness Canal, before the docks were built in the 1870s. The canal still carries commercial shipping and increasing numbers of pleasure craft. Beyond Gloucester even quite deep-draft yachts can re-join the Severn just below Ashleworth. The canalised river can take you up to Tewkesbury, Upton-upon-Severn and the attractive old city of Worcester.

Yachts outward bound from Sharpness should aim to lock out about half an hour before HW there, taking some foul tide on the downward passage to start with. Follow the upriver directions in reverse, but remember that at HW Sharpness the tide will have been ebbing down in The Shoots for nearly three quarters of an hour. By the time you get below the upper Severn Bridge the ebb will be running strongly. Once you have passed Charston lighthouse take care to stay in the

THE RIVER SEVERN FROM AVONMOUTH TO SHARPNESS

UPPER RIVER SEVERN

deep-water channel, and beware being set westwards towards Lady Bench and Gruggy shoals on the Welsh side of The Shoots.

Local pilots

Owners of leisure craft, particularly narrow boats, who may lack the experience and confidence to tackle the River Severn, are strongly advised to take a local pilot who has the knowledge to make this passage safely. For some inland waterways boats there may be insurance restrictions about operating in tidal waters and specified rivers without a pilot.

The Gloucester Harbour Trustees currently license four self-employed pilots who have formed themselves into the Gloucester Pilots Partnership. These pilots are usually available to provide services to leisure craft navigating the upper Severn Estuary and can be contacted on ☎ 07774 226143, www.gloucesterpilots.co.uk. When taking ships up or down the pilots board and land at Barry, but when piloting leisure craft they can arrange to join or leave at Bristol or Portishead Marina.

Bristol Channel and Severn Cruising Guide • 85

The Severn bridges

The two Severn bridges look awe-inspiring from deck level. Opened in 1996, the 'Second Severn Crossing' has long graceful viaducts marching out from the Welsh and English shores, meeting at two tall towers over the turbulent Shoots channel four miles above Avonmouth. The elegant cable pattern of the central span glints in the sun like a huge cat's-cradle.

Three miles further upstream, the original suspension bridge was opened in 1966 and crosses a mile-wide stretch of the river near the mouth of the Wye. Skippers passing under this venerable bridge don't usually have time to gaze around them, but are preoccupied instead with the turbulent current and a tricky turn to port into Slime Road.

The second Severn Bridge took four years to build and 1,000 men were employed in this major project. The central span over The Shoots channel is 456m long with 37m navigation clearance. The two main pylons holding the roadway are 137m high and to establish their foundations on the estuary bed the engineers used 37 specially pre-cast concrete caissons each weighing 2,000 tonnes. To place these mammoth building blocks a special flat-bed barge was used, with a computer controlled navigation positioning system that could hold the barge precisely on station to within half a metre tolerance. The positioning of each caisson had to be completed within a two-hour tidal window. Once each caisson was secured to the seabed, work could continue within it irrespective of the tides.

For the whole construction operation, a fleet of 10 specialist and highly sophisticated floating craft was required, with seven back-up barges. Working in this fast-flowing area with a tidal range of up to 14.5m imposed some very particular problems on the construction team. Altogether 30,000 tonnes of reinforcing steel and 320,000 cubic metres of concrete were used to build the Prince of Wales Bridge.

The route of the second bridge is very close to that of the Severn railway tunnel, which was built between 1874 and 1886 and is still in use today. This is also the site of the ancient Roman ferry crossing, so even with their sophisticated technology the contemporary bridge engineers reached a similar decision about where to cross the estuary. During the construction of the Second Severn crossing a fascinating visitor centre, with models, videos and illustrations about the bridges and the area was open to the public. The centre closed in 2008 but there is a very informative website run by the Severn Bridges Trust, so for more history on crossing the Severn, engineering and bridge construction visit **www.severnbridges.org**.

The original Severn Bridge now carries the M48

The Prince of Wales Bridge

SHARPNESS

Summary

The port of Sharpness lies on the east shore of the upper Severn, about nine miles above the old Severn Bridge. Sharpness Docks are still active and are situated at the seaward end of the Gloucester and Sharpness Canal, a deep, well-maintained waterway that bypasses the shallow, higher reaches of the tidal Severn. Sharpness is an interesting haven in its own right, but is also the gateway to the extensive inland waterways of the southwest Midlands. Following the Gloucester and Sharpness Canal and then the canalised Severn, quite large and deep-draft yachts can penetrate inland to Worcester basin and beyond as far as Stourport. Entry to Sharpness is via a tidal lock accessible for about one and a half hours before local HW. Once inside the docks you pass two swing bridges and turn to port into the old canal cut where Sharpness Marine have their peaceful berths.

Tides HW Sharpness is at HW Avonmouth +0040, or HW Dover –0335. Heights above chart datum: 9.3m MHWS, 0.5m MLWS, 5.8m MHWN, 0.2m MLWN.

Port Control Contact Sharpness Radio (VHF 16/13) as you pass Avonmouth and again near the upper Severn Bridge. The port of Sharpness and its lock are run by Gloucester Harbour Trustees, whose office at Sharpness Docks is usually open weekdays 0900–1700: Gloucester Harbour Trustees, Navigation House, The Docks, Sharpness GL13 9UD ☎ 01453 811913.

Tidal streams and currents The Severn ebb starts running off Sharpness soon after local HW and the flood soon after local LW. Streams are strong, up to five knots at springs, so beware the cross-set when entering or leaving between Sharpness pier heads. Further downstream in The Shoots channel, the south-going ebb stream starts running about three quarters of an hour before HW Sharpness.

Description

Sharpness is an old established port whose importance grew steadily after the completion of the Gloucester and Sharpness ship canal in 1827. This 17-mile waterway was built to bypass the tortuous higher stretches of the tidal Severn above Sharpness Point, enabling large

The piers at Sharpness entrance look a bit rickety at low water

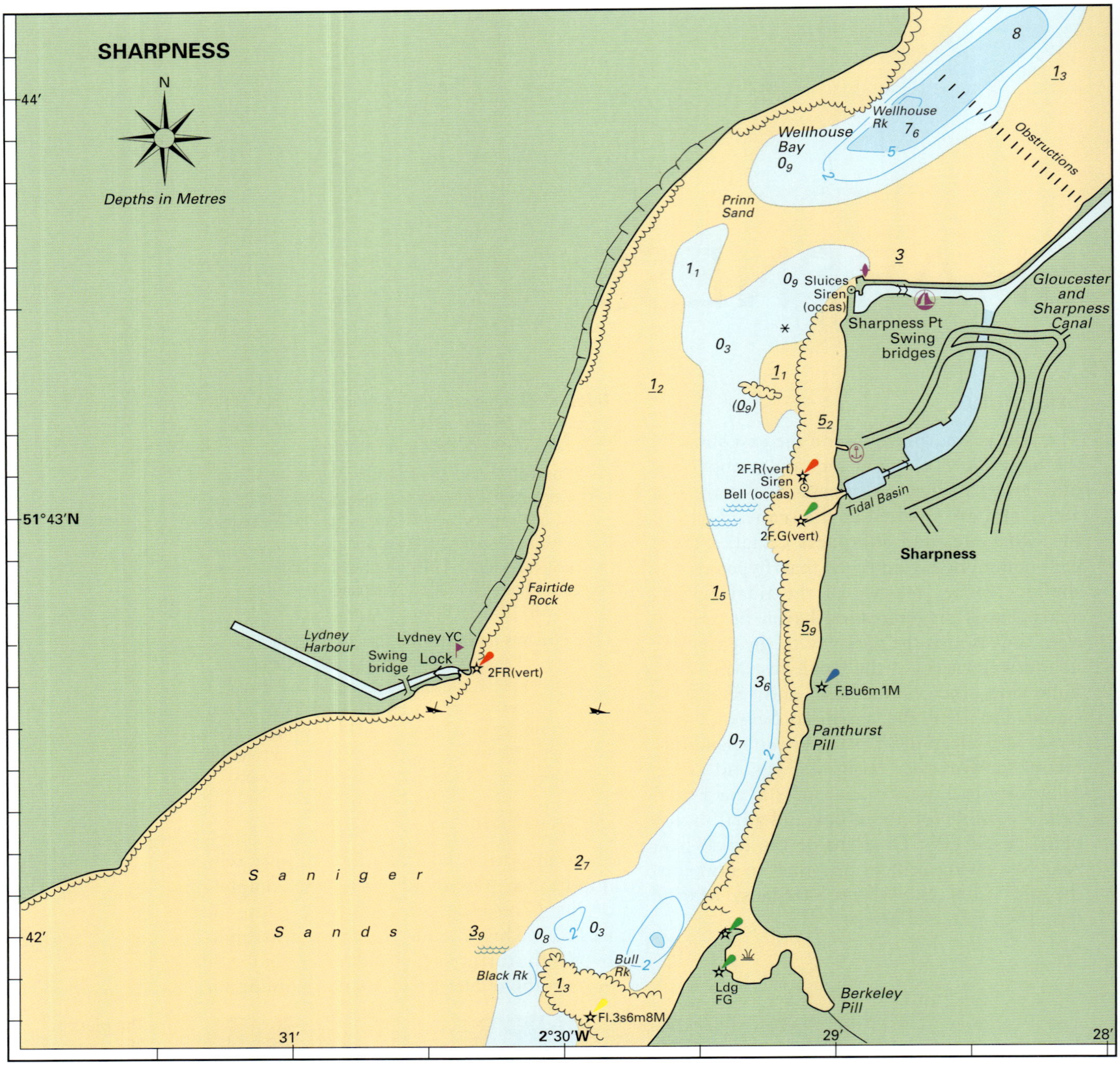

UPPER SEVERN

The moorings of Sharpness Marine are in the canal arm above the old lock

The stone tower is the remains of a pier for the Victorian railway bridge across the Severn

ocean-going ships to make the inland passage up to Gloucester. The original entrance locks once led into the now tranquil backwater where Sharpness Marine have their moorings.

Sharpness 'New Dock' opened in 1874, together with a new and larger canal entrance half a mile further downstream. The port has since seen ebbs and flows in its fortunes, but is still commercially active and remains the upstream headquarters of the Severn Pilots. Current shipping cargoes include scrap metal, grain, cement, fertiliser, timber and forest products, coal and stone. Pleasure boat traffic on the canal increases steadily each year and the trip inland to Gloucester and beyond is fascinating and most picturesque, winding through one of the most 'English' parts of England. Deep-draft yachts can cruise well up the canalised Severn to colourful Diglis basin at Worcester, and beyond as far as Stourport, which also has a large sheltered basin suitable for laying-up. Stourport is about 40M above Gloucester Docks.

The passage up the Severn Estuary from Portishead to Sharpness is tricky, and needs to be timed carefully for the last part of the flood. Sharpness locks will admit yachts for about one and a half hours before HW and Sharpness Radio controls traffic approaching the port. The lock foreman is always very helpful to yachtsmen. Inside the harbour, just beyond the docks, the visitors' berths at Sharpness Marine are quiet and sheltered, a pleasant spot for a couple of days' stay. The small town of Sharpness is a short walk from the docks area and offers reasonable shopping. Not far from Sharpness Marine you can get excellent and good-value bar food at the Salmon Inn.

Outer approaches and entry

Follow the previous chapter's directions for navigating the Upper Severn from Avonmouth to Sharpness. In principle yachts can reach Sharpness at night, since all the leading lines in this stretch of the river are clearly lit, but because of the powerful tides night navigation on this estuary is not recommended to anyone without either local knowledge or a pilot.

Berths and anchorages

Sharpness Marine These sleepy canal-side berths occupy what was once the original cut and lock basin between the tidal Severn and the Gloucester and Sharpness Canal. You can contact Sharpness Marine in advance for a berth ☎ 01453 811476 and boats can safely be wintered here or left unattended for a while. This pleasantly rural stretch of water, now a cul-de-sac, is entered by passing from the present tidal lock through Sharpness Docks, negotiating two swing bridges and then turning hard to port. Sharpness Marine have good facilities, including a comprehensive chandler, and the berths are handy for fresh water and electricity. Diesel is available from the fuel barge *Stokie No. 1* on the main canal outside Sharpness Marine – contact John Chard on ☎ 07967 960128.

Sharpness Docks Larger boats can lie alongside in the Docks by arrangement with the lock master, but the berthing is less congenial than at Sharpness Marine or alongside a little further up the canal.

Anchorages There are no safe anchorages in the River Severn near Sharpness.

Severn Bore

The tidal range in the Bristol Channel can reach a maximum of 15m, the second highest in the world after the Bay of Fundy (16.3m) between the USA and Nova Scotia. These very large ranges occur principally as a result of the local geology, a steadily funnelling shape of two coastlines. The Severn Estuary narrows from nine miles wide between Cardiff and Weston-Super-Mare down to two miles at Aust, the location of the original Severn Bridge. The Severn Bore is a natural tidal wave which, on a big spring tide, moves up the river valley like a wall of water. The largest recorded wave of the Severn Bore was 2.8m (over 9 feet) high in October 1966, just downstream of Stonebench.

The bore occurs to some degree on every spring tide, but the most spectacular tidal waves occur around the equinoxes in March and September. Barometric pressure, wind speed and direction can all increase or decrease the bore effect, as will the flow of freshwater coming down the River Severn. Low barometric pressure can result in markedly higher tide levels, and sustained westerly winds in the days before top spring tides will tend to bank up the level of the Bristol Channel and Severn estuary. Heavy rain inland, on the other hand, will cause a significant flow of freshwater downstream which can slow the incoming tide and reduce the height and speed of the bore.

The bore is less noticeable in the wide lower reaches of the estuary, but is usually most pronounced in the upper tidal stretches between Fretherne and Maisemore. The Severn Bore is quite an attraction with hundreds of people arriving at locations like Minsterworth, Stonebench and Over Bridge to watch the surfers, kayakers, canoeists and other waterborne enthusiasts trying to ride the wave. Large bores, four or five star, will be seen when the tidal range is more than 9.5m. Between Minsterworth and Gloucester the average speed of the bore is about 16 km/hr (nearly 9 knots), though on very high tides it can get up to 21 km/hr (almost 12 knots). Photos, dates and times of this well recognised phenomenon can be found on a website, www.severn-bore.co.uk.

The Severn bore sweeps up the narrowing river *Visit Dean Wye*

Riding the bore *Visit Dean Wye/Ward*

THE RIVER SEVERN FROM SHARPNESS TO STOURPORT

The Severn rises deep into Wales, 200 miles from the racing Bristol Channel. Until the 1820s, local craft traded as far upstream as Pool Quay, just below Welshpool, but today the effective head of navigation is Stourport-on-Severn, 60 miles above Sharpness. There are fully-fledged marinas at Sharpness, Gloucester, Tewkesbury, Upton and Stourport, so the Severn is no cruising wilderness. Canal and River Trust (CRT) run the locks and bridges, which open smoothly on demand. Berthing places and facilities have improved steadily in recent years, as have many of the charming waterside pubs that mark your progress.

The challenging bit is getting there, because the Bristol Channel has the most dramatic tides in Britain. The spring range at Avonmouth is 12.2m (40ft), greater than Jersey or St Malo, while the funnelling estuary causes roaring rates up to 8–10 knots locally above Avonmouth. Timing is everything, so strangers should start the last leg up to Sharpness either from Penarth Marina on the Welsh shore or from Portishead Marina just below Avonmouth. Aim to arrive off Sharpness half-an-hour before HW there (i.e. just before HW Avonmouth), leaving neither too late (you don't want to miss Sharpness lock), nor too early (the tide will be powerful and the depths more skimpy).

The estuary passage under the two Severn bridges is awe-inspiring from deck level, their great height and span magnifying the stature of the surrounding country. Just below the old (upper) bridge you pass the mouth of the Wye, while up ahead are the timeless landscapes of the Forest of Dean. To the east, the low wetlands of the Vale of Berkeley are dotted with secret villages hidden away in a remote strip of land between Bristol, the M5 and the river.

In the last reach you pass two power stations on the English side and then the Sharpness piers take shape ahead. By now the tide should be almost slack, allowing you to enter the lock without too much drama. This cavernous, rather slimy shipping lock is always a welcome haven to upcoming boats. When the gates clang shut behind you, the powerful estuary tides are safely cut off and you can look forward to 60 miles of relatively placid water, with no navigational decisions except where to pull in for lunch.

Sharpness to Gloucester

The Sharpness to Gloucester ship canal is a sympathetic waterway for seagoing boats. Creeping through Sharpness docks, you feel at ease among professional mariners, with coasters loading and unloading either side. The canal is a decent width all the way to Gloucester, with sizeable barges, old tugs and dredgers, converted fishing boats and all manner of working vessels moored to the bank. Just beyond Sharpness docks, the old entrance arm of the canal is now a peaceful marina backwater perched above the river.

For several miles above Sharpness the canal runs alongside the shallow tidal Severn, whose sinuous sandy reaches slide in and out of view. You pass the ruins of the Severn Railway Bridge, with footprints of the old pier foundations fading away across the sands. One foggy autumn evening in 1960, two estuary tankers missed the entrance to Sharpness lock and collided with the bridge, whose magnificent wrought iron spans carried a gas pipe as well as the railway. The resulting explosion destroyed two sections of the bridge and the wrecks of the two tankers can still be seen at low water.

Two bridges swing at Purton village and two miles further on there's a good berth on the south bank at Shepherd's Patch. The Tudor Arms is close by and a lane leads out to the Slimbridge Wildfowl and Wetlands Centre, established in 1946 by Sir Peter Scott. Just beyond Frampton-on-Severn you pass a fascinating boating oasis at Saul Junction,

Moorings in the heart of Gloucester

where the Stroudwater joins the ship canal between Davis and Son's boatyard and an elegant bridge-house. This is a bustling place, with all kinds of craft being renovated. You'll see several smart barge yachts luxuriously fitted out.

Above Saul Junction, the canal leaves the river for a while to cross open farming country, with striking views west towards the Forest of Dean and east to the Cotswolds. At Quedgeley you meet the outskirts of Gloucester and the last stretch of canal creeps past scruffy industrial backyards on its way to the docks. The old quays, sheds and railway sidings are steeped in trading history, but look as dismal from the water as from anywhere else. The city docks are rather different though, magnificently restored to bring their maritime and waterway past dramatically alive. Just beyond the lifting bridge, continue straight ahead to moor in the main basin, either along the west quay or at the pontoons on the northeast side.

Gloucester Docks

These grandiose docks were packed with tall-masted ships in the days of sail and the sailing barges moored here today give a flavour of how things would have looked and felt. Most of the redbrick warehouses have been carefully restored and some converted into desirable apartments with soothing quayside views. The National Waterways Museum occupies three floors of the old Llanthony Warehouse, offering visitors a compelling tour through English transport history.

Gloucester to Tewkesbury

Joining the Severn again through Gloucester lock, you follow quite a narrow section out of the city past several bridges and a winding corridor of willows. Now you feel properly inland and the salty vibes of the ship canal give way to a more rural atmosphere. There's something slightly unreal about helming a seagoing boat through such leafy surroundings, with robins chirruping and farmyard smells wafting on the breeze. Gazing ahead across the bows, you find yourself recalling more boisterous passages in open water, with heavy spray rattling the wheelhouse and nothing in view except gloomy grey sea.

These middle reaches of the Severn are what skippers dream about in the English Channel when the wind freshens unexpectedly, the seas become steeper and the whitecaps more malevolent. As crockery starts clattering dismally in the galley, you can imagine being beamed up and set down in such peaceful scenery as the River Severn between Gloucester and Tewkesbury.

This section has some memorable waterside pubs with convenient moorings – The Boat at Ashleworth Quay, the Haw Bridge Inn, the Coalhouse Inn at Apperley, the Yew Tree at Chaceley Stock and the 15th Century Lower Lode Inn just before Upper Lode lock. Many Severn pubs are located at old ferry crossings, and you can still see slipways where flat-bottomed punts once pushed their noses in.

The Severn skirts north of Tewkesbury, but you can turn into the River Avon arm and hang a left just below the Avon lock to moor at Tewkesbury Marina. The Cotterell family established this charming haven in the late 1960s and have gradually improved and landscaped the site to create a restful inland marina for 350 boats. Visitors are always welcome and there are repair facilities on hand. Tewkesbury is a traditional Gloucestershire market town with good shopping and a lively theatre. There are several good places to eat in Tewkesbury, why not try the Salerno Italian in Church Street or the Boathouse pub on its island in the River Avon.

Tewkesbury to Worcester

From Tewkesbury it's six miles to Upton-upon-Severn, a favourite stop. Upton Marina is a pleasant basin on the north shore just below the town. You enter under a footbridge with about 25ft clearance at normal river level (there's a headroom gauge outside). All kinds of boats moor in this spacious marina, which is bordered by neat grassy banks. Upton is a delightful time warp, with old family shops along a traditional high street. The Malvern Meat Company on Court Street is a must, both a butcher and café, and Upton is home to the Map Shop – which says it all. The Boathouse is a tapas and wine bar in the evenings but is also open for breakfast or brunch. Upton's famous 'Pepperpot' tower is all that remains of a 12th-century church, which took a battering during the Civil War when a group of Roundheads were pinned down there by Royalists.

As you cruise upstream from Upton past the distant Malvern Hills, the river valley feels slightly steeper and is sometimes enclosed by unexpected stretches of sandstone cliffs. This is Elgar country, as English as tea and scones. On a hot summer day, the breeze seems to sigh with those familiar tunes of the great man's Enigma. Not far below Worcester you reach some riverside berths run by Seaborn Leisure, a pleasant halt a short stroll from Kempsey village and one of the best Severn pubs. The Walter de Cantelupe Inn is run with relaxed flair by Martin Lloyd-Morris and the food is first class. If you eat here in the evenings try the Worcestershire sausages and a bottle of house Chilean red. For a hearty lunch, go for their real nostalgic 'ploughman's' and a pint of Wye Valley Bitter or Timothy Taylor's Landlord. Walter de Cantelupe has nothing to do with melons, but was a portly bon viveur Bishop of Worcester in the mid-1200s.

River moorings at Upton-on-Severn

The friendly marina at Upton-on-Severn

UPPER SEVERN

Cruising past Worcester cathedral

Riverside moorings in Worcester opposite the racecourse

A mile upstream from Kempsey you reach the pontoons and clubhouse of the Severn Motor Yacht Club, established in 1926 when Admiral Cummings was elected President. The SMYC has occupied this site since 1937. During the Second World War, the Admiralty requisitioned many club boats and several were lost on active service. Photographs in the bar show how dramatically the Severn can break its banks during wet winters. The clubhouse floods at least every other winter and a plaque near the fireplace marks the record river level of 1947.

Just upstream from the SMYC you pass under a high road bridge and start approaching the outskirts of Worcester. On the west bank, near the mouth of the River Teme, is the site where two spirited Civil War battles took place in 1642 and 1651. The Royalists won the 1642 Battle of Powick Bridge, but nine years later the Battle of Worcester was carried soundly by Parliamentarians. Half a mile beyond this now very tranquil site, the river lock at Diglis lifts you into the attractive Worcester reach of the Severn, which leads past two famous features of this ancient city – the cathedral and the racecourse.

Berthing in Worcester

Although Worcester is rather a sprawling city, the centre has some striking vistas as you cruise through. There are two possible berthing spots – the river quays on the east bank opposite the racecourse or, further downstream, Diglis canal basin. The racecourse quays are snug enough with good bollards, but are opposite the noisy A443 that invades Worcester from the north. For a more peaceful berth and a taste of old trading Worcester, follow the wide canal locks into Diglis basin a little way above the main river lock.

Here in this old Midlands port 45 miles above Sharpness, you used to see an extraordinary mix of boats moored higgledy-piggledy around the quays and wharves. Colourful narrow boats once rubbed shoulders with small cabin cruisers, traditional wooden yachts looking their age, some unlikely looking conversions and one or two sizeable seagoing boats that in their heyday had seen action and tasted real salt water. Unfortunately, property developers are in the process of transforming what was once a sleepy, pleasantly scruffy yet rather homely basin into another enclave of bijou waterside residences. They describe the new Diglis enthusiastically as ' . . . a brown field opportunity providing 421 dwellings, retail outlets, cafés and restaurants, offices, community centre and gym, via new buildings and the refurbishment and reuse of existing buildings in the Conservation Area …'. What a pity.

Strolling up the Worcester and Birmingham canal to Sidbury Lock, you can visit the Commandery, a gracious 15th century building in restful gardens, once a hospital but later involved in Civil War action when Charles II based himself here for the 1651 Battle of Worcester. Not far from here is Benedicto's Italian Restaurant, always a good bet.

Peter's favourite pub near Diglis was the Salmon Leap in Severn Street, opposite what was once the Royal Worcester porcelain works, but it no longer seems to be here. Fortunately Browns at the Quay is still on the riverside near the main Worcester bridge and they do tempting sharing platters, charcuterie, fish, mezze or vegetarian. Occupying an old corn mill, Browns has plenty of atmosphere and a deft chef. To reach it from Diglis, cross the canal entrance locks and follow the Severn path upstream past the cathedral.

Worcester to Stourport

Leaving Worcester past the racecourse and rowing station, the Severn edges away from the road into lush pasture, where cows graze along the banks. You pass three locks in succession at Bevere, Holt and Lincomb. A little way past Holt lock on the port hand, the Lenchford Inn has good pontoons and is a handy pull-in for lunch. Above Lincomb you soon reach Stourport Marina, a secluded basin on the east bank near an industrial estate. Oddly enough, this estate helps keep the marina quiet and secure, because few sightseers wander past. If you want to leave a boat at Stourport, this is

The Staffordshire and Worcestershire Canal starts at Stourport on the River Severn

the place, but for a passing visit to sample the atmosphere, press on upstream to the town quays just below Stourport Bridge. There are pontoons along the east bank by the Angel pub under the weeping willows, or you can climb through two wide locks into the upper basin.

The prominent Clock Warehouse near the top lock is the home of Stourport Yacht Club, a friendly place where seagoing cruising boats lie far inland. The basin is also packed with narrow boats, for whom the shallow Staffordshire and Worcestershire canal sets off under a tight bridge. Stourport is an odd mixture. The riverside, canal basins and locks are picturesque and fascinating to wander round, but a noisy fairground strikes a garish note just upstream from the narrow boat locks. Brummies used to catch buses out here at weekends and now they arrive in streams of cars to join the fun of the fair.

Stourport is effectively the head of navigation for the River Severn, although smaller boats with a pioneering urge can venture upstream another mile or so, usually touching bottom near Gladder Brook. When the river is high enough, shallow draught boats sometimes get up as far as Bewdley, an agreeably old-fashioned town which was once a thriving river port with quays, wharves and plenty of trade. Bewdley's surviving transport feature today is its splendidly restored station, where lovingly maintained steam trains of the Severn Valley Railway can take you another dozen relaxing miles up the river to Bridgnorth. That's beyond the latitude of Birmingham though – almost bandit country.

Maximum boat dimensions

Reached from the tidal estuary by the Gloucester and Sharpness Ship Canal, the upper Severn is navigable by sizeable seagoing boats right up to Stourport, nearly 60 miles above Sharpness. Bear in mind that boats sit 10cm (4in) lower in fresh water so remember to adjust your draught.

Gloucester and Sharpness Canal
(16½ miles)
Max boat length: 73.1m (240ft)
Max beam: 9.1m (30ft)
Draught: 3.0m (10ft)
Headroom: 32m (105ft)

River Severn – Gloucester to Worcester
(29 miles)
Max boat length: 41.1m (135ft)
Max beam: 6.4m (21ft)
Draught: 1.8m (6ft)
Headroom: 7.5m (24ft 6in)

River Severn – Worcester to Stourport
(13 miles)
Max boat length: 27.4m (90ft)
Max beam: 5.7m (19ft)
Draught: 1.8m (6ft)
Headroom: 6.1m (20ft)

The upper basin above the narrow locks at Stourport

Gloucester Docks

Gloucester has been a trading point on the River Severn for hundreds of years, certainly since Roman times, and was actually named a port by Elizabeth I in 1580. The impressive dock area that we see today goes back to the opening of the ship canal in 1827, which avoided the winding and tortuous stretch of the river from Sharpness. After this Gloucester really started to thrive and old photographs show graceful square-rigged barquentines and busy fleets of lighters rafted alongside. Cargoes could be moved from sea-going vessels to narrow boats without being transhipped in Bristol and from Gloucester there was quite rapid access to the Midlands.

The increase in trade through the Victorian era meant more quay space and warehousing was needed so the new Victoria Dock was constructed, east of the Main Basin, in 1849. The main cargoes that were stored here were corn, timber, citrus fruits, wines and spirits while the principal export was salt from Worcestershire. These wonderfully preserved warehouses found new uses in the second half of the 20th century. The development of the railways through the 1840s and 50s encouraged train companies to build branch lines into the dock and distribution of imports moved from canal boats to trains through the mid and late 1800s.

Trade continued to expand during the second half of the 19th century but this also meant the size of ships increased. With larger vessels it became more difficult for them to reach Gloucester so a new entrance and dock facilities were opened at Sharpness.

In the early 1900s, steam packets ran a daily service between Gloucester and Sharpness, calling at villages on the way. Today you can experience the trip in some luxury aboard MV *Edward Elgar*, the largest hotel boat on the inland waterways, though it is slightly more expensive than the 1s 3d second class return to Sharpness in 1907. Port traffic boomed during the 1920s when oil terminals were built and tankers shuttled up and down from Avonmouth by river and canal.

Moored these days in the living theatre of Gloucester main basin, you can feel shipping ghosts flitting about the old warehouses and almost hear the squeal of blocks and tackles swinging cargoes onto the quay. The authenticity of the docks has made them a regular location for filming period dramas such as The Onedin Line. Right on the quayside at Gloucester Docks, the National Waterways Museum occupies three fascinating floors of the old Llanthony Warehouse and has some historic boats moored alongside. Don't miss visiting this superb museum as you are passing through Gloucester, for a compelling and extremely nostalgic tour through English transport history. There is also a museum, based in the old Custom House, telling the history of Gloucestershire's regiments and soldiers.

The old warehouses in Gloucester docks have been sympathetically converted

OLDBURY PILL

This attractive rural inlet near the village of Oldbury-on-Severn is on the English side of the Severn Estuary, a couple of miles above the old (upper) Severn Bridge and not quite a mile downstream from Oldbury Power Station. Thornbury Sailing Club have their hospitable base at the mouth of the pill, where there is also a short launching jetty for sailing dinghies. The club was started in 1949 and has a fascinating history if you go to www.thornburysc.org.uk. Further in a few local boats lie on drying moorings. The pill is accessible for about two hours either side of local HW, which is about 20 mins after HW Avonmouth. Small cruising boats that can take the ground safely can settle into the mud and lie here in perfect shelter.

To reach Oldbury Pill when coming up the estuary, pass under the centre of the old Severn Bridge an hour before HW Avonmouth and make good about 070° towards an old red-brick chimney on the east shore behind Littleton Pill. When you are about two cables off the bank, turn to stay parallel with it to avoid various salmon weirs. Oldbury Pill lies a mile upstream from the chimney, and the blue and white painted clubhouse is conspicuous on its north side. When the pill is open, turn into the entrance leaving a small buoy close either side and the club launching jetty to port. Continue up the north side of the pill, leaving to starboard the moorings off the south side. Fetch up just before a floating jetty attached to the north bank. At low water keelboats can sit upright here in the soft mud. Don't venture beyond this jetty though, where there are many dinghy moorings.

Coming down the estuary heading for Oldbury Pill, leave Sharpness an hour before high water there and follow the Upper Severn directions down as far as the Counts light-float. Provided you reach this mark less than an hour after HW Oldbury, turn to steer about 140° towards a prominent tree plantation just south of Oldbury Power Station. The ebb will keep you clear of the walls of the power station cooling reservoir and carry you down towards the pill.

In practice Oldbury Pill is an unlikely port-of-call even for the most pioneering of small cruising boats, but its peaceful estuary atmosphere is rather special and the nearby Anchor Inn at Oldbury-on-Severn does excellent food and beer.

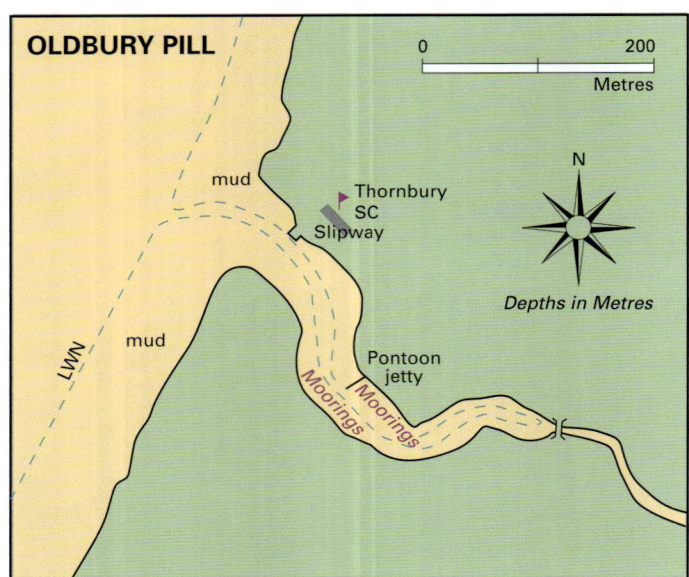

Berkeley Castle

Standing on the south shore of the Severn Estuary, Berkeley Castle is the oldest continually inhabited castle in England and has been in the same family, the Berkeleys, for 25 generations since its construction in 1117. The castle was built on the instructions of Henry II as a fortress on the border with Wales – one of the long line of March castles to keep the Welsh out of England. King Edward II was held prisoner in Berkeley Castle for 18 months before he was murdered in 1327 and the cell in which he was held can still be seen. Another suspicious death that occurred here was that of the last court jester in England, who fell to his death from the minstrel's gallery, also in the 1300s.

The Berkeley family have been close to the courts and kings and queens of England since the Middle Ages. The Barons of the West met at Berkeley Castle before setting out to meet King John at Runnymede to make him sign the Magna Carta. In the castle grounds is Queen Elizabeth I's bowling green and Shakespeare originally wrote *A Midsummer Night's Dream* for a Berkeley wedding celebration. There have been two *HMS Berkeley* ships in the Royal Navy.

The Berkeley family made their name overseas as well as in Britain, with William Berkeley becoming the first Governor of Virginia. Bishop Berkeley of Cloyne left legacies to both Yale and California Universities in the United States, lending his name to the University of California.

Berkeley Castle has one of the largest and oldest archives in the country with over 20,000 documents in safekeeping, many dating back to the time the castle was built. Amongst many of the domestic items you can see in the castle is Francis Drake's cabin chest and Elizabeth I's bedspread. The Earls of Berkeley all fought for the Kings of England in major battles and the banner the Fourth Earl took with him to the Battle of Culloden can also be seen in the castle. In the grounds is a pine tree, said to have grown from a cutting taken at Culloden.

Over the years the castle gradually transformed from a defensive fortress to a refined and elegant stately home. There are rich tapestries, fine furniture and paintings and treasures from around the world. As well as a Norman Keep there is a superb picture gallery, a great hall, dining room and medieval kitchens. The gardens contain many rare plants and a restful lily pond. The grounds reach all the way to the banks of the Severn.

Situated just over two miles from Sharpness, the magnificent castle and grounds can be visited from April to October. For details of opening times and what you can see at the castle visit **www.berkeley-castle.com**.

Berkeley Castle has been owned by the Berkeley family since its construction over 900 years ago *Deb Hopton / The Berkeley and Spetchley Estates*

THE RIVER AVON AND BRISTOL

Summary

The mouth of Bristol's River Avon lies about one and a half miles northeast of Portishead Marina, between Avonmouth south pier head and the breakwater jutting out from Royal Portbury Dock. Avonmouth and Royal Portbury are commercial docks which are normally prohibited to yachts and you should keep clear of shipping in their approaches. The River Avon practically dries at low water to thick mud, but is navigable above half-tide for six miles up to Bristol. Visitors to Bristol lock into the City Docks where there are good quayside berths and a marina. There are also drying berths at Crockerne Pill, a couple of miles into the Avon. Yachts waiting for sufficient rise of tide to enter the Avon can anchor a quarter mile northeast of Portishead Marina lock, there is nowhere to moor in the river itself so if you miss the lock you really have to return to Portishead.

Tides HW Avonmouth is at HW Dover –0415. Heights above chart datum: 13.2m MHWS, 0.9m MLWS, 10.0m MHWN, 3.5m MLWN. HW at Bristol is 10 mins after HW Avonmouth.

Port Control Port of Bristol Authority. Coming up the Severn Estuary bound for Bristol Docks, call *Bristol VTS* on 12 when you are opposite the English and Welsh Grounds fairway buoy, to inform them of your destination and ETA, Bristol Harbour Office ① 0117 903 1484. Once you are well up the River Avon at Black Rock, call *City Docks Radio* on VHF 14 or ① 0117 927 3633. 48 hours' notice is required for Plimsoll Bridge to be opened, this is necessary for all boats with more than 5.8m air draught.

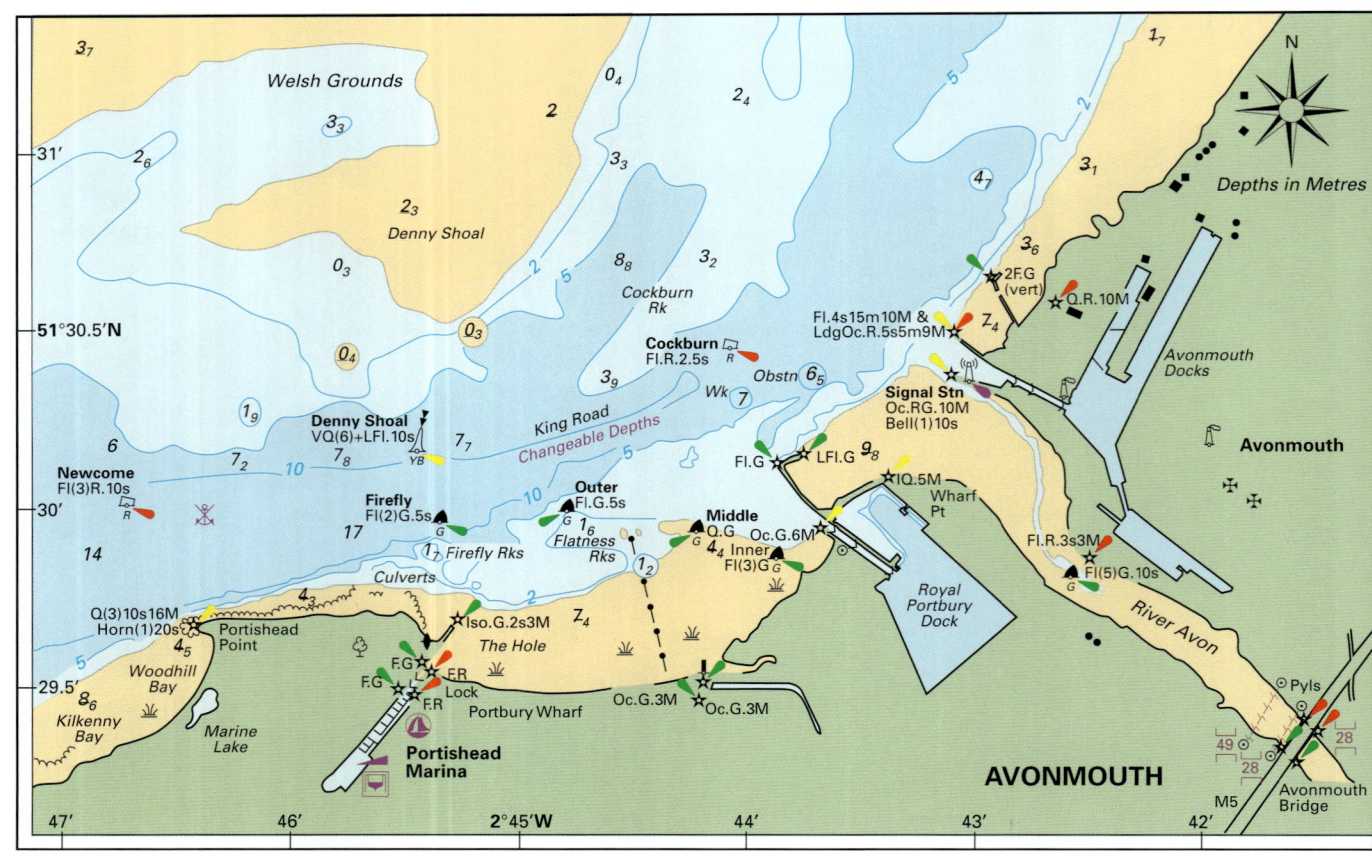

THE RIVER AVON AND BRISTOL

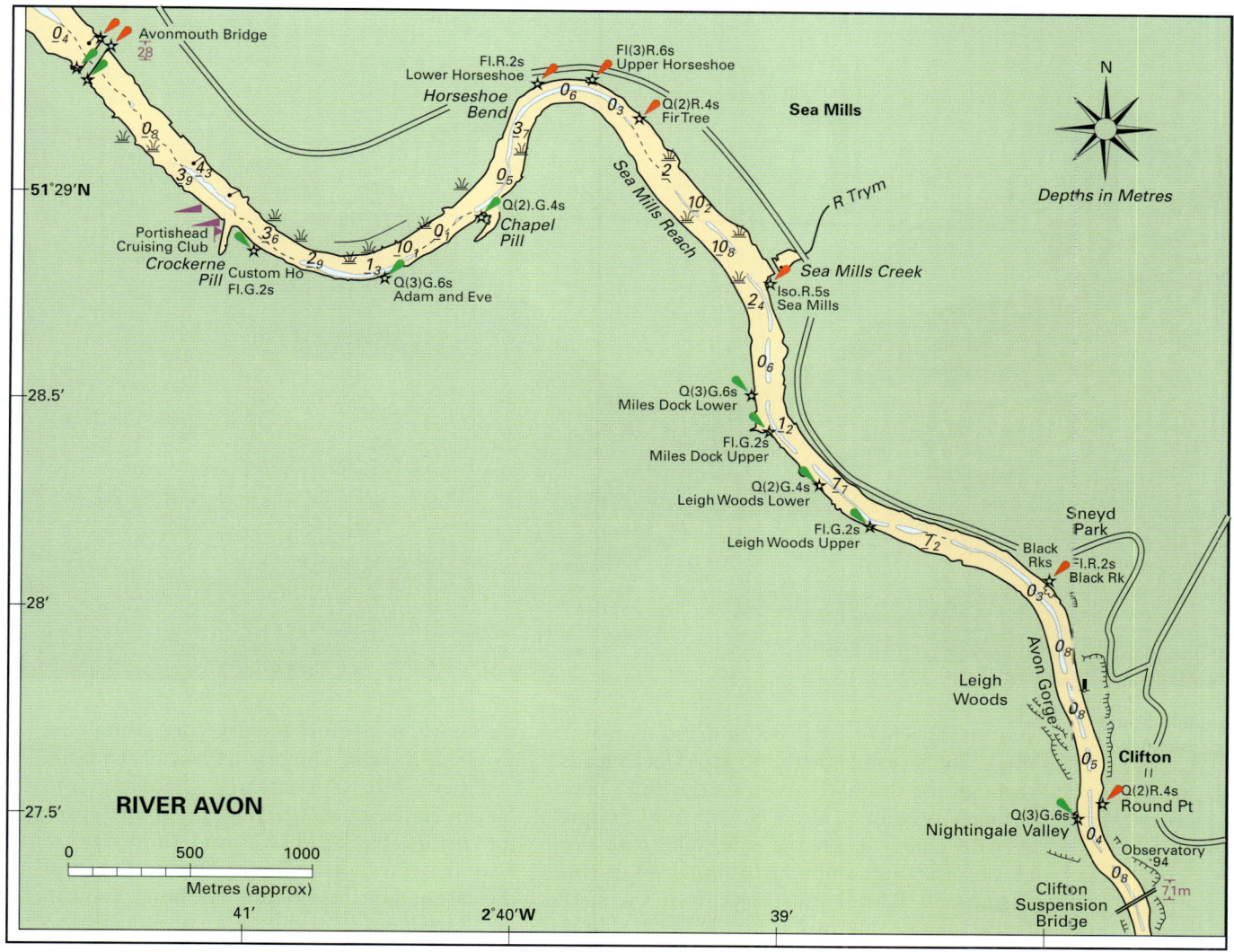

Tidal streams and currents Streams are strong in the approaches to Avonmouth, in excess of five knots on a spring flood. The tide is also strong in the Avon itself, so it's best not to enter the Avon until two hours before HW Bristol.

Description

Above Cardiff, the Bristol Channel narrows into the Severn Estuary, where Bristol Deep cuts between the Welsh and English Grounds banks. From Cardiff to Portishead is 20 miles and Portishead's snug marina is accessible for at least three and a half hours each side of high water. The dockland complexes of Avonmouth and Royal Portbury are conspicuous from the Severn estuary, and somewhere among them is the relatively narrow entrance to the River Avon. The Avon dries out at low springs, but is navigable a couple of hours before high water to the historic city and port of Bristol.

Yachts heading for the River Avon and Bristol Docks should call *Bristol VTS* on 12 in good time to inform traffic control of your destination and ETA. If you are arriving directly up-Channel, call them when you are opposite the English and Welsh Grounds fairway buoy. It is best to stay on the south side of Bristol Deep but if you do approach from the north side the recommended place to cross is just past Denny Shoal S cardinal buoy leaving Firefly G to starboard. If you are coming directly from Portishead, call *Bristol VTS* **before** locking out of the marina a couple of hours before HW Avonmouth. From Portishead you head upstream past Royal Portbury Dock before turning southeast into the Avon paying special attention to ships and tugs moving in and out of the docks.

Entering the Avon you follow the Swash Channel parallel to Avonmouth south pier and only about 75m south of it. Don't turn into the river too soon, because the Swash Bank bulges out north of Portbury Pier. Once into the Swash Channel and out of the cross-tide, follow two sets of leading marks to make a dog-leg into the river. Leave a green conical buoy to starboard as you quit the second line and then stay in midstream for the straight stretches, keeping to the outside of bends.

The valley starts to feel more attractive once you pass the M5 bridge, which has 28m clearance. Crockerne Pill opens up to

SOUTH COAST

Brunel's bridge is as amazing today as it was the day it opened in 1864

starboard, where local boats dry out in soft mud. The last mile before Bristol Docks leads through the dramatic Avon Gorge and under Brunel's elegant Clifton Suspension Bridge. As you come up on the tide, take care not to obstruct any shipping using the fairway. Visitors to Bristol must lock into the City Docks, whose entrance is on the north side of the river a quarter mile above the suspension bridge.

Bristol Marina lies on the south side of what is known as the Floating Harbour, the docks' main inner basin, but you have to pass through Cumberland Basin first. About half a mile into the Floating Harbour you'll see the marina to starboard, just before the dry-dock containing *SS Great Britain*. The marina has all the usual facilities, with a boatyard, chandlery and marine engineers on site, but very limited space for visitors. The best berths for a short stay are near the entrance to St Augustine's Reach at the east end of the Floating Harbour. You can lie alongside the southwest quays adjacent to the Lloyds Bank building, or use the southeast corner near the Arnolfini Arts Centre, handy for the old quarter of town and its pubs and restaurants.

Crockerne Pill, which dries completely to soft mud, lies on the south side of the River Avon, two miles up from Avonmouth and half

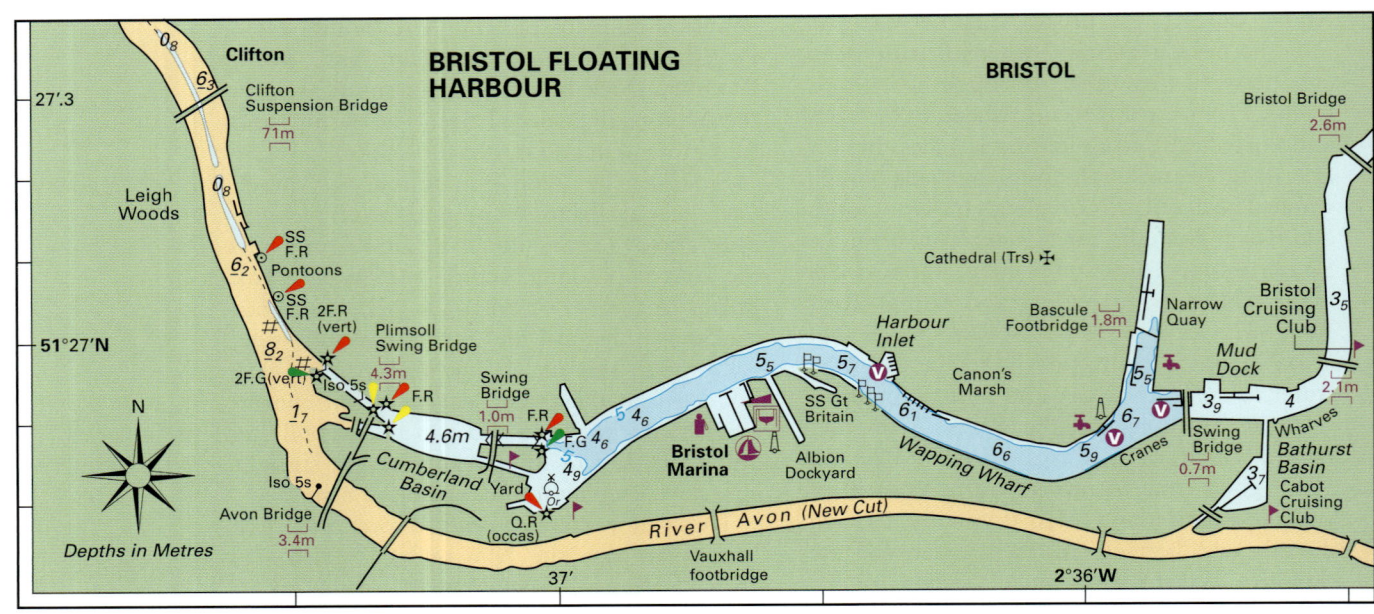

102 • Bristol Channel and Severn Cruising Guide

THE RIVER AVON AND BRISTOL

a mile above the M5 flyover. For small boats that can take the ground safely this tranquil backwater provides a retreat from the fast-flowing river and offers perfect shelter in any weather. At the head of the inlet is an attractive common with some shops nearby. Members of Portishead Cruising Club have their moorings here, and the clubhouse and slip are on the west bank of the entrance. You'll see an iron jetty and a drying grid in the southeast corner of the pill.

Outer approaches

Approaching the mouth of the Bristol Avon involves negotiating some of the fastest flowing stretches of the Severn Estuary and avoiding various extensive areas of drying sand and mud. The tide is a critical factor, whether you are coming upstream or downstream. The good news is that the approaches to the Avon are well marked, because of the considerable volume of commercial traffic using these waters, but keep well clear of any shipping manoeuvring near Avonmouth entrance.

Coming upstream from seaward, Bristol Deep is the buoyed fairway that follows the south shore of the Severn Estuary and leads broadly ENE from the English and Welsh Grounds fairway buoy LF.10s. The buoy positions you between these two shoal areas at a natural crossroads in the estuary, lying just over six miles northeast from Flat Holm island and about five miles south of the mouth of the River Usk.

If you are bound straight up the Avon for Bristol it's usually best to arrive at a position half a mile south of the English and Welsh Grounds fairway buoy about three hours before HW Avonmouth. This gives you, say, just over an hour to cover the 11 miles to Avonmouth (normally plenty of time with the powerful flood tide under you), and a similar period to make the river passage up the Avon. You need to arrive at Bristol Docks entrance at least half an hour before HW so as to catch the last inward lock opening.

Through Bristol Deep leave the North Elbow green conical bell buoy Q.G a cable or so to starboard and continue just north of east for two and a half miles to pass between Clevedon N cardinal buoy (VQ) and the East Mid Grounds red buoy Fl.R.5s. The stream along this stretch will be slightly on your starboard quarter. Two more miles at just north of east take you to the Avon green buoy Fl.G.2.5s and then you follow the line of the coast northeast past Portishead, edging closer inshore to pass Black Nore Point about a quarter of a mile off and then Portishead Point just a cable off, keeping well south of the Newcome Red buoy Fl(3)R. The stream along this stretch will be more or less astern, following the line of the estuary.

Follow the inshore route which will leave Firefly green conical buoy Fl(2)G and the Outer green buoy Fl.G.5s to port on the way. The entrance to the Avon lies not quite one and a half miles 075° from the Firefly buoy.

Coming down the Severn Estuary from Sharpness through The Shoots channel, follow the directions given in the Avonmouth to Sharpness chapter in reverse. However, the trouble with this passage is that you will have used up two to three hours of ebb by the time you arrive off Avonmouth, so the stream will be foul in the Avon with the river level falling quickly. Most boats aim to lock into Portishead Marina for a night and continue up to Bristol the next day, locking out of Portishead again a couple of hours before high water.

Entry

It's important to allow for any cross-tide on the final approach to the Avon. Yachts approaching the river bound for Bristol Docks should call *Bristol VTS* on 12 when off Portishead Point or, if coming from Portishead marina, just before locking out, to advise them of your destination.

The mouth of the Avon looks to be four cables wide between the Royal Portbury Docks pier end LFl.G.15s and Avonmouth south pier head Oc.RG with its prominent signal station. However, a wide mud bank bulges out northwards from the Portbury Pier side of the entrance and the deepest water lies in the Swash Channel, well over on the north side of the mouth as you come in. Therefore

Visitor moorings near the Arnolfini building in Bristol's Floating Harbour

SOUTH COAST

A replica of the *Matthew* offers trips around Bristol's Floating Harbour

Visitors can moor at various locations in the Floating Harbour

THE RIVER AVON AND BRISTOL

keep very close to Avonmouth south pier until St George's leading marks come into line – two white columns on the south side of the river bearing 173° (both Oc.5s). Follow their transit until you are fairly close to the south bank, when the channel curves slightly back towards the north side of the inner mouth past Nelson Point. Thereafter you can generally follow the middle of the river, but tending towards the outside of bends.

There are several other pairs of white column leading marks on the way up to Bristol, all of them lit. Crockerne Pill lies on the south side of the river half a mile above the M5 flyover. Small boats that can take the ground safely can enter this creek within one and a half hours of high water, leaving the moored boats in the centre of the pill to starboard.

If bound for Bristol, call the Dock Master on VHF 14 or ☎ 0117 927 3633 when you are at Black Rock. Tongue Head entrance lock is not far beyond the suspension bridge to port. A watch is kept from three hours before to an hour after high water, although lockings don't normally occur after high water. Normal inward locking times are 2hr 35mins, 1hr 25mins and 15mins before high water, and the lock may stay open for up to half an hour after these times if other craft are expected. Although the last inward lock is 15mins before high water, you won't be shut out if arriving a little late. If you are early or just miss a lock, moor alongside the Hotwells pontoons on the east bank 200m down from the lock.

Having locked into Cumberland Basin and passed through the entrance lock swing bridge, you then have to negotiate a second swing bridge at the 'Junction Lock' between the basin and the Floating Harbour. Bristol Marina lies about half a mile into the Floating Harbour on the starboard hand, but most visiting boats make for the east end of the harbour where you can lie alongside the southwest quays at the entrance to St Augustine's Reach or the pontoons by the Arnolfini Arts Centre.

Locking schedule

For guidance the locking schedule is as follows but can be changed by the Marine Services Supervisor. Bridges are not swung during periods of heavy traffic flow.

Times before High Water	Outwards		Inwards	
First Locking	2 hours	50 mins	2 hours	35 mins
Second Locking	1 hours	40 mins	1 hours	25 mins
Third Locking		30 mins		15 mins

Entry at night

Although not recommended for strangers, entering and navigating the Avon at night is quite feasible in clear weather using a chart plotter. The leading marks in the river are all lit and there are also numerous single lights on either bank – green lights to starboard and orange lights to port.

Berths and anchorages

Floating Harbour visitors' berths There are approximately 50 visitors' berths in the Floating Harbour with short-stay berths near the entrance to St Augustine's Reach at the east end. You can lie alongside the southwest quays adjacent to the Lloyds Bank building, or use the visitors' pontoons near the Arnolfini Arts Centre which are now secure with coded access. These are handy for the old quarter of town with its pubs, restaurants, theatres and galleries. Harbour Inlet can only be used by boats of less than 15m length and 2m draught. The Floating Harbour hosts numerous events during the year so can become quite busy, check www.bristolfloatingharbour.org.uk, for the dates of events.

Bristol Marina Situated on the south side of the Floating Harbour, between the Baltic Wharf development and *SS Great Britain*, Bristol Marina's pontoon berths offer complete shelter with ready access to boatyard facilities, a Marine Travelift up to 50 tonnes, engineers, sailmaker and chandlery. However, the marina has limited room for visitors and you should book a berth in advance ☎ 0117 921 3198. Diesel and water are available alongside. The marina is about a mile from the city centre but there are shops within a short walking distance.

Crockerne Pill This rather attractive drying inlet off the south side of the lower Avon is suitable for small boats that can take the ground safely. The name Crockerne Pill means Pottery Wharf and in the 12th century pottery was made here, examples of which can be seen at Bristol City Museum. Later, many pilots or hobblers lived at Pill and would take ships up the river to the docks in the city. The creek is the headquarters of the long-established Portishead Cruising Club, who always welcome visitors. It's a good idea to contact the secretary in advance at: The Clubhouse, Pump Square, Pill, Bristol BS20 0BG ☎ 01275 373988 (Wed. evenings), www.pccsail.com. The waterside clubhouse on the west side of the creek entrance is open every Wednesday evening. Visitors can make their way upstairs to the bar and introduce themselves to the bar staff.

SOUTH COAST

Bristol Marina has only limited space for visitors

There's lots of boating activity in the harbour

Enter near high water if possible, or at least within one and a half hours of high. You take the ground in soft mud, whether you use a vacant mooring or go alongside the iron jetty in the southeast corner of the pill. There's a water tap close to the jetty and local shops nearby.

Scouring operations

To maintain the depth in the Floating Harbour scouring operations take place about twice a month. Details of when this will happen are posted in Local Notices to Mariners which can be found on the Bristol Harbour website which also contains a lot of useful information
www.bristol.gov.uk/streets-travel/bristol-harbour

106 • Bristol Channel and Severn Cruising Guide

Historic Bristol Docks

In the days of sail the old quays of Bristol Docks would have been double-banked with trading clippers, barquentines and brigantines from around the globe. Naval ships, small coasters and fishing boats would have jostled for space in the harbour.

Then, as now, ports were intriguing places, but they were also dens of iniquity, hopefully less so today. There were the waterfront inns where the press gang roamed freely to keep the Navy manned in the long battle against Napoleon. You would also find all the practical trades and suppliers associated with shipping – the chandlers, sailmakers, rope makers and shipwrights.

There were coopers who made the countless wooden barrels used for storing water, salted meat or gunpowder. There were the unsung firms that slaughtered the pork and beef and then salted the meat down into the tough pickled joints that seafarers became accustomed to. There were the biscuit-makers, who baked the hard ships' biscuit that could survive months at sea so long as you knocked the crusts on the table before eating to drive the weevils out.

Supporting these ships and seafarers were countless skills and crafts that were part of Bristol's everyday life but have now passed into history. Yachtsmen can probably appreciate their demise as well as anyone. Even in the short history of production yachts, experts that were once a normal part of the sailing scene have now become quaint reminders of a bygone era. Not many yachtsmen can tuck a splice these days, or need to, even whipping a rope's end has given way to heat sealing.

Probably the strongest vibes of history in Bristol Docks now come from the dry basin on the south side of the Floating Harbour where SS Great Britain lies as a proud monument to the first days of steam. Designed by Isambard Kingdom Brunel, Great Britain was built in 1843 at Bristol's Great Western Dockyard. Built to serve the growing transatlantic passenger trade, she set off for her maiden voyage to New York on 26 July 1845, a passage completed in an astounding 14 days. This achievement marked the beginning of a new era in nautical history and SS Great Britain was one of the technological forerunners of modern shipping. Still looking elegant in her dry dock, Great Britain also seems to exemplify the industry and inventiveness of the Victorian era and the birth of international passenger travel.

It was no mean feat to reach Bristol docks in a large sailing ship, unlike today in an easily handled boat with an engine. The narrow winding river with fluky wind would have been a challenge for any ship's master. Although the river mouth was wider in those days, without Avonmouth or Portbury docks, ships would try to approach the Avon at high water slack.

The lower reaches of the Avon were deeper then, and once in the river large sailing ships would moor opposite Broad Pill, just below where the motorway bridge is now, and further up on the outside of the next bend, below Ham Green to wait for the next high water before making the last leg up to Bristol.

Except in highly favourable conditions, ships would have been towed slowly upriver by a couple of 'hobblers', the traditional longboats of about 25ft pulled by four or six oarsmen. These boats were based at Pill and plied an active trade in the busy days of sail. The tide provided the motive power and the hobblers kept the ship heading in the right direction. The trick was always to use the elements to best advantage, softly softly, waiting a tide if necessary. Brute force was not employed until steam tugs arrived on the scene.

The Avon Gorge is the most dramatic stretch of the river, in the last mile before Bristol lock. The Clifton suspension bridge harmonises perfectly with this natural cut. It is a truly graceful piece of engineering, another of Isambard Kingdom Brunel's creations but not completed until 1864, five years after his death. The elegant catenary seems perfectly to complement your gradual transition from river to city.

SS Great Britain is a great visitor attraction

PORTISHEAD

Portishead Marina is a friendly location

Summary

Now well established in the old Portishead dock, the spacious 356 berth Boatfolk Portishead Marina has become an important base for Bristol Channel cruising, strategically placed to take advantage of the powerful tidal escalator downstream and handy for making a passage upstream to Sharpness. The marina entrance, partly protected by a jutting pier, lies seven cables east of Portishead Point and about one and a half miles WSW of the mouth of the Avon. The marina is entered through a tidal lock and is accessible for at least three and a half hours each side of high water. Pay-at-Pump diesel and petrol are available alongside, just inside the lock to port, opposite is a black water pump out station. The marina has plenty of room for visitors, is within easy walking distance of the town and, surrounded by new waterside properties, is developing a restful, residential atmosphere. There are several restaurants and bars along the quay on the north and east sides serving Italian, fish & chips and modern European dishes.

Tides HW Portishead is at HW Dover −0415, i.e. at the same time as HW Avonmouth. Heights above chart datum in Portishead Pool: 13.1m MHWS and 9.9m MHWN.

Port Control Portishead Marina, Lock control building Portishead BS20 7DF. Call *Portishead Marina* on VHF 80 or ☏ 01275 841941.

Tidal streams and currents Streams are moderate in the bay between Portishead pier and Royal Portbury Dock,

but strong further out in King Road. A local eddy sets west towards the pierhead for most of the flood. Close inshore off Portishead Point, the stream turns west-going about two hours before high water.

Description

Once an active trading port, Portishead was gradually eclipsed by Avonmouth and Royal Portbury, so that Portishead dock became very run down until the marina was developed there. Now Boatfolk Portishead Marina is an important base and staging post for Bristol Channel cruising, while many Bristol owners keep their boats there. The marina has excellent facilities, with good showers, water and electricity at the pontoons, and a fuel berth supplying both diesel and petrol, black water pump out, hard standing and boatcare repair facilities are available in its two yards. There is a 35 tonne hoist and private slip suitable for trailer boats up to 7m and max 1.5 tonnes. Not far away there are pubs, restaurants and shops – the Royal Hotel is five minutes' walk on Pier Road and you'll find a Waitrose supermarket and a leisure centre just outside the marina.

Surrounding the marina there's a great choice of bars and restaurants, try Searock where you can either have fish and chips to take back to the boat or eat in their restaurant overlooking the marina. Just past Waitrose you can visit the Port Bar in the Precinct which offers coffee and breakfast, lunches or supper and craft beers. At the south end of the marina Aqua has a first class menu and Hall and Woodhouse are on the quay. From the marina you can set off to explore the nature reserve and there is a good bus service into Bristol which takes about 40 minutes.

The marina entrance faces northeast, partly sheltered from the north and west by a quay and then a jutting pier. The area just outside the lock gates to the east is known locally as 'The Hole', once quite a pronounced muddy gully scoured by a drainage sluice serving the low-lying land to the south. This area now dries to soft glutinous mud for about two and a half hours each side of low water and yachts can anchor in The Hole or sometimes use one of the private buoys there if vacant. The soft mud is quite safe for a keelboat to sink into and, before the marina was open, this relatively sheltered area was once used regularly as a staging anchorage by boats on passage up or down the estuary. Boats waiting for the marina lock to open can either jill about or else anchor for a while on the south edge of Portishead Pool, roughly a cable northeast of the pier head in about three metres datum depth.

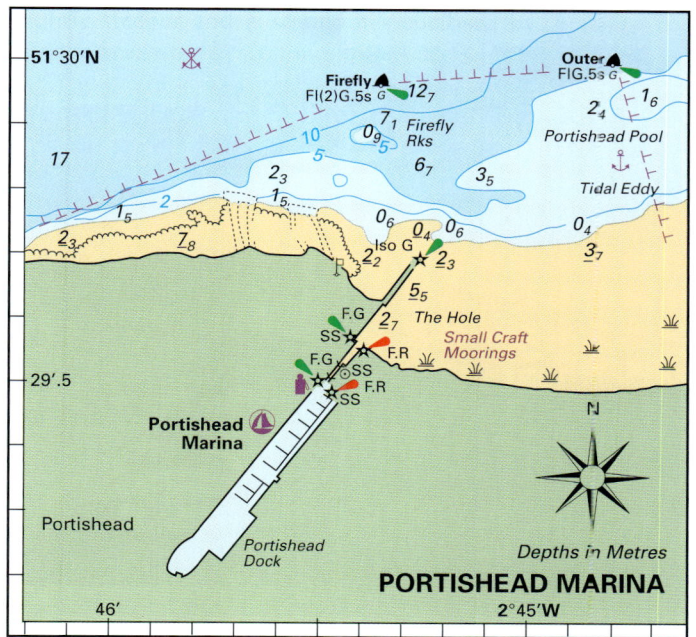

The tide runs away quickly outside the lock at Portishead

SOUTH COAST

Cruisers and narrow boats mingle at Portishead

Approach and entry

Coming up the estuary, follow the directions for the River Avon but then turn south towards Portishead pier and the marina entrance immediately after rounding Firefly green buoy Fl(2)G.5s. Firefly rocks, with only 0.9m depth at datum, lie about 100m south of the buoy. Watch for the west-going eddy setting towards the pier as you approach.

Coming down the estuary from Sharpness or across from the River Avon, pass just west of the Outer green buoy Fl.G.5s before heading towards Portishead pier and the marina entrance.

Entry at night

Portishead can be approached at night near high water, so long as you take care to counteract first the main tidal stream and then the west-going inshore eddy that sets towards the pier. Portishead pier head has an isophase green light and you'll see port and starboard lights at the entrance to the lock. The marina traffic control signal lights are just off the outer lock gates and follow the normal IALA international standard.

Berths and anchorages

Boatfolk Portishead Marina Visitors berth as directed in the marina and you'll receive instructions in the lock (or call on VHF 80). The marina has comprehensive facilities and is a snug and attractive place to lie.

Anchoring outside the marina lock Boats waiting for the Portishead marina lock to open can anchor for a while about a cable northeast of the pier head in about 3m datum depth.

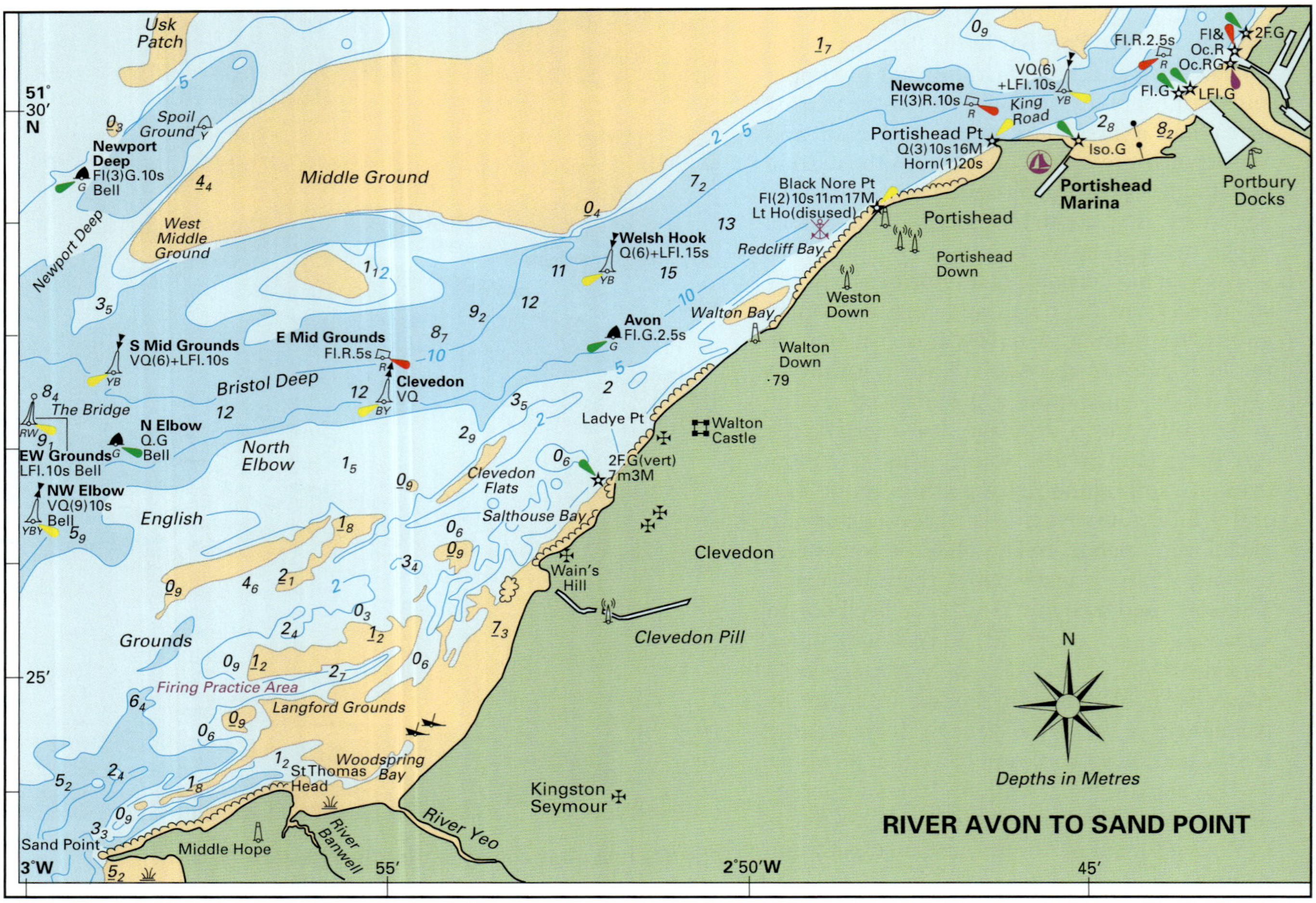

110 • Bristol Channel and Severn Cruising Guide

WALTON BAY

The fast-flowing Severn Estuary and upper reaches of the Bristol Channel have relatively few naturally sheltered coves or bays where you can tuck close in on a whim and drop the hook, but Walton Bay is one of them. Little more than a slight indent into the rolling Somerset shore, this anchorage is nevertheless a pleasantly remote spot where you can fetch up well inshore out of the worst of the tide, given the right weather conditions. Only two and a half miles southwest along the coast from Portishead Point, Walton Bay lies opposite the small village of Farley, a couple of cables up-Channel from a conspicuous disused tower on the coast just below Walton Down. This tower is the old Walton signal station that was once manned by watch-keepers to keep an eye on shipping movements up and down the Channel. Flag signals were flown to ships and barges anchored inshore of this stretch of coast to inform masters that berths were ready for them up at Bristol or, after 1908, the Royal Edward Dock at Avonmouth. Now the tower carries radar scanners used by *Bristol VTS* for watching traffic.

Walton Bay is a gentle and straightforward part of the coast and the low cliffs, slightly crumbling, are uncomplicated with only a few rocky ledges fringing the shore. In the days of sail, barges and coasters used to fetch up here if they ran out of tide on the way up to Bristol. A wide drying shoal northeast of the bay affords some natural protection as the ebb falls away,

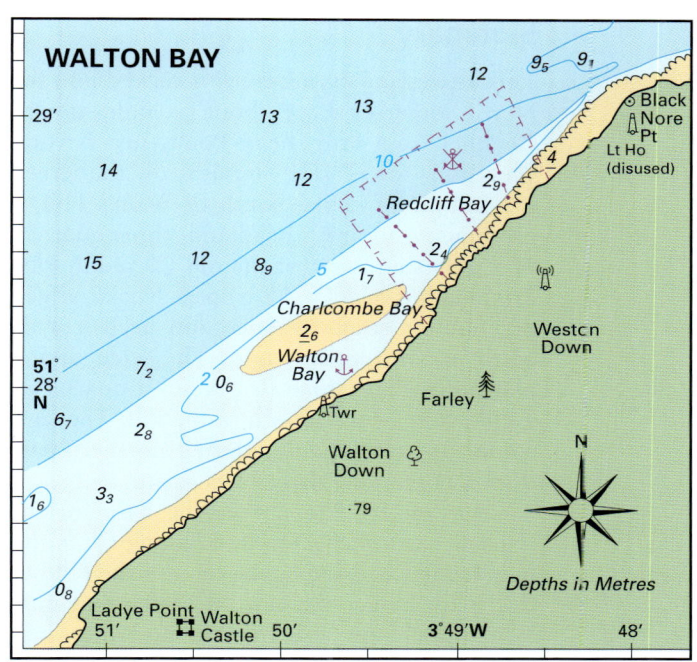

as does a drying bank a little way offshore 3–4 cables west of the bay. Charlcombe Bay is just a quarter of a mile northeast of Walton Bay and a small rocky ledge juts out slightly between them.

At neaps, and partway between neaps and springs, most yachts will be able to anchor and stay afloat in Walton Bay, but at dead springs low water depths are skimpy and you have to anchor further out to stay afloat.

Bristol Channel and Severn Cruising Guide • 111

CLEVEDON PILL

Summary

This interesting drying creek is tucked into the North Somerset shore about six miles down-Channel from Portishead Point, just beyond Clevedon town. The mouth of the creek is a couple of cables south of Wain's Hill, a prominent humped headland three-quarters of a mile southwest of the old Clevedon Pier. Fringing this headland are Spear Rocks, which dry out for some distance and need a wide berth as you come round. The wide drying plateau of Blackstone Rocks lies a quarter of a mile west of the mouth of the Pill. They are completely unmarked and their northern part dries a potentially dangerous 5.2m.

Clevedon Pill used to be the base for the cruising section of Clevedon Sailing Club and they maintained some moorings in the Pill but this is no longer the case. It seems that only local boats now use the Pill and there are doubts about the reliability of any markers indicating how to enter the creek.

Clevedon Sailing Club has its premises on the Marine Parade along Clevedon seafront and they have a useful website, www.clevedonsailingclub.com, if visitors are cruising in the area. Most of the cruising members now keep their boats rather more remotely. Club members recommend that entering the Pill should only be undertaken with local advice. There is still a sketch chart in the BCYA handbook for approaching the Pill and the following directions Peter researched for the last edition of this book.

Tidal streams and currents Off the entrance to Clevedon Pill and close off Wain's Hill, the tide turns about 20 minutes before slack water out in the estuary. The streams run broadly NE–SW and reach three and a half knots at springs. The last of the Channel flood starts turning to set offshore near Blackstone Rocks. The ebb coming down past Clevedon also tends to set slightly offshore.

Approach and entry

Strangers should only approach Clevedon Pill in a shallow draught boat and during the last two hours before high water. However, while Blackstone Rocks are an obvious hazard, they also create a substantial natural breakwater that protects the creek from the west. Further shelter is given by the extensive drying sands well out to the west and southwest, the outer cordon being the long narrow banks of the English Grounds.

The tortuous channel through the Clevedon Pill saltings is marked rather enigmatically by perches, but entering slowly in quiet weather on the last of the flood you can't come to much harm even if you mistake a mark. Near the head of the creek you can find good shelter by taking the ground in the narrow fairway between the salt marshes. Lie either to fore-and-aft anchors or use a vacant local mooring.

Apart from Wain's Hill, the coastline here is rather low-lying, close as it is to the Somerset Levels. At the head of Clevedon Pill is a Flemish-looking dyke with a drainage sluice, and the inlet itself is fringed with salt marshes. The Pill is occupied by mostly shoal draught local boats, and its upper part offers good shelter in almost all conditions. The creek is only vulnerable at high water springs in a fresh north-westerly, when the saltings are covered and the protection they give to the narrow winding channel is temporarily removed. There are shops about half a mile away.

Coming up the estuary In quiet weather only, strangers should pass about a quarter of a mile off Sand Point no earlier than one and a half hours before high water. Then make good about 055° across Langford Grounds, which in practice means heading for the coastline receding beyond Clevedon. Langford Grounds will be well covered at this state of tide but the flood stream may create some eerie swirls and eddies. Four miles on from Sand Point you'll see Wain's Hill coming up on the starboard bow, but be sure to stay outside Blackstone Rocks by keeping distant Ladye Point well open of the end of the old Clevedon Pier.

When Wain's Hill bears 095° turn straight towards it. This clearing line will keep you safely north of Blackstone Rocks, but you must also avoid Spear Rocks that fringe the west and northwest sides of the Wain's Hill promontory. Drawing closer inshore towards the mouth of Clevedon Pill, you should be able to see an outer post with two smaller perches beyond it. These three marks lie close off the southwest side of Wain's Hill. The post should be left close to starboard while the two outer perches are left to port. Then identify the next perch, which is left to starboard as the channel makes a tight turn west and then southwest, with three more perches being left to port. Opposite the last of these three is another perch on the west side of the channel, marking the point at which the deep water makes a right-angle turn to the southeast. Thereafter you leave all perches to port and wind your way up between the salt marshes.

Coming down the estuary Between Portishead and Clevedon the coast is reasonably clear of dangers save for the long sandbank (drying 1.2m) off Walton Bay. A useful offing mark is the Avon green conical buoy (Fl.G.2.5s) which lies just over a mile N by E from the end of the old Clevedon Pier. From the Avon buoy make good about 200° for two miles, passing the pier a good three cables off. This track takes you to a position close WNW of Wain's Hill, which you should round a cable off before proceeding as above.

Entry at night

Definitely not recommended for strangers.

Berths and anchorages

In the Pill Work into the Pill between the salt marshes and look for a clear spot where you can lie in the channel between fore-and-aft anchors. If possible you should ask a local before taking the ground – it's important not to obstruct the fairway, and in any case you may be able to use a vacant mooring. Wherever you come to rest, stay well away from the steep banks because you'll dry out at an uncomfortable angle if you tuck in too close. There are various small wooden landing stages in the upper part of the Pill, a concrete slip and a couple of sets of steps.

Clevedon Pill may be an acquired taste

LANGFORD SWATCH

In quiet weather, the shallow inner channel known as Langford Swatch makes an interesting shortcut between Clevedon and Sand Point, inside the well-drying sands known as Langford Grounds. The Swatch also provides access to anchorages in Woodspring Bay. Imray's electronic chart shows the general line of this inner passage, which only dries about five feet at MLWS and is available for most of the tide at neaps. As the ebb falls away the streams broadly follow the line of the Swatch and can reach three knots, especially when Langford Grounds are uncovered.

Coming down-Channel, say from Clevedon Pill, steer SSW from a position a couple of

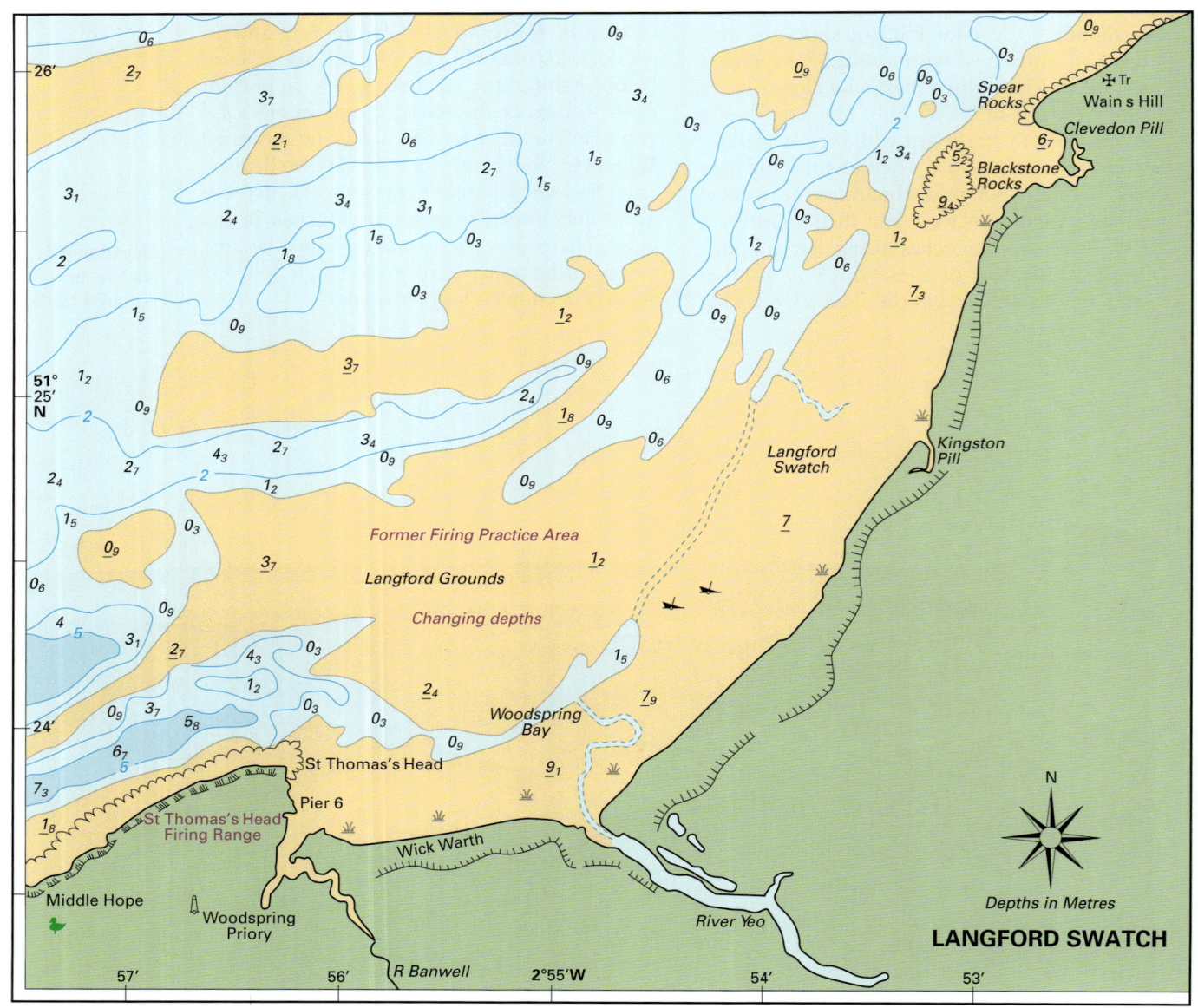

cables or so outside Blackstone Rocks. This course leads between the hard, gently shoaling sand of Langford Grounds and the steeper but softer mud fringing the coast. Keep towards the mud rather than the sand. About one and a half miles downstream from Blackstone you'll see two above-water wrecks a quarter of a mile off the beach. Pass close outside these wrecks and follow the trend of the shore. Off the mouth of the River Yeo, when St Thomas's Head bears about 265°, steer towards St Thomas's at first and then edge offshore to clear the point by two cables. Finally hug the Middle Hope shore about two cables off emerging into the main Bristol Channel again off Sand Point.

Langford Swatch should only be taken in quiet weather when there's no swell. The ideal conditions would be light southeasterly winds when the tides are near neaps.

Bristol Channel Yachting Association

The Bristol Channel Yachting Association acquired its present name in 2003, but before the change of identity this long-running organization was known as the Bristol Channel Yachting Conference. For over 50 years the BCYC was an active forum for advancing the interests of all those folk who enjoy boating, sailing and cruising the Bristol Channel, and its strong contacts and regular liaison between so many local clubs was, and still is, rather unique in the boating world.

Over the years the membership base of the BCYA has expanded to include associate membership for marinas and yacht class associations. This allows all members and berth holders of these organisations to benefit from the network of knowledge and contacts within the association. It also means that many thousands of sailors can proudly fly the distinctive BCYA house flag – red for Wales, blue for the Bristol Channel and white for England.

The 21st century BCYA has a user-friendly website for everyone using these waters, **www.bcya.org.uk**. The site incorporates the latest news; details of its practical conservation scheme, *BCYA Blue*; weather and navigation; up to date contact details for clubs, marinas and harbours; a guide to anchorages; an online shop; a list of the year's events all over the channel plus an active social media presence. In addition the BCYA produces *The Blue Book* – an A5 spiral bound book of contacts and sketch charts which is a must for every chart table. And don't forget a copy of the songbook for those impromptu meetings on the water.

The BCYA runs three Channel rallies every year, each tying in with major shoreside events. Entry is free and if any encouragement to attend is needed there's a free drinks reception. The Welsh Coast Rally, which takes place in July, is the occasion for the presentation of trophies, a large silver cup for the Bristol Channel Yachtsperson of the Year and a framed certificate to the Bristol Channel Club of the Year.

This invaluable organisation is run on a completely voluntary basis so if you cruise the Bristol Channel be sure you support it.

BCYA Rally in Cardiff, July 2022 *Gordon Craig*

WOODSPRING BAY

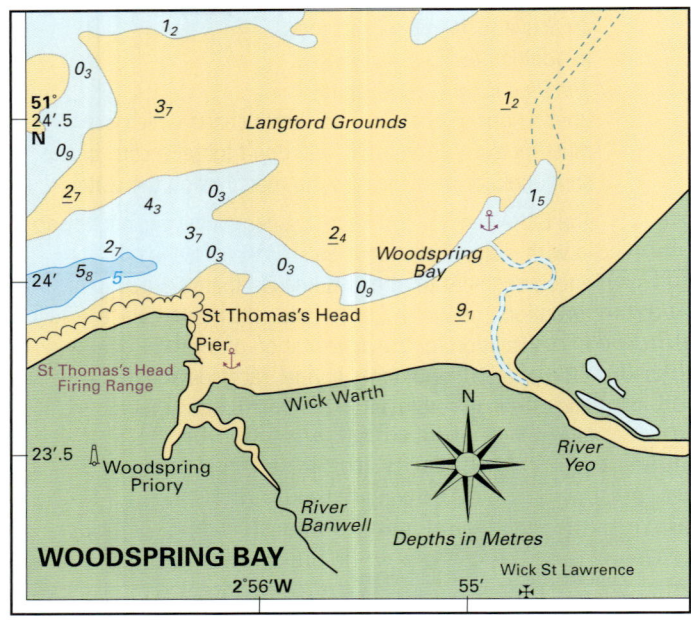

In quiet settled weather or with offshore winds, moderate draught yachts passing through Langford Swatch can find a snug passage anchorage in Woodspring Bay off the mouth of the River Yeo, which meets the Bristol Channel not quite a mile east of St Thomas's Head. Except at low springs moderate draught boats will just stay afloat in the Swatch itself, or you can tuck further in out of the tide and sit in the mud off the mouth of the river. The same applies to the mouth of the River Banwell, just southeast of St Thomas's Head off the old MOD jetty. These are both peaceful get-away-from-it-all spots with no facilities ashore. From St Thomas's Head a path leads inshore to Woodspring Priory, a striking, ecclesiastical looking building with an ornate square tower, owned and restored by the Landmark Trust.

On some charts, Woodspring Bay is still shown as a firing practice area and St Thomas's Head is marked as a firing range. However, it's only occasionally that this lonely, atmospheric stretch of the Somerset coast is used by the RAF for target practice and the anchorages in Woodspring Bay described above can be safely visited during the summer months with peace of mind.

The church at Woodspring Priory *Landmark Trust / John Miller*

WESTON-SUPER-MARE

Summary

Weston-super-Mare is a traditional seaside resort at the north end of Weston Bay. Knightstone Harbour lies close southeast of Anchor Head which, together with Birnbeck Island and its access pier, forms the north extremity of the bay. The harbour area is rather exposed to the south, partly protected from the southwest by its sea wall, and reasonably sheltered from other directions by the land. The firm sandy bottom allows keelboats to dry out on legs or against two wooden piles at the quay. Knightstone is accessible for about two hours each side of high water, but neaps restrict movements to shoal-draught boats. Weston Bay is fringed with fine sandy beaches, although further out the bay dries for over a mile at datum to mud.

Tides HW Weston-super-Mare is at HW Avonmouth –0020 or HW Dover –0435. Heights above chart datum: 12.0m MHWS, 0.7m MLWS, 9.0m MHWN, 2.7m MLWN.

Port Control Knightstone Harbour is managed by North Somerset Council at Tropicana Office, Marine Parade, Weston-super-Mare, BS23 1BE, ☎ 01934 626982.

Tidal streams and currents There is always a south-going stream in Weston Bay, strongest at half ebb and flood. At the south end of the bay the tide sets west along Brean Down, causing overfalls off Howe Rock in fresh westerlies. The strong streams off Birnbeck Island can also cause overfalls.

Description

The broad expanse of Weston Bay faces due west and is bounded on the north by Anchor Head and Birnbeck Island, and on the south by the distinctive two-humped promontory of Brean Down. A few miles offshore are the two prominent islands of Steep Holm and Flat Holm, while the Cardiff Bay barrage locks are less than nine miles across the Bristol Channel from Weston-super-Mare. Weston Bay dries completely for over a mile at low springs, to sand close in and mud further out. Around the fringes of the bay are Weston-super-Mare's popular beaches. Weston feels like a seaside time warp, with its grand pier, donkey rides and fish-and-chip shops, but its drying harbour at Knightstone is fun to visit near high water.

Tucked into the northeast corner of Weston Bay, close to the town centre, Knightstone Harbour is partly protected from the southwest by the curve of the sea wall, the southwest end of which is referred to as Knightstone Pier. The harbour has a firm bottom, is reasonably sheltered except in winds from between south and southwest and can generally be entered two hours either side of HW. Knightstone Harbour is simply a relatively protected area of firm drying sand where local boats moor. Tripper boats and ferries for Steep Holm island pick-up and land at the quay steps.

Two cables south of the harbour, Weston Grand Pier is a prominent mark from offshore and is left a cable to starboard on the way in. The pier acts as a partial breakwater from the south and should not be approached too closely because the tide sets strongly through it. Weston, as a bustling seaside resort, is not one of the more tranquil havens of the Bristol Channel, but it does have all the facilities of a large town and its summer holiday atmosphere can be infectious.

Outer approaches

Four miles out in the Bristol Channel, opposite Weston Bay, are the two islands of Flat Holm and Steep Holm. Flat Holm has a lighthouse Fl(3)WR.10s and several old farm buildings. Steep Holm is maintained as a nature reserve and is unlit. Both are steep-to and can be approached safely provided that due allowance is made for the strong tidal streams out in mid-channel. From Steep Holm, Brean Down bears about 115° distant two and a half miles, while the entrance to Knightstone Harbour bears about 080° distant four and a half miles.

SOUTH COAST

Six miles WSW of Steep Holm is the East Culver E cardinal buoy Q(3)10s, which marks the east end of the Culver Sand, a narrow shoal not quite two miles long and with only 2.2m LAT depth at its shallowest part. Except in very quiet weather you should give this sandbank a wide berth when approaching Weston from down-Channel. The West Culver W cardinal buoy VQ(9)10s lies just over two miles west of the East Culver buoy.

Approach and entry

Strangers should only approach Weston Bay near high water, preferably on the last of the flood when the Bristol Channel streams are dying down.

From down-Channel Clear Brean Down by at least half a mile to avoid the sometimes boisterous overfalls off its west tip, and then head northeast for Anchor Head, keeping Birnbeck Island on your port bow and Weston Grand Pier fine to starboard. When entering Weston Bay remember that the stream will begin to set south as you draw inside Birnbeck. The final approach line is about 080° leaving Weston Grand Pier a cable to starboard and Knightstone Pier to port. A post beacon marks the end of a short causeway extending out

WESTON-SUPER-MARE

from Knightstone pier head. Round up into the harbour and either anchor or go alongside the quay.

From up-Channel Give a wide berth to Birnbeck Island with its overfalls and strong tidal sets. Then head southeast to round Anchor Head before approaching Knightstone Harbour as above.

Entry at night

Remember that Steep Holm, Brean Down and Birnbeck Island are unlit. The short pier on the north side of Birnbeck Island sometimes shows two fixed vertical green lights, but don't confuse Birnbeck with Weston Pier, which reliably shows two bright fixed vertical greens that are the only useful approach lights for Knightstone Harbour. Approaching or leaving Weston Bay at night, it's important to keep a close watch on your tidal set by taking frequent bearings of lights you can identify with certainty – Flat Holm island Fl(3)WR.10s and, in clear visibility, Monkstone Rock lighthouse Fl.5s over on the Welsh side of the Channel.

Berths and anchorages

Knightstone Harbour Yachts with legs or bilge-keel boats can dry out on a firm sandy bottom east of Knightstone pier head. There are numerous mooring chains in the harbour so anchors should be buoyed. Keelboats may lie alongside the two wooden dolphins at the quay, by arrangement with the council. You can land with a dinghy at the steps or the pier head slipway, but take care not to obstruct local boatmen. Shops are nearby and you'll find a water tap on the pier head slipway.

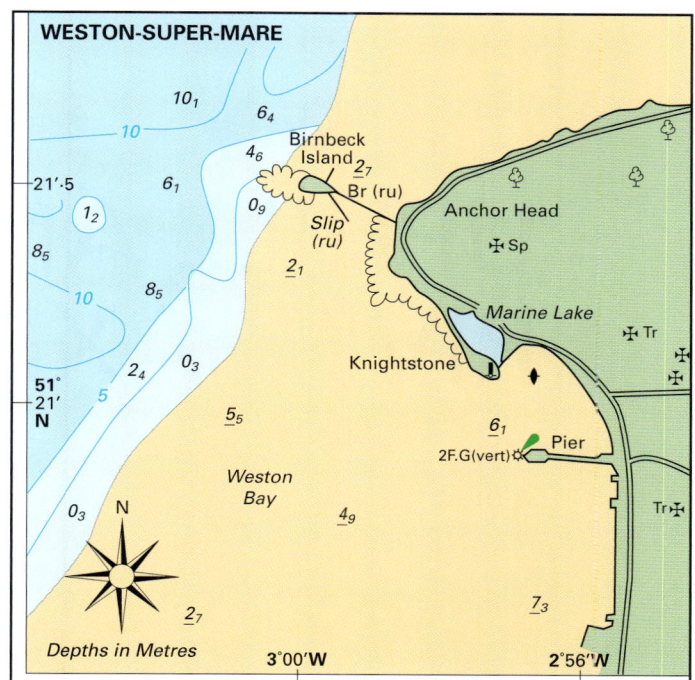

Above:
Knightstone drying harbour at Weston-super-Mare

Left:
Weston-super-Mare's famous pier

UPHILL AND THE RIVER AXE

Summary

The shallow River Axe flows into the southeast corner of Weston Bay and in reasonable weather can be entered for about 1¾ hours each side of high water. You approach from a position about four cables north of Brean Down and the outer mark is Juicy red and white buoy which is on the edge of the mud bank. The channel is not dredged so can move. Initially steer towards Black Rock then you should start to pick up the port-hand marks. Inside the river mouth the banks are marked by port and starboard hand marks. The river contains numerous local moorings, especially in the first half mile. There are no visitors' berths as such, but the Weston Bay Yacht Club can usually find a vacant mooring for a night or two. Uphill, an attractive small village on the outskirts of Weston-super-Mare, lies on the east shore of the Axe.

Tides As for Weston, i.e. HW at the river mouth is at HW Avonmouth –0020 or HW Dover –0435. Heights above datum: 12.0m MHWS, 0.7m MLWS, 9.0m MHWN, 2.7m MLWN.

Port Control Weston Bay Yacht Club leases the River Axe from the Environment Agency and the club controls all the moorings from near their clubhouse upstream to the Brean Road sluice. Contact the Moorings Master ☎ 07519 804588. The moorings in Uphill Pill are managed by Uphill Wharf, ☎ 01934 418617.

Tidal streams and currents The stream is always south-going in Weston Bay, turning west-going along the north shore of Brean Down as it flows out into the Bristol Channel. There are often overfalls off the west tip of Brean, where this local current meets the main Channel tide.

Description

The River Axe is narrow, shallow and extremely muddy, but has a rather wild, salty and attractive atmosphere that will appeal to all those who enjoy winding creeks surrounded by salt marshes and open country. The whole area around the Axe and the Pill is an SSSI. The Axe is well packed with boats of all sorts and several sailing clubs operate from Uphill Sands, at the mouth of the river, where there are small boats drawn up on the beach and storage huts for gear. Weston Bay Yacht Club, which was established in 1932 and used to be based at Knightstone, have their wooden clubhouse at Uphill Sands. The river contains numerous local moorings, especially in the first half mile before Uphill Pill. There are no visitors' berths as such, but members of Weston Bay Yacht Club are always helpful and can usually find you a vacant mooring for a night or two and the club has a pontoon at the entrance to the river.

This southeast corner of Weston Bay is dominated by Brean Down, a long narrow peninsula with two distinctive 'humps', that juts out for almost a mile to form the south arm of the bay. Brean looks like an island from a distance, since the surrounding land is low-lying.

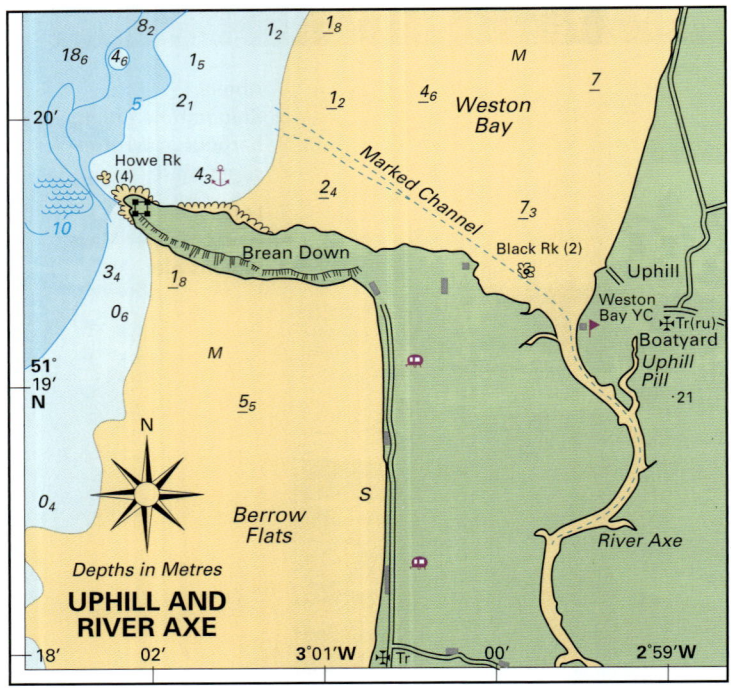

UPHILL AND THE RIVER AXE

The River Axe has a loyal boating fraternity

About half a mile up the Axe, the narrow creek known as Uphill Pill joins the main river from the Uphill side. The pill winds a short way north through the saltings as far as the Uphill Wharf Marine Centre. This busy little yard can be reached near high water, has a good range of facilities and can handle boats up to about 35ft. Their travel-hoist can lift up to 10 tons and the yard has good workshops for repairs and servicing. Chandlery, clothing and marine electronics are available on site.

Picturesque Uphill village is only a short walk from anywhere on the Axe, with two useful shops for stores and a couple of convivial pubs – the Dolphin and the Ship – that serve excellent food. You'll also dine well at La Cucina, an Italian restaurant on Uphill Way.

Approach and entry

Coming into Weston Bay, first make for the north side of Brean Down, steering for the 'saddle' between its two distinctive humps. About four cables north of Brean, more or less opposite the saddle, a locally maintained red and white buoy marks the outer bar of the River Axe. This buoy, called rather oddly 'Juicy', should be left close to port. Edging slightly closer to the Brean Down shore at first, steer towards Black Rock, an above-water rock right in the southeast corner of the bay at the mouth of the river, making good about 125° as far as the first port-hand mark – a red buoy with a topmark not quite half a mile away. The north side of this stretch towards Black Rock is marked by withies and, depending on the height of tide, the tips of these withies may still be poking above water and should be left close to port.

At the first red buoy, a cable or so from Black Rock, the channel dog-legs sharply to starboard towards the next red buoy, leaving the rock rather further to port than Brean Down to starboard. You leave this second red buoy close to port and then turn to port into the river, whose line will be obvious. Above this point the banks are marked by perches with port and starboard topmarks. Simply

SOUTH COAST

The entrance to the River Axe at low water

keep in midstream until you find a convenient buoy or, as a last resort, room to anchor. If you follow these directions from the Juicy buoy, the River Axe approaches should never carry less than about six feet depth at half-tide.

Although locals will approach the Axe soon after half-flood, strangers should wait until about one and a half hours before high water, when there is more depth to play with. Entry on the ebb is not advisable – you'll meet a fast current coming out! Fresh winds from between north and northwest can kick up a nasty sea on the bar, and in strong southerlies savage down-draughts are often experienced from Brean Down.

The Weston Bay Yacht Club website has a lot of useful information and a video which gives you a good idea of the lie of the river, its muddy banks and the moorings, www.westonbayyc.co.uk.

Entry at night

Not recommended for strangers.

Berths and anchorages

River Axe Dry out in the soft mud but don't lie too close to the steep banks or you'll end up at a perilous angle. It's best not to anchor unless absolutely necessary, because of the numerous ground chains. Secure to a vacant mooring initially and ask at the Weston Bay Yacht Club. Once you are safely inside, the Axe offers good shelter in all conditions, especially further upstream.

Uphill Pill This narrow creek is used by craft bound to or from Uphill Wharf Marine Centre and just below the yard there are a few drying pontoon berths to which visitors may sometimes moor. Uphill Wharf Marine Centre is quite a busy place with all kinds of boats moored at the drying pontoons there. The yard has comprehensive repair facilities and there are full services on site, including power, fresh water, a waste pump-out system and a shower block.

Close north of Brean Down In moderate winds from between WSW and south you can find a reasonable anchorage in a shallow bay on the north side of Brean Down, about four cables east of the old ruined fort.

BURNHAM-ON-SEA & THE RIVER PARRETT

Summary

Burnham-on-Sea lies at the head of Bridgwater Bay, a wide drying bight in the Somerset coast nearly eight miles across between Brean Down in the north and Hinkley Point in the south. Burnham itself is approached across a bar four miles offshore, then over and between the extensive drying banks known as Gore Sand and Stert Flats. A buoyed channel and sector leading light are maintained for the coasters and sand dredgers that still ply up the River Parrett as far as Dunball Wharf. Strangers should only approach Burnham in settled offshore weather and during the last hour and a half of flood. The Somerset coast here is low and rather featureless, but in quiet conditions those who enjoy unusual out-of-the-way havens can anchor behind Stert Island opposite Burnham-on-Sea Motor Boat and Sailing Club, where all boats will settle safely at low water in the soft mud. Landing on the island is not permitted as it is part of the Bridgwater Bay National Nature Reserve and WWT Steart Marshes site. By arrangement with the club you can also dry out alongside the southwest side of an excellent long pontoon in the River Brue where members of the club keep their boats and welcome visitors. The surrounding country feels refreshingly remote and unspoilt.

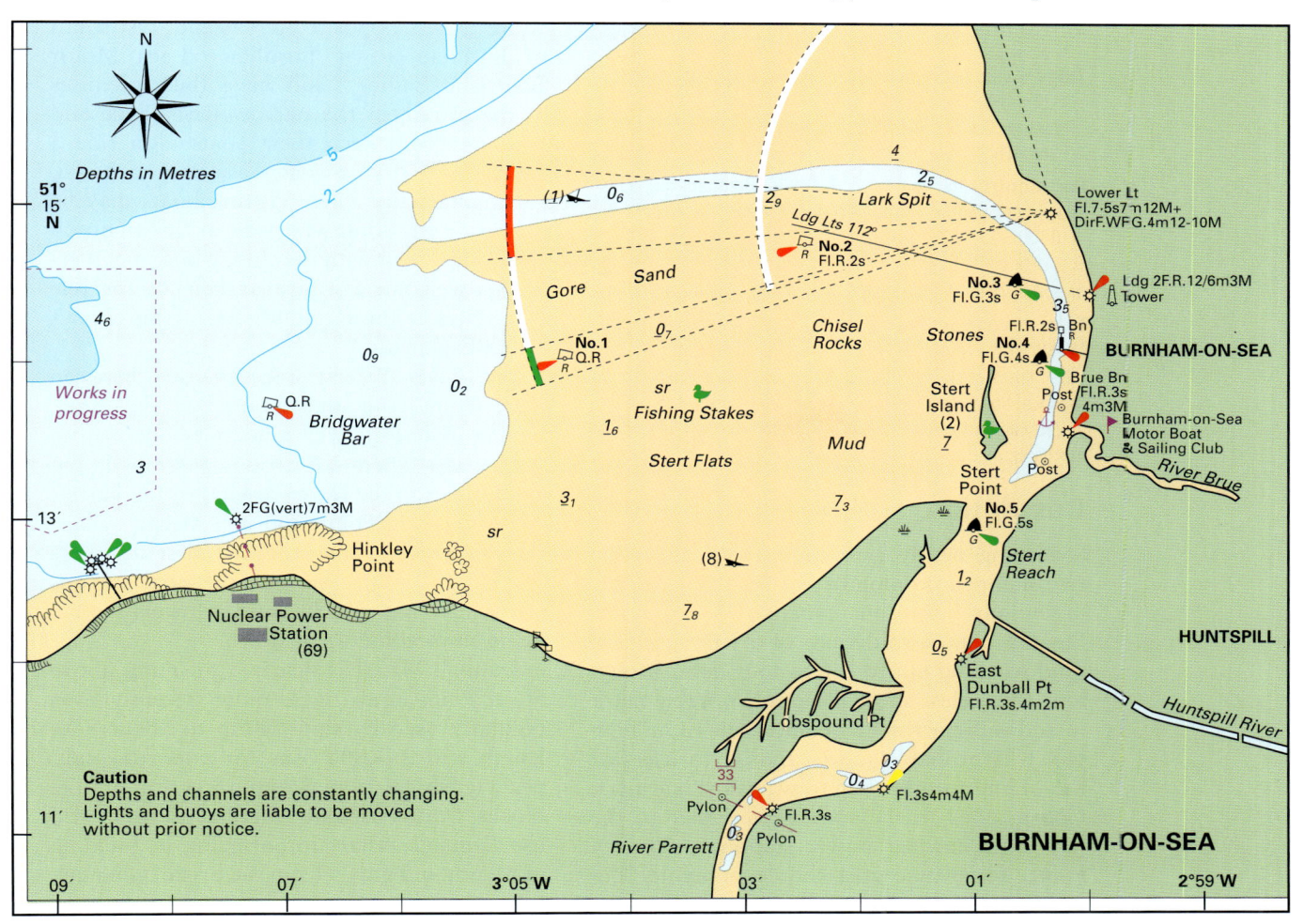

Bristol Channel and Severn Cruising Guide • 123

The Burnham-on-Sea club pontoon, just into the River Brue

At the beginning of 2022 the Government approved a proposal for a tidal barrage on the River Parrett. This latest plan was proposed after the severe flooding in Bridgwater and the Somerset Levels in 2014. The barrage will be located about halfway between Dunball wharf and the town, roughly between The Express Business Park and the village of Chilton Trinity. At the time of writing the completion of the structure was supposed to be 2024 but a rather longer time scale has now been suggested.

Tides HW Burnham (or Bridgwater) is at HW Avonmouth –0020 or HW Dover –0435. HW Bridgwater Bar is about 10mins earlier. Heights above chart datum at Burnham: 10.9m MHWS, –0.2m MLWS, 8.1m MHWN, 2.1m MLWN.

Port Control The harbour authority for Burnham-on-Sea is Sedgemoor District Council. Contact the harbourmaster on ☏ 0300 303 7799 or harbour.master@sedgemoor.gov.uk. The local pilots listen on VHF 16/08 when ships are expected or about to leave, which is only near spring high waters.

Tidal streams and currents The streams flow roughly NE-SW in the offing outside Gore Sand, reaching three and a half knots at springs. Further inshore towards Burnham, the local flows into and out of the River Parrett are more discernible and below half-tide tend to follow the line of the north channel.

Description

Stretching nearly eight miles SSW from the two-humped promontory of Brean Down, the potentially hazardous expanse of Bridgwater Bay is a remote wilderness of drying sand and mud reaching out for up to four miles from a low, featureless shore. The only notable mark inland is Brent Knoll, a conical hill 133m high which is probably more familiar to users of the M5 motorway than to wayward mariners. Conspicuous in the southwest corner of the bay is the nuclear power station at Hinkley Point. The whole area should be avoided in any fresh west or northwesterly winds, or in poor visibility.

The unassuming seaside town of Burnham-on-Sea fringes the head of Bridgwater Bay and is partly sheltered from the west (especially below half-tide) by a narrow off-lying dune known as Stert Island. In quiet weather between springs and neaps, moderate draught yachts can either just stay afloat or settle in very soft mud between the dune and the shore. More or less opposite Stert Island, just south of Burnham town, Burnham-on-Sea Motor Boat and Sailing Club have their premises at the mouth of the narrow River Brue and club members keep their boats alongside a long, sturdy drying pontoon in this sheltered, rather attractive inlet. Visiting boats may lie alongside the southwest side of this pontoon by arrangement with the club, whose members always welcome new faces at their comfortable clubhouse at the far south end of Burnham's South Esplanade.

The River Parrett joins the sea between Stert Point and the mouth of the Brue, having wound its way nine miles down from Bridgwater. There are various possible drying anchorages in the lower reaches of the Parrett between Stert Point and the sleepy village of Combwich. Neap tides are best for these anchorages, partly because the tidal streams are gentler but also because at neaps there'll be no ships going up or down.

Dunball Wharf is nearly eight miles above Stert Point and until quite recently was regularly used by ships of up to about 85m length and 2–3,000 tons for importing salt, peat, fertilisers from Scandinavia and granite blocks from Portugal. Suction dredgers still use Dunball Wharf for bringing in building sand, grit and gravel from the Bristol Channel.

BURNHAM-ON-SEA & THE RIVER PARRETT

Further downstream at Combwich, a specialist Ro-Ro terminal is used by barges for bringing in heavy machinery, parts and equipment for Hinkley Point power station. Shipping movements at Burnham and in the Parrett all happen around spring high tides and the local pilots are constantly monitoring the changing depths and line of the channel in the river. Quite a few small local boats are kept at Combwich, drying out in mostly soft mud.

Outer approaches

Out in the offing, Steep Holm island (unlit) lies two and a half miles WNW of Brean Down. Six miles WSW of Steep Holm and just over seven miles northwest of Hinkley Point, the East Culver E cardinal buoy Q(3)10s guards the east end of the Culver Sand, a narrow shoal not quite two miles long and with only 2.2m LAT depth at its shallowest part. Except in very quiet weather you should give this sandbank a wide berth when approaching Bridgwater Bay from out in the Channel. The West Culver W cardinal buoy VQ(9)10s lies just over two miles west of the East Culver buoy. The nuclear power station on Hinkley Point is prominent from offshore, as (in clear visibility) is Brent Knoll, a distinctive conical hill two miles inland from Burnham.

Approach and entry

The Burnham-on-Sea Motor Boat and Sailing Club, who know these waters well, recommend two alternative approaches to Burnham – the north channel north of Gore Sand, which carries the deepest water, or the south channel south of Gore Sand that ships take at night using the sector leading light. Both routes can be followed on your chart plotter and with an echo sounder.

On their friendly website, Burnham-on-Sea Motor Boat and Sailing Club publish useful pilotage notes and WGS84 waypoints that lead through these two channels. The waypoints are updated when the channel shifts so it is best to go to the website to ensure you have the current coordinates, www.burnhamonseamotorboatandsailingclub.co.uk/pilotage. In practice moderate-draught yachts approaching Burnham near high water will have plenty of depth pretty much everywhere.

If you use the club's waypoints you should plot them on your plotter to verify their suitability. Whether using the north or the south channel, strangers should only approach Burnham in quiet weather, reasonable visibility and between one and a half and two hours before high water.

North Channel This line of approach follows the narrow non-drying tongue of water shown on charts, although the mouth of this channel isn't buoyed and its outer end is roughly 3½M slightly north of west of the lower light. The club's suggested approach route follows this channel more or less due east, skirting north of Gore Sand and then north of Lark Spit.

There are no leading marks for this route but following the recommended line you'll see Burnham lower lighthouse fine on the

Left: The distinctive lower leading light

Right: Coming and going near the Burnham club pontoon

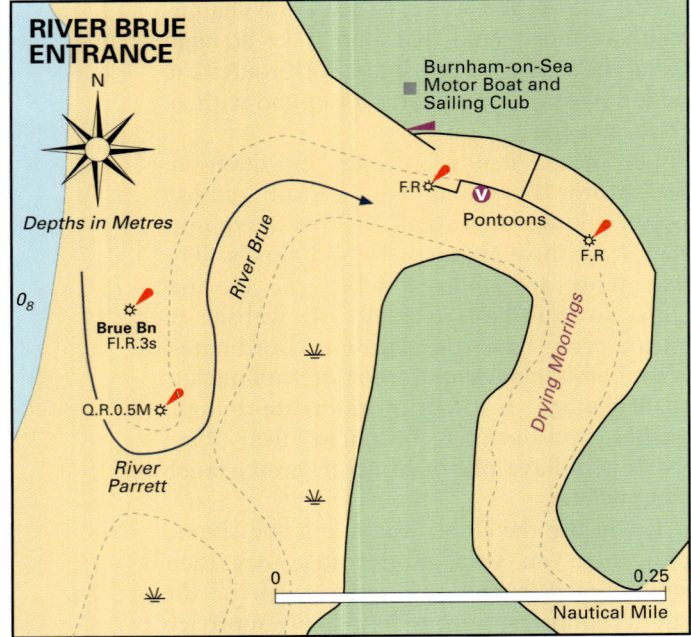

starboard bow, standing just off the Burnham shore. This lighthouse is on the port bow on the next leg, and then you'll leave it a quarter of a mile to port when you can use the club waypoints for the final approach. The last leg takes you just east of south past Burnham church tower and then you follow the shore past the jutting out slipway to the mouth of the River Brue, just beyond the clubhouse.

South channel This lit approach to Burnham starts south of the Gore red-and-white fairway buoy Iso.5s Bell, which lies one and three quarter miles northwest of Hinkley Point and its conspicuous power station. From the outer position about ¾M south of the Gore bell buoy, where you pick up the first waypoint on the club list, head due east for a mile then 070° and when you are about a cable south of No. 1 red buoy (QR) edge further east towards the lower light on 076°. This takes you to a turning point about four cables NNW of No. 2 green buoy Fl.G.5s where you turn roughly ESE for another mile. Keep the church tower in line with a red line on a white background, or 2F.R at night. From here you head south, following the Burnham shore, to the mouth of the River Brue, just beyond the clubhouse, be sure to keep clear of the fixed light at the end of the jetty. The Brue beacon marks the edge of the River Parret and not the entrance to the River Brue.

Entering the River Brue

As you draw south past the Burnham-on-Sea Motor Boat and Sailing Club and the end of Burnham sea wall, look out for the red Brue beacon Fl.R and the withies beyond it that mark the south tail of a shallow marshy spit that partly encloses the mouth of the River Brue. Two sets of local leading marks take you into the Brue – the first set leads southeast through the narrow entrance gap and the second set turns you northeast behind the tail of the spit. Thereafter, follow the suggested track shown on the sketch chart, curving fairly close to the north shore of the river mouth and heading for the outer face of the nearest length of pontoon. Once you've made fast, make your number ashore at the clubhouse.

Entry at night

This is not really recommended for strangers although Burnham is actually one of the better lit approaches along the south shore of the Bristol Channel. The south channel approach is lit by the fixed white sector of the Burnham lower light Fl.7.5s and DirF.WRG.12–10M. From a position about a mile north of Hinkley Point Power Station you follow this fixed white sector at 076° until you turn ESE, steering on two fixed red leading lights near the church tower in transit at 112°. Once you reach the red beacon by the slip Fl.R.2s you are in the main outer channel of the River Parrett and can anchor behind Stert Island until daylight.

Berths and anchorages

Anchoring off Burnham The area between Burnham seafront and Stert Island doesn't quite dry and a shallow tongue of water remains even at MLWS. Yachts can anchor in this area behind Stert Island, either just staying afloat at low water or settling into soft mud, depending on the tide and your draught. Near high water when the stream is fairly slack, you can land at the slip on Burnham seafront.

River Brue pontoon By arrangement with the Burnham-on-Sea Motor Boat and Sailing Club, visitors can moor alongside the southwest end of the club's sturdy long pontoon just into the mouth of the River Brue, settling into soft mud at low water. This snug spot is protected by the marshy spit that partly encloses the mouth of the river and by Stert Island further out. It is best if visitors contact the club in advance if they would like to use the pontoon, ☎ 01278 792911 or 07885 397691.

River Parrett Near neap tides you can anchor and dry out in soft mud in the lower reaches of the River Parrett, between Lobspound Point and Combwich village. Neap tides are best for these anchorages, partly because the tidal streams are gentler but also because at neaps there'll be no ships going up or down. The pronounced bay close west of Lobspound Point is a good spot.

BURNHAM-ON-SEA & THE RIVER PARRETT

Combwich Pill Visitors can sometimes use a drying mooring up at Combwich, by arrangement with the Combwich Cruising Club. The narrow drying creek known as Combwich Pill dries out to soft mud. You'll find a useful general store in Combwich village and the Anchor Inn on the riverside.

Note Bridgwater Marina is not accessible by lock from the River Parrett. The old lock gates are disused, which is rather a shame because the marina basin is an attractive spot with the Admirals Landing pub on the south quay.

Bridgwater Bore

Like the Severn itself the River Parrett also experiences a bore on certain big tides. This can be seen from bridges in the town. It is rather less dramatic than the main Severn bore but is an interesting phenomenon.

The landlocked basin at Bridgwater is the end of the canal and not accessible to the River Parrett

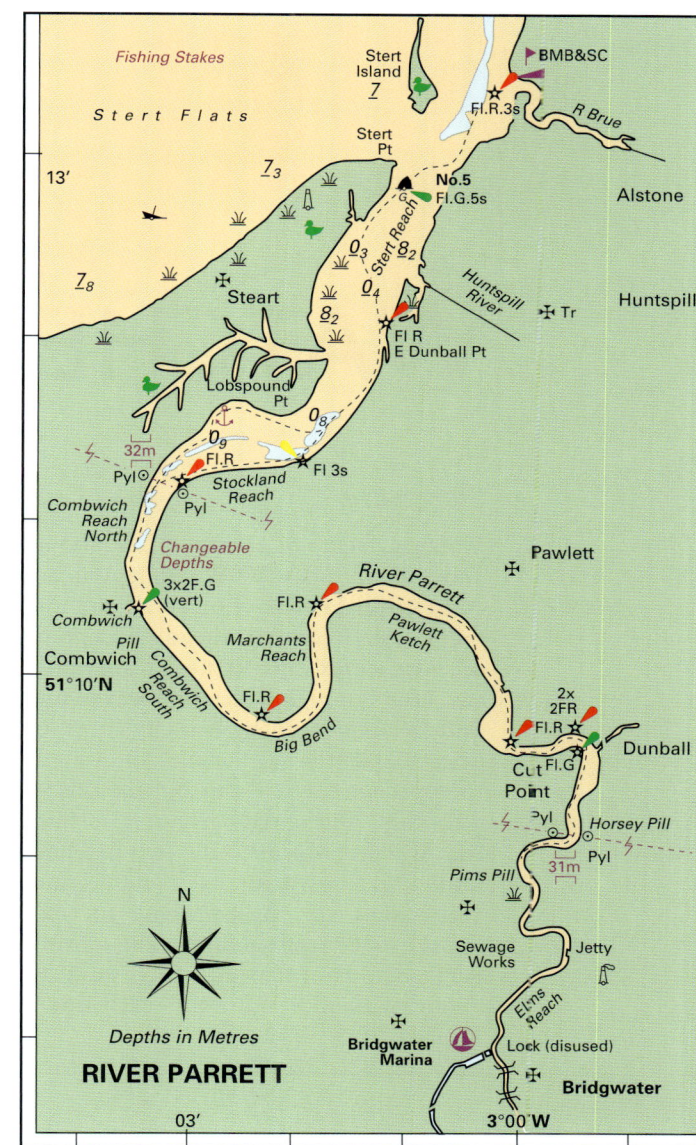

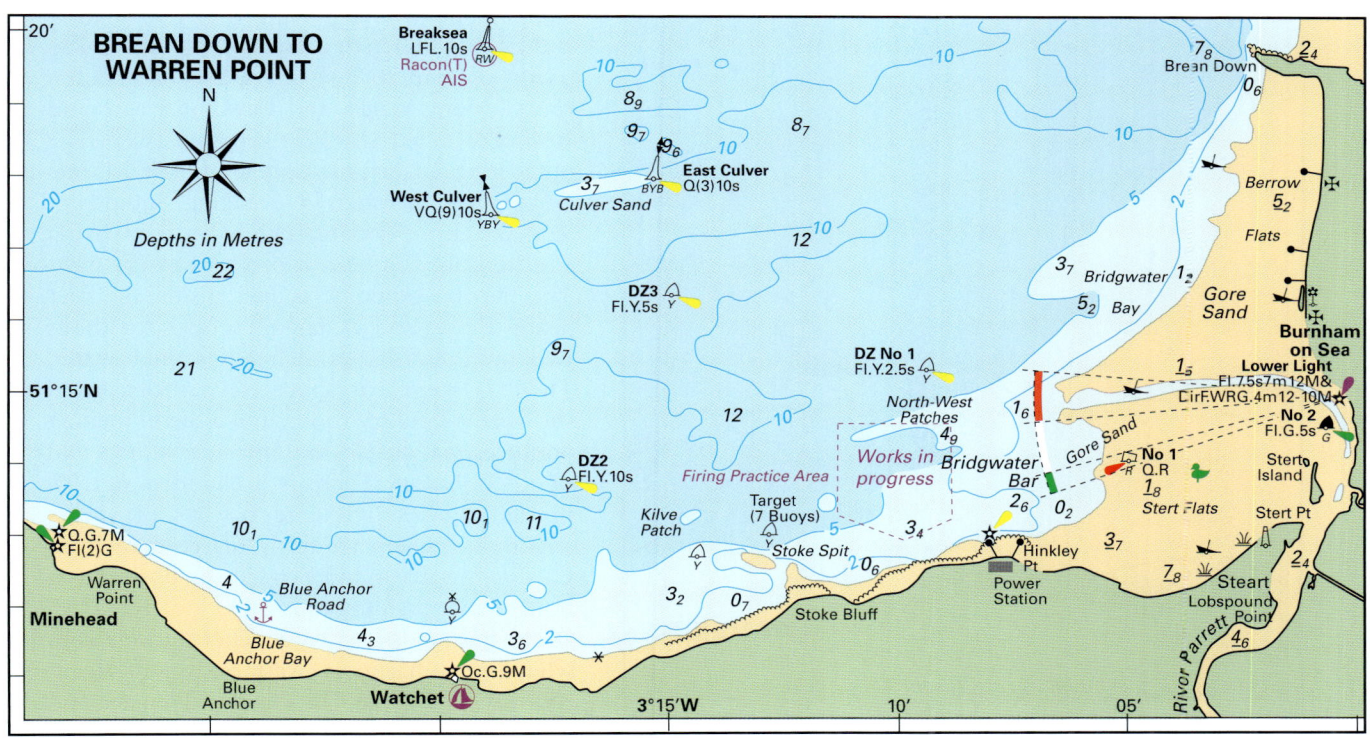

Bristol Channel and Severn Cruising Guide • 127

WATCHET

Summary

Watchet harbour entrance lies about seven and a half miles WSW along the Somerset coast from Hinkley Point and not quite six miles ESE from Minehead. Except in fresh onshore winds, entry is straightforward within two hours of high water, but bear in mind that Watchet is fringed by a rocky foreshore that dries for nearly half a mile, so don't attempt to approach the harbour outside this window of access. The outer harbour also dries right out. Watchet Marina, now part of The Marine Group, is known for its friendly atmosphere and makes an excellent base for exploring the upper Bristol Channel. The marina basin is reached via a flap-sill which stays open for about two and a half hours each side of high water. There's plenty of room for visiting boats up to about 15m length.

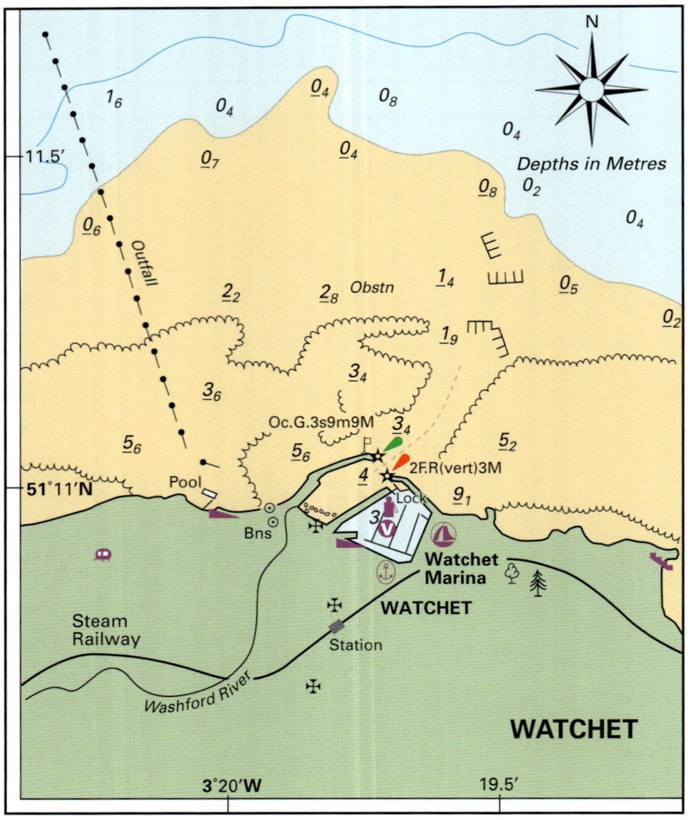

Tides HW Watchet is at HW Avonmouth –0040 or HW Dover –0455. Heights above chart datum: 11.3m MHWS, 1.0m MLWS, 8.5m MHWN, 3.6m MLWN.

Port Control Watchet Marina – Call VHF 80 or ☏ 01984 322230.

Tidal steams and currents Off Watchet, the west-going stream begins about one and a quarter hours after local high water and runs for five hours. The east-going stream begins soon after local low water and runs for nearly seven hours. Rates off Watchet entrance can exceed four knots at springs so it's important to allow for any cross-tide when entering the harbour.

Description

Until the marina was opened in 2001, Watchet was one of the smallest Bristol Channel harbours working commercially and 200ft ships used to negotiate the narrow entrance, spring through 180° and then fetch up alongside the East Quay. Nowadays there's no shipping into Watchet and the friendly marina is the focus of activity. Two sturdy outer piers partly overlap to give good shelter and the rocky drying ledges and foreshores east and west of Watchet also help keep out swell. The outer harbour dries to soft mud. The Marine Group has invested in dredging equipment to maintain reasonable depths in the marina as silting up has been a problem in the past. The marina entrance is just inside the pier heads to port and its flap-sill is open for about two and a half hours each side of high water. There is plenty of space for visitors, good showers, a laundry room, and a diesel fuelling pontoon just inside the entrance at the end of 'C' pontoon. There is a chandler nearby. In the summer, weekend flotillas of yachts and motor boats regularly arrive here from Cardiff, Swansea and Penarth or down from Portishead and numerous other locations.

The marina is next to Watchet station, from where the charming West Somerset Steam Railway runs along the coast to Dunster and

Minehead or inland to Taunton. The attractive town has narrow winding streets and a fine Esplanade. Watchet Boat Museum tells the story of this tiny port's maritime history. There are several good pubs, of which the Bell Inn and Star Inn on Market Street are both sound bets for supper and Pebbles Tavern specialises in cider. For an excellent and good-value lunch make for Sam's Deli and café in Swain Street. In the evening, wandering along the Esplanade, pop into the Esplanade Club and see their fascinating collection of old photos of Watchet, especially those of the harbour in the days long before the marina was here. The new East Quay development has galleries, a café which is open for breakfast, lunches and teas, there are also artists' studios and self-catering accommodation at the top.

Approach and entry

The outer approaches to Watchet are navigationally straightforward, except that Culver Sand should be avoided when coming across the Bristol Channel from Barry or Cardiff Bay. The West Culver W cardinal buoy lies six and a half miles just east of north from Watchet harbour entrance. The strong tidal streams out in the Channel provide the most significant pilotage factor.

Strangers should only approach Watchet within two hours of high water. The lighthouse and flagstaff on the west pier head are conspicuous from seaward. Stay at least half a mile offshore until the pier heads bear about SSW and then head straight for the entrance, allowing for any cross-tide. The ebb stream can be particularly vicious off the west pier head. Once through the pier heads, turn hard to port for the marina entrance. Signal lights control access through the marina flap-sill – three vertical green lights mean that craft can proceed through the gate with caution and three vertical red lights mean that access is closed.

Entry at night

Approaching and entering Watchet at night is quite feasible for strangers, provided you are sure of your position in the offing and that you allow carefully for the tidal set. The west pier head lighthouse Oc.G.3s has a nine-mile range

The friendly marina at Watchet

SOUTH COAST

and the east pier head light 2F.R(vert) has a three-mile range. Signal lights control access through the marina flap-sill – three vertical greens allow craft to proceed through the gate with caution and three vertical reds mean the gate is closed.

Berths and anchorages

Watchet Marina There is plenty of space available for visitors but you should call Watchet Marina on ☎ 01984 322230 or VHF 80 for directions.

Blue Anchor Road This traditional shipping anchorage lies 2–3 miles WNW from Watchet entrance. The broad sweep of Blue Anchor Bay is reasonably sheltered from due west, but open from northwest through north to east. Much of the bay dries at LAT, but you should edge as far inshore as draught and tide allow. The mud bottom provides good holding.

The Ancient Mariner

The marina basin is behind an automatic sill

Watchet's distinctive entrance light

130 • Bristol Channel and Severn Cruising Guide

MINEHEAD

Summary

Minehead is a popular seaside holiday town six miles WNW along the coast from Watchet. Its small drying harbour, which can be crowded with local boats during the season, is formed by a single stone pier and is accessible for about two and a half hours each side of high water. The best approach is from the NNW between a red and a green spar beacon. The harbour is sheltered from north through west to SSE, but exposed to the east. The sand and mud bottom slopes gently upwards from the entrance, so bilge-keelers or keelboats with legs can dry out on the firmer inner part – ask the harbourmaster for directions before settling down. During the season three pairs of drying fore-and-aft visitors' buoys (white, yellow and orange) are laid off the harbour entrance just east of three wooden posts that were once used for springing sailing vessels in or out of the harbour. The town centre is a short walk from the harbour.

Tides HW Minehead is at HW Avonmouth –0035 or at HW Dover –0450. Heights above datum are approximately: 10.8m MHWS, 0.9m MLWS, 8.2m MHWN, 3.5m MLWN.

Port Control The Harbourmaster has his office on the inner part of the pier ☎ 07799 456128. He can also be contacted VHF 12 while he is on duty.

Tidal streams and currents Streams off Minehead can be strong, reaching four or five knots at springs a mile offshore. The west-going stream begins one and a quarter hours after local HW and runs for about five hours. The east-going stream begins soon after local LW and runs for nearly seven hours.

Description

Although Minehead is a rather hectic resort with its Butlins holiday park nearby, its small drying harbour is set back from the main rough and tumble of dubious seaside delights and is a congenial place to lie for a night. Bilge-keelers, centre boarders or keelboats with legs may all take the ground on the firm bottom, although boats using legs are better off in the inner part of the harbour on firmer sand. A substantial stone pier curves east and southeast to provide good shelter from north through west to SSE. However, Minehead is open to the east and it's unwise to enter the harbour in easterly winds or to dry out there if easterlies are forecast.

At the end of the pier, on the inside face, are the landing steps used by the numerous tripper, day-fishing and hire launches which provide plenty of fascinating activity for anyone with time to sit and watch. These boats operate so long as there's enough water at the steps – normally anytime above half-tide for their modest draught. Most yachts will be able to enter the harbour for two hours each side of high water, although those drawing more than about one and a half metres should wait until near high water.

On the quayside is a pleasant pub, The Old Ship Aground, where you can sit on the terrace and watch all the harbour comings and goings. You'll find a water tap near the harbourmaster's office, and another tap and an electricity point halfway along the

You have to be prepared to take the ground at Minehead

SOUTH COAST

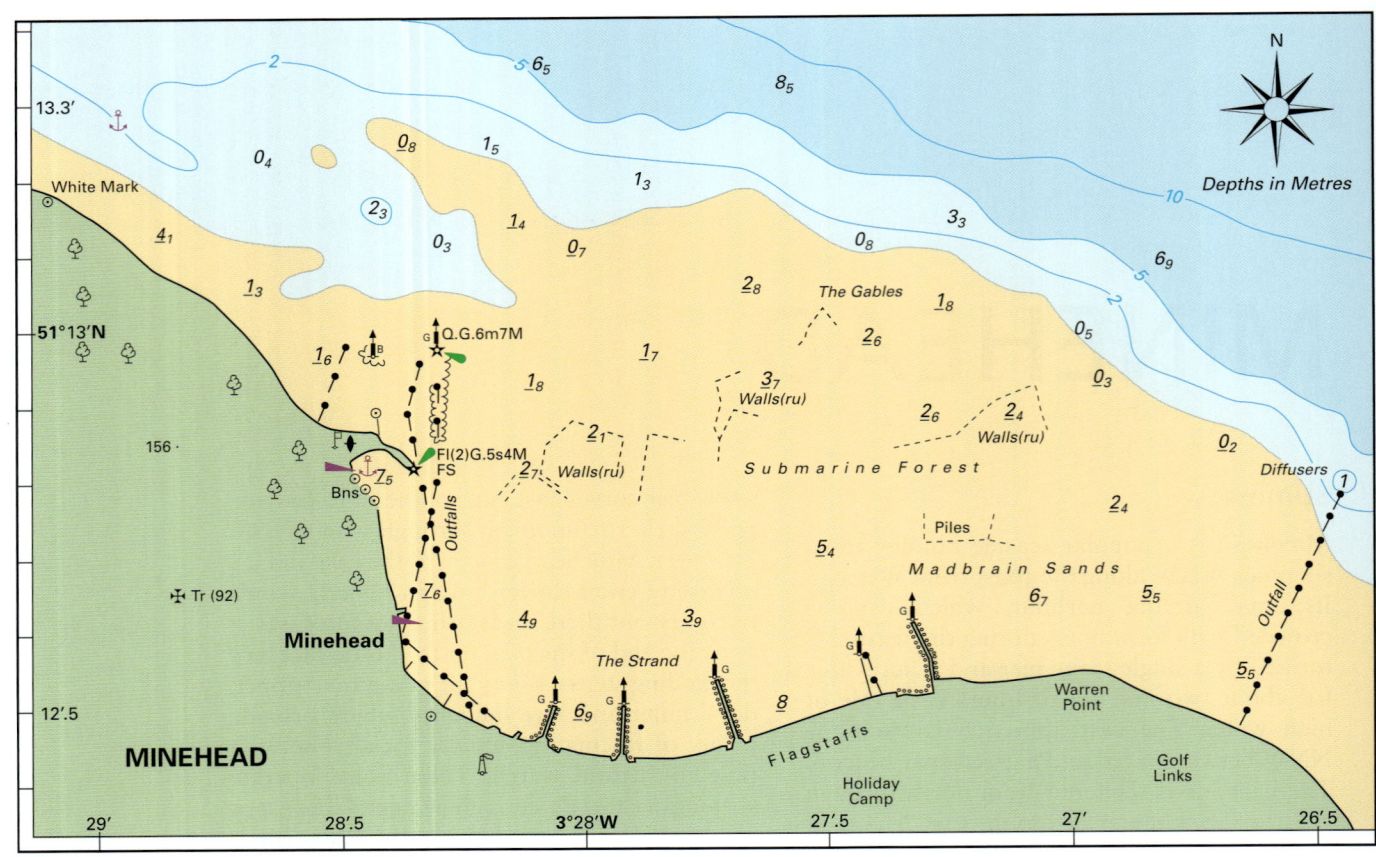

quay. The town centre, with plenty of shops and a garage for fuel, is 10 minutes' walk from the harbour. The town is usually over-populated during the summer, being swamped periodically by the Butlins inmates from the famous holiday camp just across the bay from the harbour. Minehead started to grow as a holiday resort after the original West Somerset Railway extended the line from Watchet and built a station near what was originally a small fishing village. After Billy Butlin built one of his holiday camps here in 1962, Minehead was never quite the same. The West Somerset Steam Railway is now run as a tourist line and the trip along the coast through Dunster to Watchet station is most picturesque.

Outer approaches

Coming from the east The wide drying coastal flats extending east and seawards from Minehead harbour are cluttered with a good many obstructions, so it's best to stay well offshore until you are in a position to approach the harbour from the NNW. Pass Warren Point and its conspicuous holiday camp a good mile off and make for an outer 'fairway' position about three quarters of a mile NNW of the pier head. There's a white mark low down on the cliff abreast this approach waypoint and if the tide is too low to enter Minehead, you can anchor opposite this mark about a quarter of a mile offshore in three and a half metres, i.e. roughly midway between Greenaleigh Point and the two post beacons off Minehead harbour.

Coming from the west Approaching Minehead from the west is relatively straightforward, but pass Foreland Point at least one and a half miles off to avoid the worst of its overfalls. If there's not enough rise of tide to enter Minehead, anchor about half a mile ESE of Greenaleigh Point abreast the white mark low down on the cliff.

Wave-rider buoy Note that a yellow spherical 'wave-rider' buoy is moored north of Minehead harbour pier head, 51°13'.68N 3°28'.15W. This buoy is used to measure wave heights for oceanographic research and should be avoided when you are approaching from eastward or from out in the Channel. Sometimes the buoy can be partly submerged on a fast spring tide and difficult to spot.

Entry

Only approach Minehead within two hours of high water, watching the echo-sounder carefully on the way in. From the outer fairway position three quarters of a mile NNW of the pier head (see waypoint below), head towards the green beacon post that stands not far north of Minehead harbour and then pass between this post and a black spar beacon a cable west of it. From here simply continue just east of south for the harbour pier head and then round up behind it into the harbour.

MINEHEAD

Half-tide at Minehead harbour

Minehead outer 'fairway' waypoint 51°13´.504N 003°28´.848W (WGS84).

Entry at night

Entering Minehead at night is perfectly feasible by GPS in quiet weather and good visibility, although a paucity of navigation lights can make it tricky to gauge your distance off visually. Make for the fairway position by GPS and/or by bringing Minehead pier head light Fl(2)G.5s onto a safe bearing of 155° while you are still a mile offshore. Then simply approach the pier head along this line, watching the echo-sounder as you go, but edge to port and steer for the green beacon post Q.G until you are quite close to it, turning south at the last moment for the harbour pier head to pass between the green post and the black post (which is unlit) standing a cable west of it.

Berths and anchorages

Minehead Harbour Go alongside the pier initially, clear to the west of the landing steps, and ask the harbourmaster for directions. The inner part of the harbour is firm enough to dry out on legs. There are five drying visitors' buoys, three are located in front of the slip and two are just outside the two half-tide marker posts on the edge of the harbour entrance.

Anchorage outside the harbour The waiting anchorage between Greenaleigh Point and the two post beacons is sheltered from due west through south to SSE. On neap tides, shallow-draught boats can fetch up further towards Minehead, between the white mark and the two post beacons.

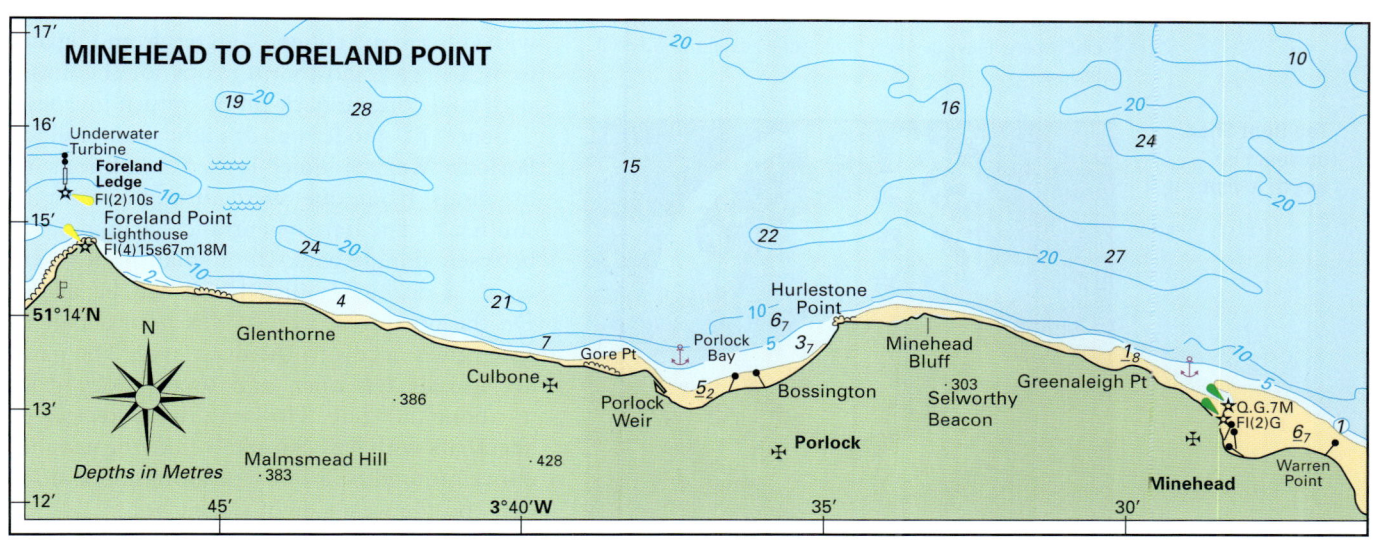

Bristol Channel and Severn Cruising Guide • 133

PORLOCK WEIR

Summary

This fascinating miniature harbour lies in the southwest corner of Porlock Bay, six miles west along the coast from Minehead and a similar distance ESE from Foreland Point. The tiny 'dock' can be entered for an hour or so each side of high water via a short channel and a pair of gates. The gates are usually left open and the harbour allowed to dry, but there's a firm bottom for taking the ground and a quay to lie alongside. The swing bridge into the inner harbour is not opened very often so you should make arrangements in advance. The dock provides good shelter from all quarters, although fresh east or northeasterly winds send in a swell near high water. Just outside the gates is a small pool retained by a shingle bar at the outer end of the entrance channel, with about a metre depth at low water.

Tides HW at Porlock Weir is at HW Avonmouth −0045 or HW Dover −0500. Heights above chart datum: 10.2m MHWS, 0.8m MLWS 7.8m MHWN, 3.4m MLWN.

Port Control The Porlock Weir Harbourmaster's office is on the west side of the entrance gates ☎ 01643 863187, or the harbourmaster on ☎ 07423 283405.

Tidal streams and currents The streams are moderate in Porlock Bay, but stronger (up to four or five knots) in the offing. When approaching Porlock Bay from the west, note that spring streams can also reach five knots off Foreland Point, where heavy overfalls often extend over a mile offshore.

Description

Porlock Bay's shingle foreshore represents the first sign, as you work west along the English side of the Bristol Channel, that this cruising ground is not composed entirely of drying sand and mud. As you round Hurlstone Point from the E, the coast begins to undergo a subtle but discernible change. It will soon become higher, more rugged and generally steep-to, the elusive shifting shoals of the upper reaches giving way to hard, tangible rock. The tides will still be fast, but not so savage as further up-Channel.

Porlock Weir, tucked into the southwest corner of Porlock Bay, is a picturesque and delightfully salty little haven, overlooked by gentle wooded slopes, the prominent hotel and some charming old cottages once occupied by fishermen and local pilots. This stretch of coast is on the fringes of Exmoor, where steep wooded valleys wind down to the sea. Porlock is one of the most atmospheric ports of call on the English side of the Bristol Channel, especially if you can get into the dock area and dry out. From this surprisingly snug haven you can hear the sea breaking on the beach outside. This is one of many corners of the Channel with strong vibes of seafaring history. There was much trade between England and Wales in the days of sail and old photographs show Porlock Weir's miniature harbour packed with ketches and cutters. Cargoes from England to Wales were mostly pit props for the mines with coal coming back on the return journey.

Boats of moderate draught can call at Porlock Weir in quiet settled conditions or in winds from due west through south to southeast. The narrow entrance channel leads between shingle banks to a small pool where up to a dozen smallish boats can lie afloat. On the northwest side of this pool a pair of gates gives access to the dock area. The gates are usually left open and so the dock dries at about half-tide. However, bilge-keelers or keelboats with legs can safely take the ground, either moored to a buoy or alongside a stone quay on the west side of the harbour.

The Boat Shed museum is worth a visit

PORLOCK WEIR

Enigmatic withies lead you into Porlock Weir

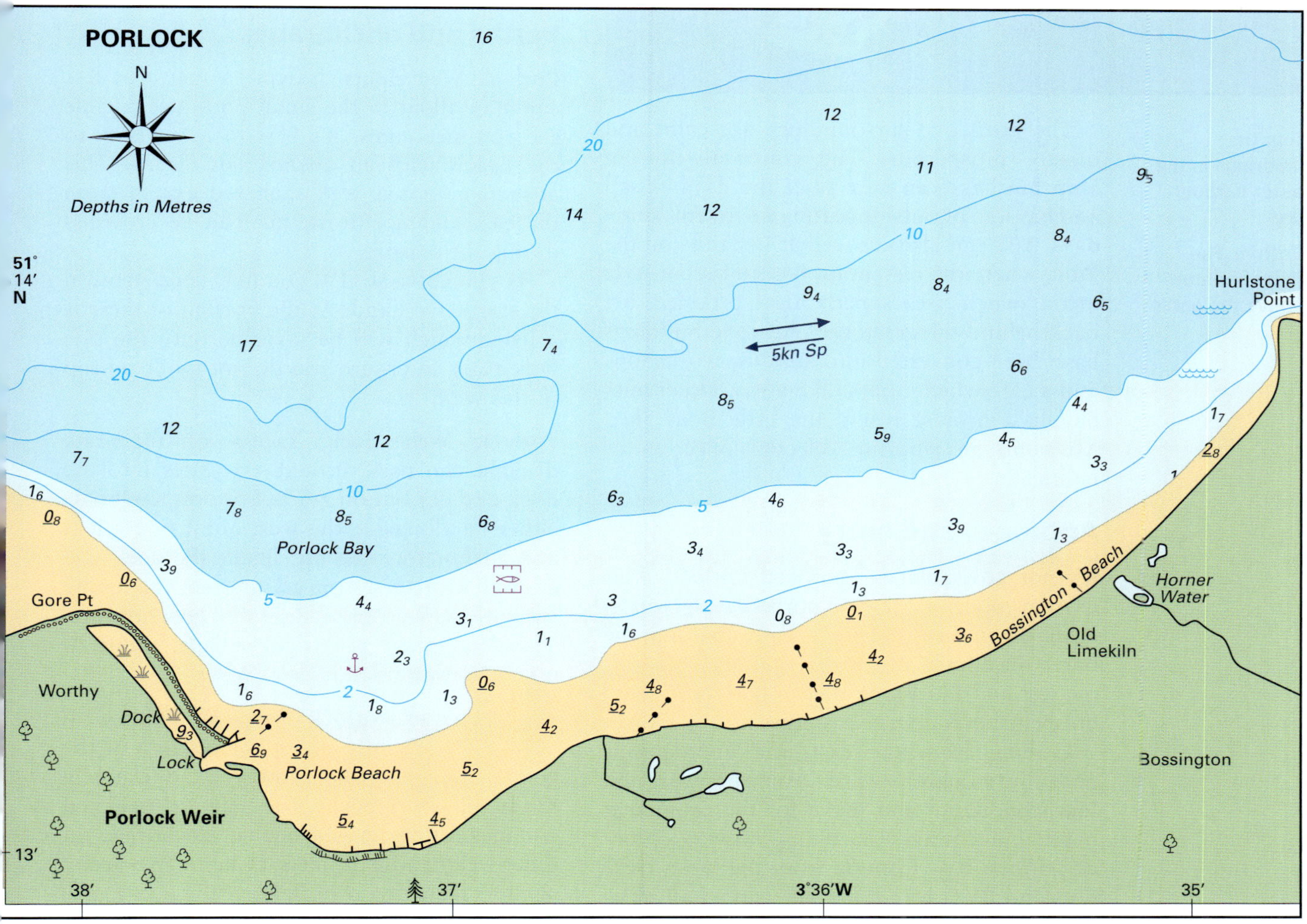

PORLOCK

Depths in Metres

Hurlstone Point

5kn Sp

Porlock Bay

Gore Pt

Worthy
Dock
Lock

Porlock Weir

Porlock Beach

Bossington Beach

Horner Water

Old Limekiln

Bossington

Bristol Channel and Severn Cruising Guide • 135

SOUTH COAST

Top: The moorings in the outer harbour dry

Bottom: The inner harbour above the gates

The attractive surroundings are calm and quietly prosperous. The convivial Bottom Ship Inn has been here since the days of sail and has lots of outside seating for warm sunny days. You can also eat well at Locanda on the Weir, where the restaurant has an Italian style menu which uses superb local produce. Set back behind the green the old stone buildings have been converted into studios, workshops and a café which offers take-away. Don't miss having a browse round the little Boat Shed Museum, an amazing eclectic collection of nauticalia.

Approach and entry

It's not advisable to approach Porlock Weir in even moderate east or northeasterly winds. Both the narrow harbour entrance and the outer anchorage are very exposed from this quarter and Hurlstone Point offers practically no shelter, even in true easterlies.

Coming from the east, the approach is perfectly straightforward. You simply round Hurlstone Point and make for the prominent hotel and cottages in the southwest corner of Porlock Bay. Coming from the west, clear Foreland Point by a good one and a half miles to avoid the worst of its overfalls, passing a mile outside the platform that stands off the headland. Just west of Porlock Bay, stay well off the drying rocky spit that extends a good three cables northwest of Gore Point.

In quiet weather, if early on the tide, you can anchor over shingly sand just north of the Porlock Weir entrance channel, opposite the line of thatched cottages. Don't leave this anchorage until about an hour before high water, when you can enter between the two tallest withies at the east end of the channel. Leave all other withies close to port as you pass between the shingle banks to the inner pool.

If you draw a metre or less you can stay afloat in the pool, if there is room. Otherwise carry on through the gates into the dock area. You may have to put someone ashore first to ask the harbourmaster to roll the footbridge aside.

Entry at night

Not recommended for strangers since the entrance is unlit. Foreland Point is the nearest light Fl(4)15s, six miles to the west. But in quiet settled weather and good visibility, you can enter Porlock Bay using GPS and echo-sounder, anchoring just north of the entrance channel about 300 metres offshore. The lights of the hotel can sometimes help you in.

Berths and anchorages

Porlock Weir Boats drawing a metre or less can stay afloat in the small pool just outside the entrance gates. It's best to moor bow to the beach with an anchor out astern. This attractive spot is well sheltered except from the east and northeast, but can be crowded during the season.

As you enter at HW you may spot steps on the starboard hand. At the bottom of these is a ledge which will be invisible until the tide falls away so ensure you do not moor on top of this wall.

Porlock Weir dock Yachts of moderate draught can pass through the gates into the dock and dry out on a firm bottom. Keelboats either lie alongside the west quay, or rig legs and anchor fore-and-aft. Inside the dock you are well protected from all quarters and handy for Porlock Weir's hostelries and general store. There's a garage at Porlock village, about 20 minutes' walk inland.

Anchorage in Porlock Bay The holding in the bay is generally very poor because of the coarse shingle bottom. However, the relatively sandy patch opposite the line of thatched cottages offers a reasonable anchorage in quiet weather. It's prudent to lie to two heavy anchors if staying overnight.

FORELAND POINT

This steep, rather gaunt headland juts into the Bristol Channel six miles west from Porlock Bay and a dozen miles east from Ilfracombe. Foreland Ledge, a narrow rocky bank two miles long, lies between half a mile and a mile north of the Foreland. The combination of jutting headland, relatively shallow ledge and strong tidal streams often produces heavy overfalls off the Foreland over a mile offshore, particularly on the ebb with the wind in the west. It's therefore advisable to clear Foreland Point by at least one and a half miles. Foreland Ledge has a least depth of 7.2m.

Just over half a mile NNW of Foreland Point, a prominent red-and-black steel tower surmounted by a lit platform Fl(2)10s marks an experimental underwater turbine that generates power from the powerful tides. The tower and platform were installed in the early summer of 2003 as part of a long-term project to assess the viability of tidal generation of electricity. Although this tower is essentially an isolated danger mark and you can pass through the half-mile gap between it and the Foreland, this should only be done in calm weather when the tide is fairly slack, otherwise there's a risk of being set dangerously close to the platform.

Close west of Foreland Point, Sand Ridge is a narrow shoal about a mile long with a least depth of two metres towards its east end. The west end of Sand Ridge is guarded by a green conical buoy Q.G, which lies about one and a half miles just north of west from Foreland Point. Although there's a narrow passage between the Foreland and the shallowest part of Sand Ridge, it's usually best to pass the Foreland a good mile and a half offshore, keeping safely clear of the turbine platform, Foreland Ledge and its overfalls, and Sand Ridge and its green buoy.

Foreland Point lighthouse
Chris Ware

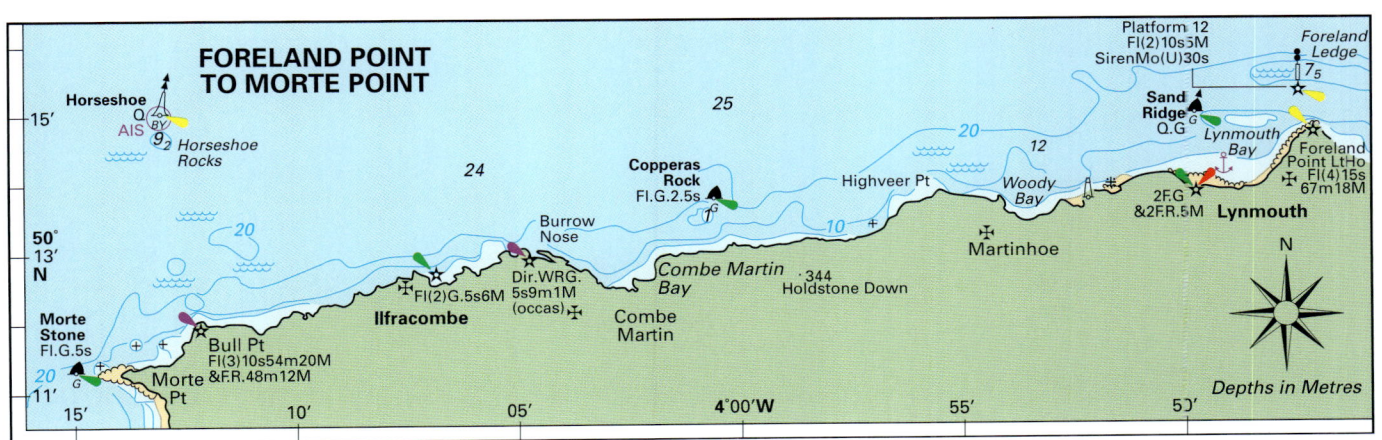

Bristol Channel and Severn Cruising Guide • 137

LYNMOUTH

Lynmouth Bay curves west from Foreland Point towards Lynmouth, where a fascinating small harbour lies at the end of a steep wooded valley next to where the shallow River Lyn flows into the Bristol Channel. In quiet weather near high water, shallow-draught boats can follow a trail of posts towards Lynmouth before entering between two stone piers. Make sure you turn to port into the harbour because you won't want to find yourself edging up the river. There's not much room for visitors to stay, but sometimes you can lie to a vacant mooring and dry out amongst the local boats or lie alongside the east quay. There is no harbourmaster and you need to be well provisioned as the nearest fuel is up in Lynton. The harbour has a little over 4m depth at MHWS but beware going too far in if you arrive at HW as you don't want to find yourself neaped.

The picturesque village is popular with holidaymakers who wander round the quays in this unusual, very tucked away place that seems in a world of its own beneath high enclosing hillsides. An amazing cliff railway, opened in 1890 and powered by the weight of water tanks, can lift you from the quayside up to the neighbouring village of Lynton. Lynmouth has several pubs and the Esplanade Fish Bar does first class fish and chips. The Ancient Mariner is set slightly above the harbour in Lynmouth Street and serves breakfast, lunch and evening meals from an eclectic menu, it's the place to head for if you are a gin aficionado. There is also a fascinating collection of nautical curios.

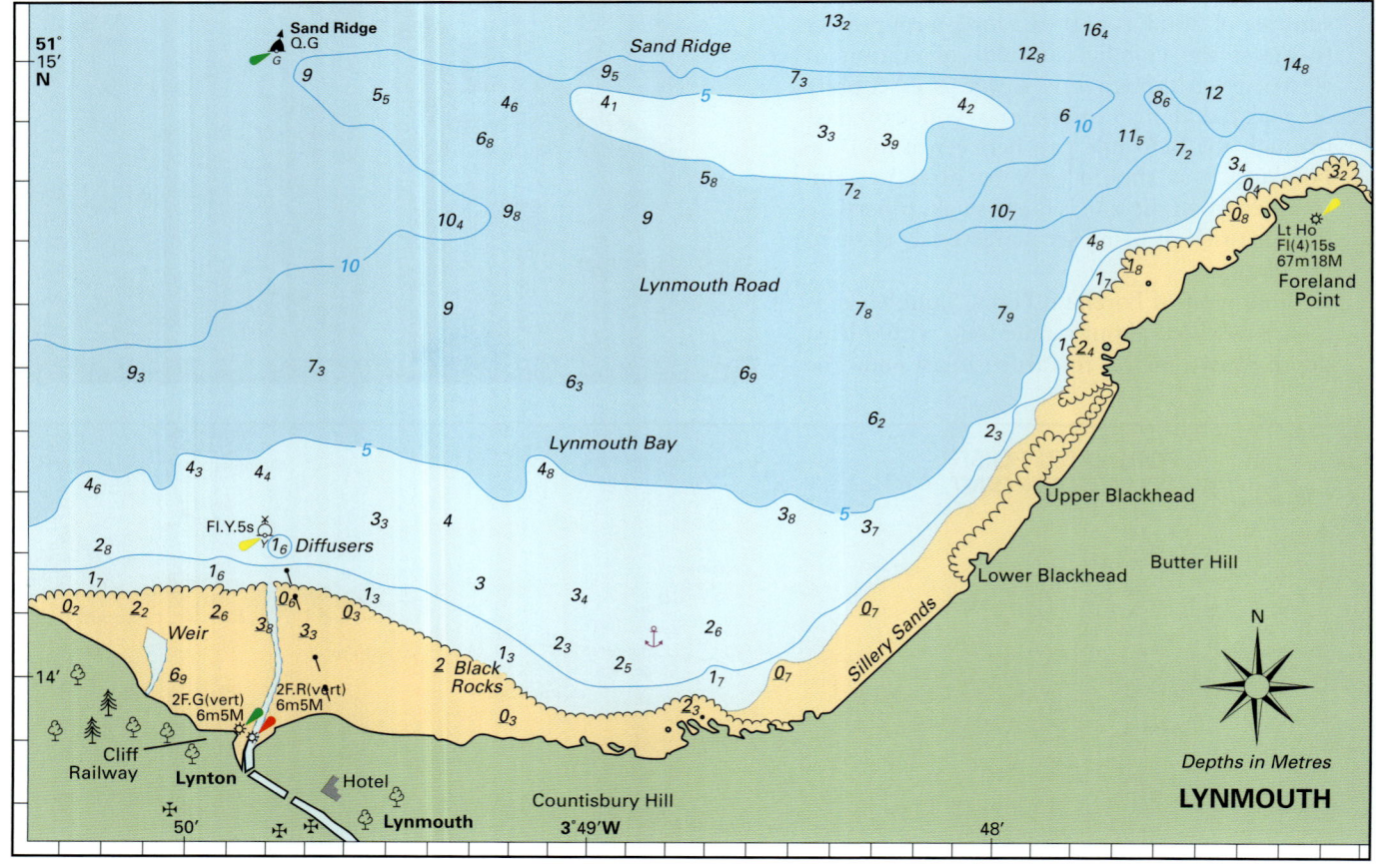

LYNMOUTH

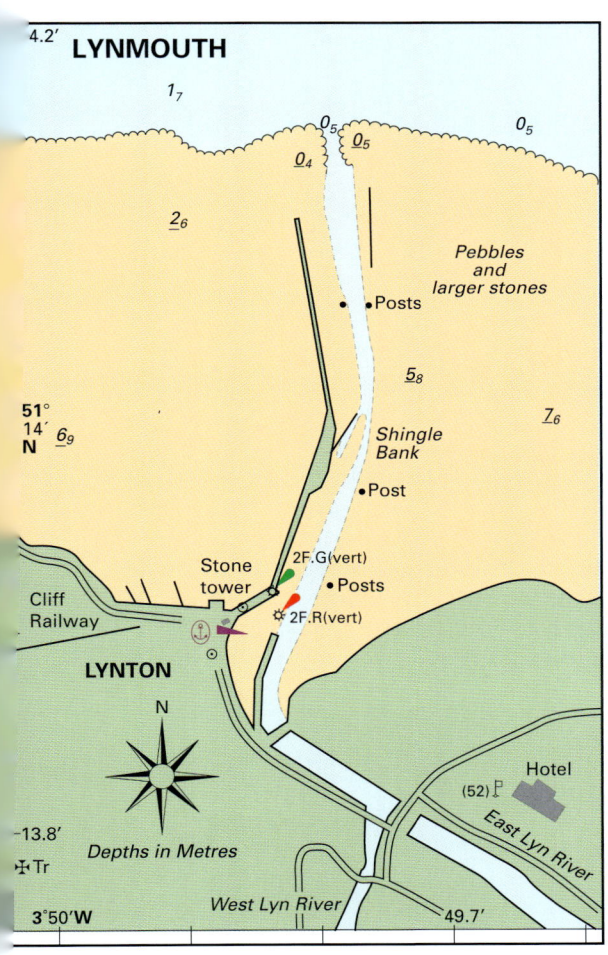

Top: The tricky entrance to Lynmouth harbour

Middle: The funicular railway links Lynmouth and Lynton

Lynmouth harbour at half-tide

The Rhenish tower on Lynmouth breakwater

Bristol Channel and Severn Cruising Guide • 139

The Lynmouth floods

On the night of 15th August 1952, the small Bristol Channel town of Lynmouth was hit by floods on a terrible and dramatic scale. There had been continuous heavy rain all that day and the East and West Lyn Rivers, which meet at Lynmouth, were being remorselessly filled with run-off waters from a wide catchment area up on Exmoor. By evening the levels in the two rivers were rising rapidly and at about 9.30pm the West Lyn burst its banks and millions of gallons of water swept down through Lynmouth, carrying large boulders and rocks in a deadly cascade, destroying houses, roads and bridges on the way. Many people lost their lives on that terrifying night, hundreds were left homeless, water supplies, gas and electricity were cut off and all the local boats in the small harbour were either sunk or swept out into the fast-flowing Bristol Channel.

The army was called in and news photographs of this stunning disaster were sent all around the world. Afterwards, people living in the West Country would always remember where they were and what they were doing when they heard the news about the Lynmouth floods. The devastation of the village by such raw natural forces seemed all the more shattering because Lynmouth was normally such a peaceful, picturesque place that holidaymakers loved to visit on warm summer days.

In an almost uncanny echo of these 1952 floods, the much smaller Cornish village of Boscastle was devastated by flash floods on 16th August 2004, virtually 52 years to the day after the Lynmouth disaster. Three inches of rain, the August average total for this area, fell in just two hours, causing two nearby rivers to burst their banks and a torrent of water to sweep through Boscastle's quaint main street. Cars were carried down and piled up near the village's tiny harbour. It was later estimated that two million tons of water had poured down through Boscastle but mercifully on this occasion nobody was killed or seriously hurt, an extraordinary stroke of luck.

The 1952 floods caused devastation in the village *Tim Prosser*

COMBE MARTIN

This picturesque coastal village is tucked into the North Devon coast ten miles west from Foreland Point and about three miles east from Ilfracombe. The pronounced bay can provide quite a snug and useful passage anchorage off Combe Martin in any winds with some south in them. The holding can be a bit dodgy and the bay is susceptible to swell and not suitable for taking the ground. In quiet conditions you can land by dinghy at a quay near the village. Anchor as far into the bay as depth and your draught allow, but watch out for the drying rocky ledges which extend seawards from either side of the entrance to the inlet that leads to the village.

Pilotage into Combe Martin is straightforward. You come directly in from seaward but make the final approach towards the village from

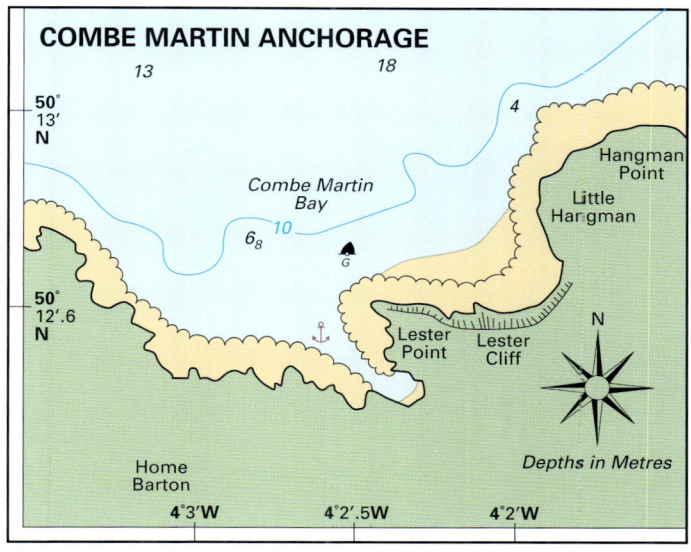

Looking into the bay at Combe Martin

The anchorage at Combe Martin can be a bit rolly and is popular with canoeists and windsurfers

the northwest, giving a wide berth to the rocky promontory on the north side of the inlet. Keep an eye on the echo-sounder as you draw into the bay. When arriving from the east, keep clear of Copperas Rock, with only 1.4m over it, that lies one and a half miles ENE of the Combe Martin anchorage and is marked on its seaward side by Copperas green conical buoy (unlit). Except for the two pier head lights shown from Lynmouth's tricky drying harbour 2F.R(vert) and 2F.G(vert), there are no navigation lights along this stretch of coast between Foreland Point Fl(4)15s18M and Ilfracombe's Lantern Hill Fl(2)G.5s6M.

Combe Martin is an attractive Devon village on the edge of Exmoor National Park. The parish church dates back to the 12th century and the village's enviable position in a sheltered valley or 'combe' gives it a particularly mild climate for the Bristol Channel coast. Combe Martin is well known for the succulent strawberries grown on terraces cut into the valley hillsides and there is still a strawberry fayre on the first Sunday in June. Silver mining became popular here in the 16th century and evidence of these mines can still be seen. Don't miss visiting the Combe Martin Museum in Cross Street, it has the most amazing collection reflecting the life and work in the village over the centuries.

Combe Martin has several pubs, but the Focsle Inn is right on the beach and from here you will see the fabulous sunsets, it also has a collection of old photos showing quite large sailing ships dried out by the quay. There's a good bakery and tea room in King Street and further along the King Street Stores that is open till really late.

WATERMOUTH COVE

Summary

The narrow, partly drying inlet known as Watermouth Cove lies a mile west of Combe Martin and a similar distance east of Ilfracombe, practically hidden from seaward behind enigmatic cliffs. You enter this fascinating natural haven between Widmouth Head and Burrow Nose, ideally near neaps at low or high water when the Channel streams are slack. During the strongest hours of tide there's often broken water off Watermouth entrance, especially on a weather-going ebb when the cross-stream can be powerful. Inside the cove you'll find good shelter in all but strong north or northwesterly winds and, even then, a low half-tide breakwater well into the cove affords fair protection. Watermouth mostly dries, but you can settle down on a firm bottom. At neaps boats of moderate draft can stay afloat in the outer part near the entrance.

Tides HW Watermouth is at HW Milford Haven −0010 or HW Dover −0520. Heights above chart datum: 9.2m MHWS, 0.7m MLWS, 6.9m MHWN, 3.0m MLWN.

Port Control Watermouth Cove is privately managed and for the use of one of the visitors' moorings contact the harbourmaster, Rob Lake, whose office is at the head of the cove ☎ 01271 865422. The Watermouth Yacht Club members always welcome visitors at their clubhouse near the launching ramp.

Tidal streams and currents The streams can be strong immediately off the entrance, up to four knots at springs, and a weather-going tide often causes broken water. The east-going stream begins about an hour after local low water and the west-going stream an hour after local high water.

Description

Just over a mile east of Ilfracombe, Watermouth Cove is a charming and unexpected natural inlet about a quarter of a mile long, entered between the high cliffs of Widmouth Head to the west and a lower promontory known as Burrow Nose to the east. The coast is fairly steep-to from either direction and when approaching from seaward the trick is simply to find the entrance. Some white Coastguard cottages stand high on Rillage Point, not quite half a mile west of Watermouth entrance. An old pill-box on Burrow Nose can be identified two cables east of the entrance, a useful mark when approaching Watermouth from the east. From offshore you'll see Combe Martin village a mile up the coast to the east.

You can enter Watermouth at practically any state of tide, although at low springs the cove dries out almost to the end of Burrow Nose. Neaps are best for exploring this stretch of coast and a dead low neap is a good time to enter Watermouth, with minimal cross-tide across the entrance. You then know exactly how far to edge in before anchoring. Watch out for crab-pot floats each side of the entrance.

Watermouth practically dries at LAT to a firm bottom of sand and shale, but makes a quiet and pleasant overnight stop for boats

The 'Storm-in-a-teacup' Boat Café at Watermouth

SOUTH COAST

You need to be able to take the ground to appreciate Watermouth Cove

Near high water in the outer part of the Cove

WATERMOUTH COVE

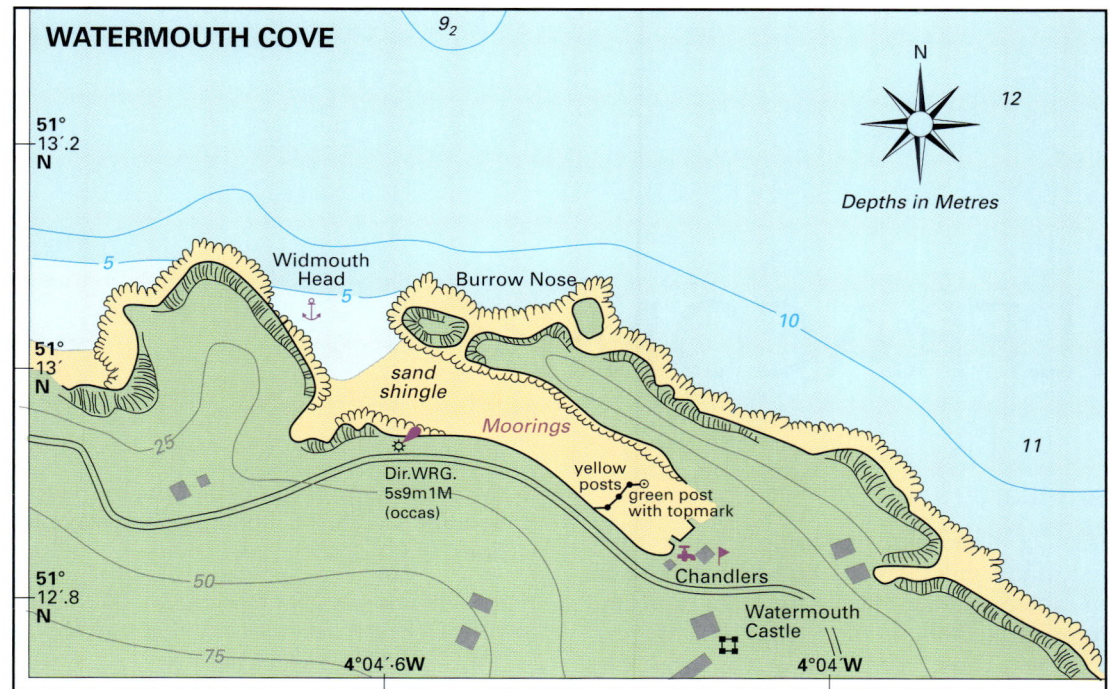

that can take the ground easily. The cove offers good shelter in all but strong north or northwesterly winds, although even under these conditions a half-tide breakwater, which partly divides the inlet, helps provide a fair degree of protection. This breakwater is marked by two yellow spar beacons and has a green spar beacon at its northeast. There's also a tide gauge close southeast of the green beacon. For use of one of the visitors' moorings, ask at the harbourmaster's office at the head of the cove. Water and diesel are also available.

At the head of the cove, the beach gives way to a low quay, a launching ramp and the friendly clubhouse of the Watermouth Yacht Club, whose members are always pleased to welcome visitors. Behind the club is the Watermouth Cove holiday park and camping site. The Watermouth Cove Yacht Club is open on Friday and Saturday evenings. From your boat the surroundings are impressive and when the sun shines, the sheer stature of this secret corner of the North Devon coast is oddly reminiscent of parts of Spain. Beyond the mouth of the cove, the restless channel tides ebb and flow swiftly, while now and then a ship passes close inshore, bound for Avonmouth or Sharpness.

Approach and entry

The entrance to Watermouth can be difficult to identify from offshore, but the gap between Widmouth Head and Burrow Nose is just a quarter of a mile east of the coastguard cottages above Rillage Point. You'll also see a small ruined pillbox on Burrow Nose not far east of the entrance. Strangers should only approach Watermouth in quiet conditions and ideally near a neap high or low water when the tidal streams are fairly slack off the entrance. There are often boisterous overfalls outside the mouth of the cove during the strongest part of the tide, although the entrance between Widmouth Head and Burrow Nose is clear of dangers. Unless you arrive near slack water, be prepared to allow for a powerful cross-set when lining up to come in. Entering under sail can be tricky because of the unpredictable down-draughts from Widmouth Head. Once into the inlet, the cross-tide will switch off and you can turn southeast towards the mooring area and the head of the cove, watching the echo-sounder as you go.

Entry at night

Definitely not recommended for strangers.

Berths and anchorages

At neaps and in quiet or offshore weather, moderate draught yachts can lie afloat at anchor in the outer part of the cove. There are several drying visitors' moorings on the outer side of the half-tide breakwater and towards the north side of the cove, which have red buoys with yellow handles. If you use one of these moorings report your arrival to the harbourmaster as soon as possible. Keelboats can dry out safely on legs so long as there's no swell. The best shelter is obtained inside the half-tide breakwater, and if there's room you may be able to dry out here by arrangement with the harbourmaster. You enter this inner area by leaving the green spar beacon on its northeast end to starboard. Chandlery is available through the harbourmaster who has a Facebook page for updates.

ILFRACOMBE

Summary

Friendly Ilfracombe harbour lies just three and a half miles east of Bull Point about 12 miles west along the coast from Foreland Point. Ilfracombe is often used as a staging-post by yachts, being one of the safest and most accessible havens on the south shore of the Bristol Channel, completely sheltered from the west and a snug port of refuge in southwesterly gales. The inner harbour dries and is protected from the east by a breakwater. It can be entered from two to three hours each side of high water, depending on your draught. The outer anchorage can be entered at any state of tide and offers good shelter except from between north and ENE. The attractive lively town has all facilities and the hospitable Ilfracombe Yacht Club always welcomes visitors.

Tides HW Ilfracombe is at HW Milford Haven −0015 or HW Dover −0525. Heights above chart datum: 9.2m MHWS, 0.7m MLWS, 6.9m MHWN, 3.0m MLWN.

Port Control Currently North Devon District Council. The Harbourmaster's office is on the Pier and can clearly be seen on your starboard side as you approach the inner Harbour ☏ 01271 862108, listening watch VHF 16, working channels 12 and 14.

Tidal streams and currents Streams can reach three and a half knots off the entrance at springs, and there may be overfalls up to half a mile west of Rillage Point especially on the ebb. The east-going stream begins about an hour after local low water and the west-going stream an hour after local high water.

The breakwater between the inner and outer harbour at Ilfracombe

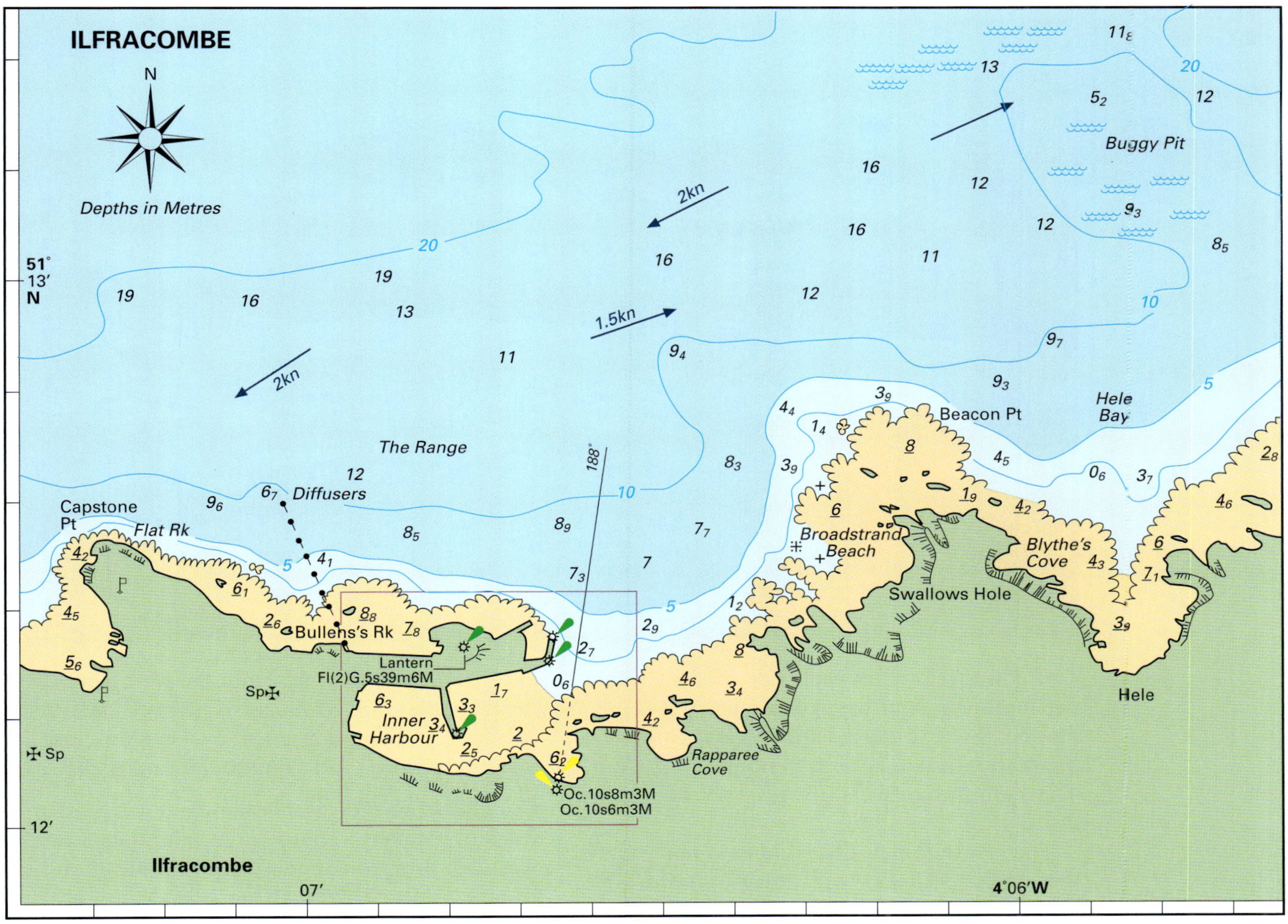

ILFRACOMBE

Description

Huddled behind Compass and Lantern Hills, Ilfracombe's attractive half-tide inner harbour probably offers the best shelter on the south shore of the Bristol Channel. There have been several proposals for a marina in this charming place, but so far none have come to fruition. Ilfracombe has always been a strategic staging post for yachts, being one of the safest and most accessible havens on the south shore of the Channel. Completely sheltered from the west, Ilfracombe is a reliable refuge in southwesterly gales. The Lundy Island supply ship regularly berths alongside the Pier near high water during the summer season.

The inner harbour dries but the outer harbour area can be entered at any tide just over a cable to the east of Lantern Hill. Here you are well protected from the south and west but rather exposed to the northeast. Visitors often raft alongside the short spur at Old Quay Head quay on the north side of the outer harbour and there are visitors' buoys just east of Old Quay Head, which dry at springs but where moderate draught boats can just stay afloat at neaps. There are drying visitors' berths in the southwest corner of the Inner Harbour, accessible between

Ilfracombe has an active yacht club

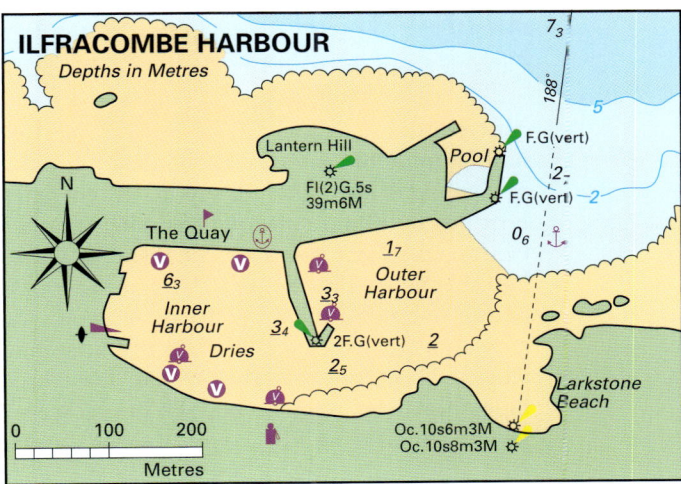

Bristol Channel and Severn Cruising Guide • 147

SOUTH COAST

Boats dried out in the inner harbour at Ilfracombe

two and three hours each side of high water, depending on your draught, and also a limited number of wall berths for fin and long keel boats should you be brave enough to dry out. The harbourmaster is always very helpful to visitors.

The hospitable Ilfracombe Yacht Club welcomes visitors and their comfortable lounge bar has fine views over the harbour. There are plenty of bistros along Fore Street – try the excellent fish at The Capstone on St James' Place. Ilfracombe has a good selection of shops and is busy during the holiday season, but not so frantic as the larger resorts of Minehead and Weston-super-Mare further up-Channel. There are useful facilities for yachts, including marine engineers, although there is no longer a chandler. You'll find quayside power and water points on the south side of the Inner Harbour – contact the harbour office in advance for shore power connection, which is always much in demand here.

Approaches

Coming from the west Pass well outside Morte Stone green conical buoy (unlit) to avoid Morte Stone ledge itself and Rockham shoal half a mile to the northeast. A potentially savage tidal race extends up to three miles north of Bull Point, although in quiet weather near slack water you can cut inshore within half a mile of Bull Point to dodge the worst of the overfalls. In heavy weather avoid the race altogether by passing north of Horseshoe Rocks N cardinal buoy, which lies three miles north by west of Bull Point. However if, in quietish weather, you happen to be approaching Ilfracombe from the west against a west-going tide, you can sometimes catch a favourable east-going eddy by keeping close inshore between Bull Point and Lantern Hill.

Coming from the east Pass outside Copperas Rock green conical buoy (unlit) and then steer west by south to round Widmouth Head and Rillage Point. There can be boisterous local overfalls up to half a mile west of Rillage Point, especially during the middle hours of the ebb.

Entry

Ilfracombe entrance lies a short half mile east of Capstone Point and a cable east of Lantern Hill, recognised by the small chapel on its summit. Make the final approach from just east of north so as to leave the Pier fairly close to starboard as you follow round to the west to enter the harbour, thereby avoiding the drying ledges that fringe the southern part of the bay. Watching the echo-sounder, anchor on a line ENE of the inner breakwater head, edging as far in as depth allows. There is now a Damien Hurst sculpture on the end of the pier which is hard to miss but not to everyone's taste. You can use one of the visitors' buoys just east of the breakwater, depending on your draught. Check the www.northdevon.gov.uk website which has a plan showing the location of visitors moorings and general harbour plans. There's a least depth of about one and a half metres in the outer harbour two hours after MLWS. The inner harbour can be entered from two to three hours each side of high water, depending on your draught.

Entry at night

Coming from the west First pick up Bull Point light Fl(3)10s and note that its fixed red sector shines over the Morte Stone and Rockham Shoal when bearing between 058°–096°. Bull Point's main flashing light is obscured from inside Barnstaple Bay but the fixed red sector shines out towards Lundy Island. Horseshoe N cardinal buoy is lit (Q), three miles just west of north from Bull Point. As you approach Ilfracombe, pick up Lantern Hill light Fl(2) G.5s and keep it on your starboard beam until you pick up the leading lights Oc.10s just to the east of Lantern Hill.

Coming from the east The last main coastal light east of Ilfracombe is 12 miles away at Foreland Point Fl(4)15s. About one and a half miles west of Foreland Point you'll see Sand Ridge green buoy Q.G half a mile offshore and, just opposite on the coast, the pier head lights for Lynmouth's drying harbour 2F.R and 2F.G. Along this whole 12-mile stretch between the Foreland and Ilfracombe, keep well offshore at night until you can identify Lantern Hill light Fl(2)G.5s not far west of Ilfracombe harbour entrance.

Final approach When entering Ilfracombe at night, come in from just east of north on the Larkstone leading lights Oc.10s, keeping them in transit at 188° until the inner pair of vertical fixed green lights on the pier is close abeam to starboard. Then head WSW into the outer harbour, steering towards the two vertical fixed green lights on the end of the inner breakwater.

Berths and anchorages

Ilfracombe Outer Harbour There's a least depth of 1.8m off the southeast corner of the pier and then the bottom shoals gradually to dry 1.5m about 100m east of the breakwater. If you come in not long after low water, watch the echo-sounder carefully and anchor well away from the pier and clear of the fairway leading to the inner harbour. Remember that some fairly shallow draught local boats will be able to move further into the harbour before a deepish keel yacht. Although the visitors' buoys just east of the breakwater dry at springs, moderate draught boats will just stay afloat here at neaps.

Note that Ilfracombe Outer Harbour remains a busy place with commercial traffic passing through it all day, and sometimes trawlers landing their catch through the night. It's recommended that you use a kedge anchor astern so that your boat always lies facing east/west, thus allowing the free movement of commercial traffic and the lifeboat. Always use an anchor light at night.

Ilfracombe Inner Harbour Dries to a firm sandy bottom and you can enter as soon after half-tide as your draught permits. The fairway dries to about 2.5m just south of the inner breakwater head, so deeper draught yachts should delay entry until two hours before high water. It's advisable to contact the harbourmaster to request a berth before entering the harbour. There are a few visitors' moorings in the southwest corner of the harbour or you can dry out alongside the south quay, but be sure not to obstruct the slip.

Just above half-tide in the outer harbour

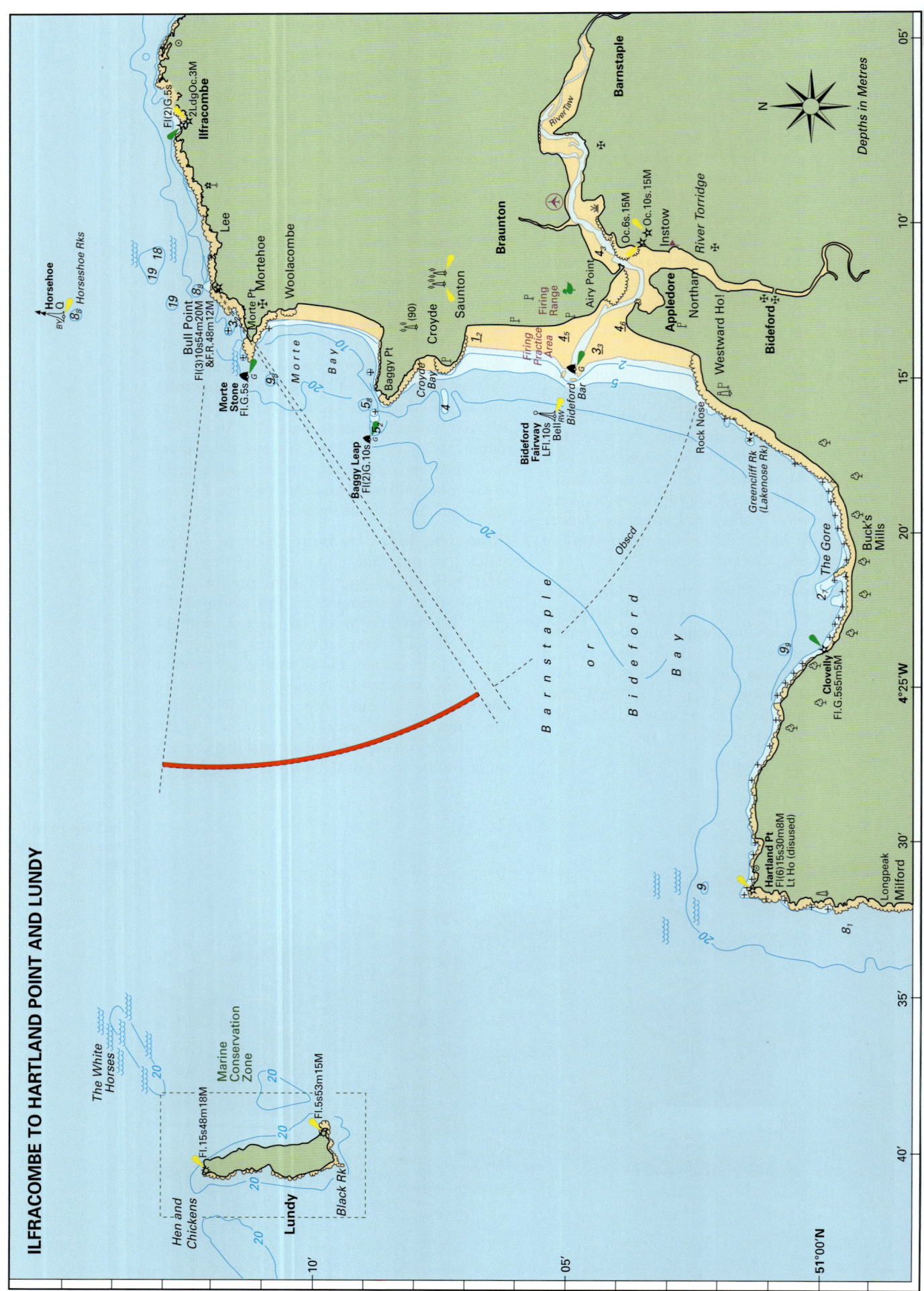

PASSAGE-MAKING FROM ILFRACOMBE

Heading down-Channel

If you are bound well down-Channel from Ilfracombe, aim to leave about an hour *before* local high water. You'll push some foul tide for an hour or so, but the stream will be easing as you come up with Bull Point and the overfalls there, which can extend up to three miles north of Bull Point, should be settling down. As you cross Barnstaple Bay the tide should be fairly slack, but about to turn in your favour to carry you nicely round Hartland Point and set you well on your way down the North Cornwall coast. The streams are much weaker beyond Hartland and it's much more feasible further down the coast to press on against the new flood.

Heading for Appledore

If you are bound round the corner for Appledore and the River Torridge, leave Ilfracombe about half an hour before local low water. This means coming out of the inner harbour before half-ebb and anchoring in the outer harbour for a while in sufficient depth. Outside Ilfracombe you'll carry a fair tide at first, but the stream will be falling off as you reach Bull Point and the race with it. You should then have more or less slack water round Morte Point and Baggy Point, and once you are well into Barnstaple Bay the tides are much weaker anyway. You must not cross Bideford Bar until about two and a half hours before the next high water, so you may have some time to kill in Barnstaple Bay.

Heading for Lundy Island

If you are going out to Lundy Island, a distance of about 21 miles from Ilfracombe, the best time to leave depends a good deal on the weather conditions and your likely speed. To maximise the fair stream, leave Ilfracombe just before half-ebb to carry about three and a half hours of west-going tide across to the anchorage on the southeast corner of Lundy. However, if conditions are such that the Bull Point race is likely to be boisterous, it's better to be passing Bull Point near slack water, just after high water, which would mean leaving perhaps an hour or an hour and a half *before* high water if you expected to sail west at between 5–6 knots. You would then clear Bull Point before the west-going stream stirred up the race again and should carry a fair stream across to Lundy. In this case though, it would be worth approaching the east shore of Lundy more or less in the middle near Tibbett's Point, thus avoiding the overfalls around the southeast corner of the island off Rat Island. From Tibbett's Point it's then easy to follow the coast of Lundy close inshore down to the anchorage north of Rat Island.

Heading up-Channel

If bound well up-Channel from Ilfracombe, leave an hour before local low water, pushing the last of the foul ebb tide but then picking up nearly seven hours of the new flood.

The broad sweep of Bideford Bay is quite exposed to the west

APPLEDORE, INSTOW AND BIDEFORD

Summary

The combined estuary of the Taw and Torridge rivers opens into the east side of Barnstaple Bay three and a half miles south of Baggy Point and 11 miles ENE of Hartland Point. Drying sands fringe the estuary mouth for up to a mile offshore and entry involves crossing Bideford Bar, which is dangerous in heavy onshore weather, but no problem in quiet conditions on the last of the flood. A buoyed channel leads to the small shipbuilding town of Appledore, on the west side of the River Torridge near the entrance. Instow village has some drying moorings opposite Appledore on the east side of the Torridge, while the market town of Bideford is two miles further up on the west bank, just below an old arched bridge. The River Taw joins the estuary north of Instow at Crow Point and shoal-draught boats with local knowledge can reach Barnstaple town, six miles upstream, on a spring high water.

Tides HW at Appledore or Bideford is at HW Dover –0525. Heights above chart datum at Appledore: 7.5m MHWS, 0.2m MLWS, 5.2m MHWN, 1.6m MLWN. HW Barnstaple is about 15mins later than HW Appledore.

Port Control Torridge District Council is responsible for both Appledore and Bideford Harbourmaster ☏ 01237 475834 or 428700, harbour.master@torridge.gov.uk. For the Appledore Pilot ☏ 01237 477928 or call on VHF 16/12 within two hours of high water.

Tidal streams and currents Although the streams in the outer approaches can be strong (up to three knots at springs off both Hartland Point and Morte Point), they are considerably weaker in Barnstaple Bay. However, a hard current runs in the lower Torridge through Appledore Pool, especially near half-ebb. Out at Bideford Bar once the tide starts ebbing, breakers soon form in the entrance channel between the shallowest part of the bar and Middle Ridge green buoy.

Description

The shallow estuary of the Taw and Torridge rivers meets Barnstaple Bay between extensive areas of coastal dunes – Braunton Burrows to

Instow village on the east side of the River Torridge

APPLEDORE, INSTOW AND BIDEFORD

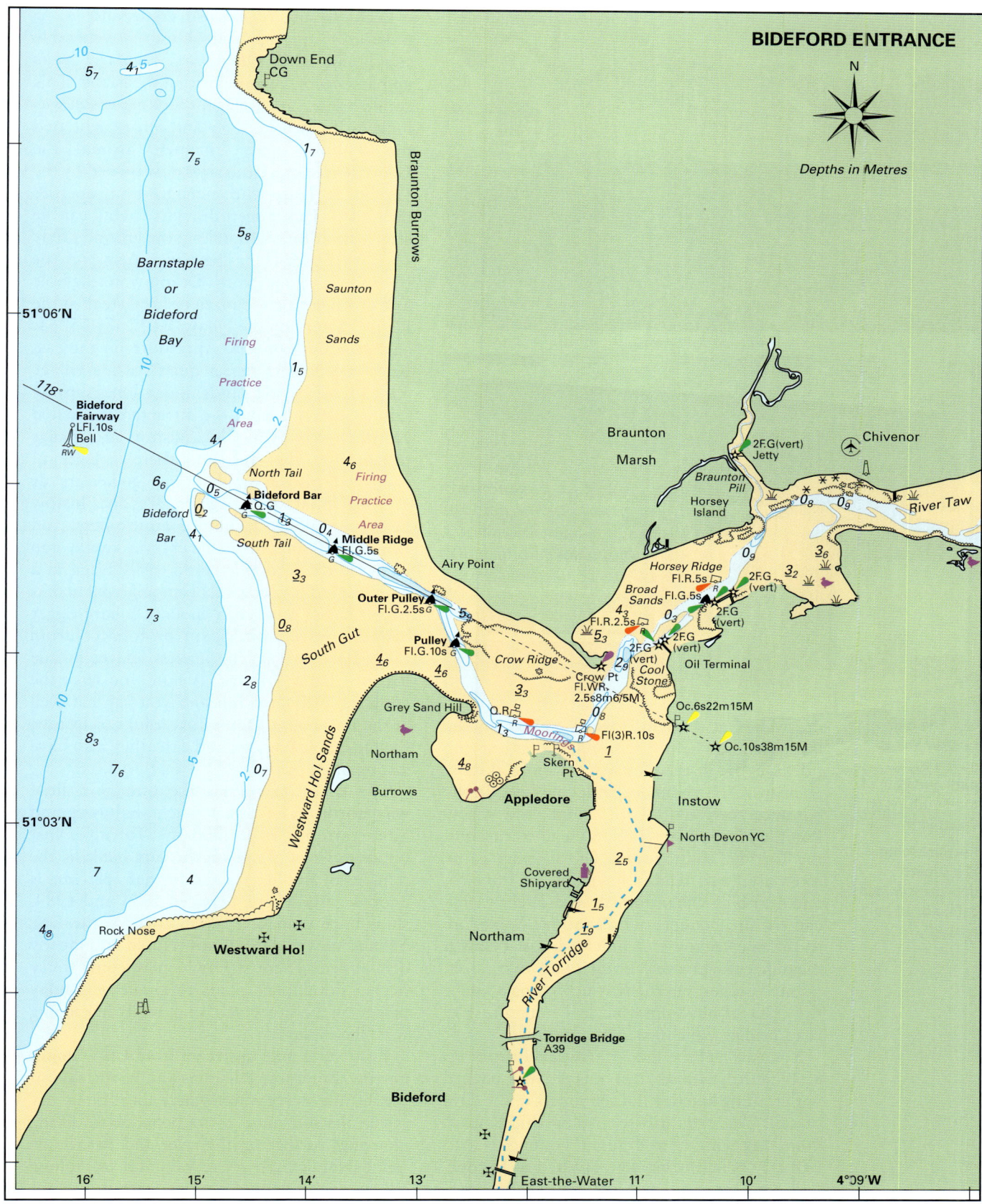

the north and Northam Burrows to the south. Just inside the entrance on the south side, the salty town of Appledore has a long history of seafaring and shipbuilding. Yachts and fishing boats lie to moorings in Appledore Pool just off Skern Point and in the river off the town's sheltered waterfront. Appledore Shipyard has turned out some fine vessels between various financial crises, including some notable superyachts.

The buoyed entrance channel into the estuary is dangerous in strong onshore winds

Top: The old railway line is now a cycle path and part of the South West Coast Path

Bottom: Johns is a superb delicatessen and café, not to be missed

or swell, but straightforward enough in the last two hours before a reasonably high spring tide. Depths in the channel are more skimpy at neaps. The channel divides just inside the entrance between Skern Point and Crow Point, with the River Taw to the northeast and the Torridge to the south. The Torridge is the most used and readily navigable of the two, and near high water quite deep-draught yachts can venture a couple of miles above Appledore to the market town of Bideford, just below a magnificent old stone bridge with two dozen pointed arches. On the way up you pass under the graceful but somewhat less romantic A39 road bridge, which has 24m clearance.

You can feel the flux of nautical history up at Bideford, whose river quays were packed with trading ketches and schooners in the days of sail. The port still sees some ships, up to 90m long with 4.5m draught, coming to load ball clay which is mostly exported to Europe. Ball clays are very fine grained, sedimentary materials of plastic consistency used in a wide range of ceramic products. Genuine, high quality ball clays are quite rare and some of the best deposits are mined in the Petrockstowe Basin, not far south of Bideford, so exporting directly by ship makes good commercial and environmental sense.

Local fishing boats also come and go at Bideford's quays, and Lundy's venerable supply ship, MS *Oldenburg*, regularly picks up passengers who are visiting the island. This comfortable, rather elegant looking vessel was built in Bremen in 1958 and once negotiated the shallow sandy channels around the German Frisian Islands, it is now owned by the Landmark Trust who manage the properties on Lundy. Quite deep draught yachts can lie alongside at Bideford, taking the ground safely soon after half-ebb. The Kings Arms on the riverside is a good North Devon watering hole and you'll get a good pizza or local steak at the Flame Factory on the Quay, ☎ 01237 475261.

Instow lies opposite Appledore on the east bank of the Torridge, a quiet seaside village with broad drying sands and a long slipway jutting well out from the attractively situated North Devon Yacht Club. Visitors are always welcome at the club and there's plenty of room on Instow sands for bilge-keelers or even keelboats with legs to dry out. Instow has a restful, old-fashioned atmosphere, and being dried out here as the ebb runs away you feel as if the next tide could easily bring in a couple of sailing coasters bringing coal across from Wales, or even a modest square-rigger carrying wool from Spain or tobacco from the Caribbean. It's a timeless place, a true Bristol Channel retreat. Ashore you have the convivial Wayfarer Inn and you can eat well at the Boathouse. Don't miss John's of Instow, the most amazing deli and café, they also have a shop at Appledore.

The River Taw joins the estuary a little way north of Instow, a much shallower and more tortuous river than the Torridge. Just opposite Crow Point on the east bank, is the remains of an old jetty and further upstream is another jetty where, between 1955 and 1984, ships once unloaded Welsh coal for the East Yelland power station, now closed and mostly dismantled. There is now a new controversy over a developer's plans to create a holiday village on the site which is not really in keeping with the estuary.

Just over a mile upstream from Crow Point, narrow Braunton Pill joins the north side of the Taw, a secret water where local boats dry out in the soft mud. More boats lie to drying moorings further up the river and Barnstaple quay, six miles above Crow Point if you follow the channel, sometimes sees an intrepid visitor alongside in a shoal-draught boat. But the depths are thin and unpredictable up here and there are no reliable charts with soundings above Braunton Pill. Although Barnstaple is an interesting and attractive town, strangers are advised not to attempt the passage up the Taw without reliable local knowledge.

APPLEDORE, INSTOW AND BIDEFORD

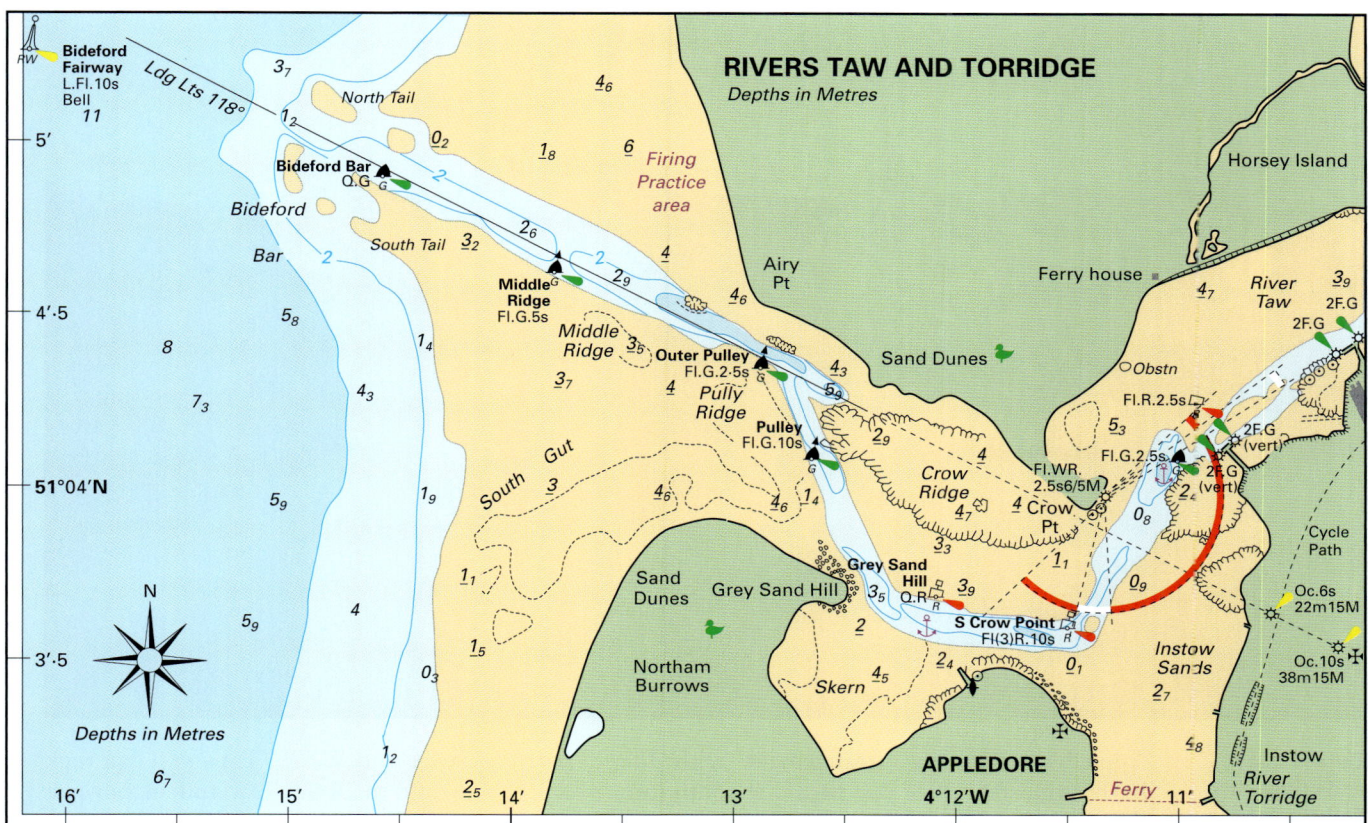

Outer approaches

Coming down-Channel Aim to arrive off Bull Point near slack water low, when the overfalls should be fairly quiet. Morte Point is one and a half miles WSW of Bull Point and the shore between the two is patchy with off-lying rocks. Avoid Rockham Shoal half a mile northeast of Morte Point, and pass outside Morte Stone green conical buoy (unlit) which marks the ledge extending westward from Morte Point.

The coast now trends south into Barnstaple Bay, past sandy Morte Bay and the high, imposing promontory of Baggy Point. Baggy Rock lurks four cables northwest of this headland, guarded by Baggy Leap green conical buoy (unlit). From the Baggy Leap buoy, make good just east of south for three and a half miles to locate Bideford red-and-white fairway buoy LFl.10s. If you were off Bull Head at slack water low, you'll probably arrive off Bideford fairway too early for the entrance channel – don't attempt to enter the estuary until two hours before high water. In quiet weather you can anchor four cables due east of the fairway buoy in about 9m LAT, sand and mud. In any winds from south of west there's a useful anchorage off Clovelly Bay, seven miles southwest of the Bideford fairway buoy in about 7m over mud.

Coming up-Channel The race off Hartland Point is the main hazard. In quiet weather you can pass about three quarters of a mile off the headland to cut inside the worst of the overfalls. Otherwise stay 3–4 miles off, outside the race.

The timing for rounding Hartland Point and entering the Torridge can be tricky when you are carrying a fair stream up the Bristol Channel. To arrive off the Bideford fairway buoy two hours before high water, most sailing boats would have to be rounding Hartland four hours before high water, which wouldn't give you much favourable tide on the way up the coast. If the weather serves, a practical plan is often to round Hartland at high water slack when the race is quiet and then tuck round the corner to anchor off Clovelly until the next tide. Leaving Clovelly at half-flood will then get you to Bideford fairway buoy at about the right time for negotiating the entrance channel.

Entry

Never try to enter the Torridge estuary in poor visibility or in fresh onshore winds or swell. Otherwise, at two hours before high water, you can leave Bideford fairway buoy two cables to starboard and make good 118° for a mile to leave Bideford Bar green buoy Q.G 100m to starboard, continuing on the same track for just over another mile to leave the Middle Ridge Fl.G.5s and Outer Pulley Fl.G.2.5s green buoys to starboard. At the Outer Pulley buoy, turn SSE and make good 157° for three quarters of a mile to leave the Pulley green buoy Fl.G.10s close to starboard and the end of Grey Sand Hill dunes 100m to starboard before turning to port at just south of east to follow the line of moorings round Skern Point and into the Torridge. It's usually possible to use an RNLI mooring in

SOUTH COAST

The old quay and bridge at Barnstaple sees little boating activity now

Appledore Pool by arrangement with the harbourmaster. Once you turn due south into the river, the deepest water lies close along the Appledore shore as far as the covered shipyard.

Entry at night

Not recommended for strangers, but Bideford fairway buoy is lit LFl.10s and Instow leading lights (*Front* Oc.6s, *Rear* Oc.10s) take you as far in as the Outer Pulley buoy QFl.G and then the Pulley buoy is lit Fl.G.10s.

Berths and anchorages

Appledore Pool Keelboats can anchor and stay afloat in the pool between Grey Sand Hill and the drying west edge of Instow Sands. The tide can run strongly through this area, especially near half-ebb, and you'll find better holding at the east end, upstream from the large mooring buoys. It's a good idea to buoy your anchor as there are numerous old cables on the bottom. Around neaps, moderate draught boats can anchor and stay afloat on the west side of the river opposite Appledore town. Land at Appledore Quay, near where the ferry comes across from Instow. Good shops and pubs in the town.

The North Devon Maritime Museum is in Odun Road, a little way back from the Quay. It has lots of interesting exhibits including model ships, boat building tools, the story of a Second World War French frogman and the history of Sir Richard Grenfell, a 16th century Bideford sailor.

Mouth of the River Taw Appledore Pool can be uncomfortable in fresh winds from between north and WNW. Then you can tuck a little way into the River Taw and anchor just northeast of Crow Point and its lighthouse Fl.WR.2.5s. You'll find moderate holding here in fine sand and the pool off Crow Point is about as far into the Taw as you can easily go without grounding at low water.

Instow In reasonable weather bilge-keelers can dry out on the south part of Instow Sands or in the shoal area opposite Instow Quay. You can either anchor or use a vacant mooring by arrangement with the North Devon Yacht Club. Instow Quay can be reached when the height of tide is more than about 4.6m and keelboats can take the ground alongside by arrangement with the club. Shops are handy at Instow village and there is fresh water at the quay.

The River Torridge There are various drying anchorages in the river between Appledore and Bideford. Northam is a sheltered and attractive spot, half a mile above Appledore shipyard on the west side of the river.

Bideford Quay The quays up at Bideford have been improved in recent years and visiting yachts are welcomed. To reach Bideford, leave Appledore an hour or two before high water and keep broadly to the west side of the river. Yachts can moor alongside the town quay by arrangement with the harbourmaster, whose office is in the square (☎ 01273 428700). It's important to check with the harbourmaster where to lie in case any ships are expected, but also because in some places the bottom slopes outwards and in others the mud is very soft. The attractive old town is nearby and there's fresh water at the quay.

APPLEDORE, INSTOW AND BIDEFORD

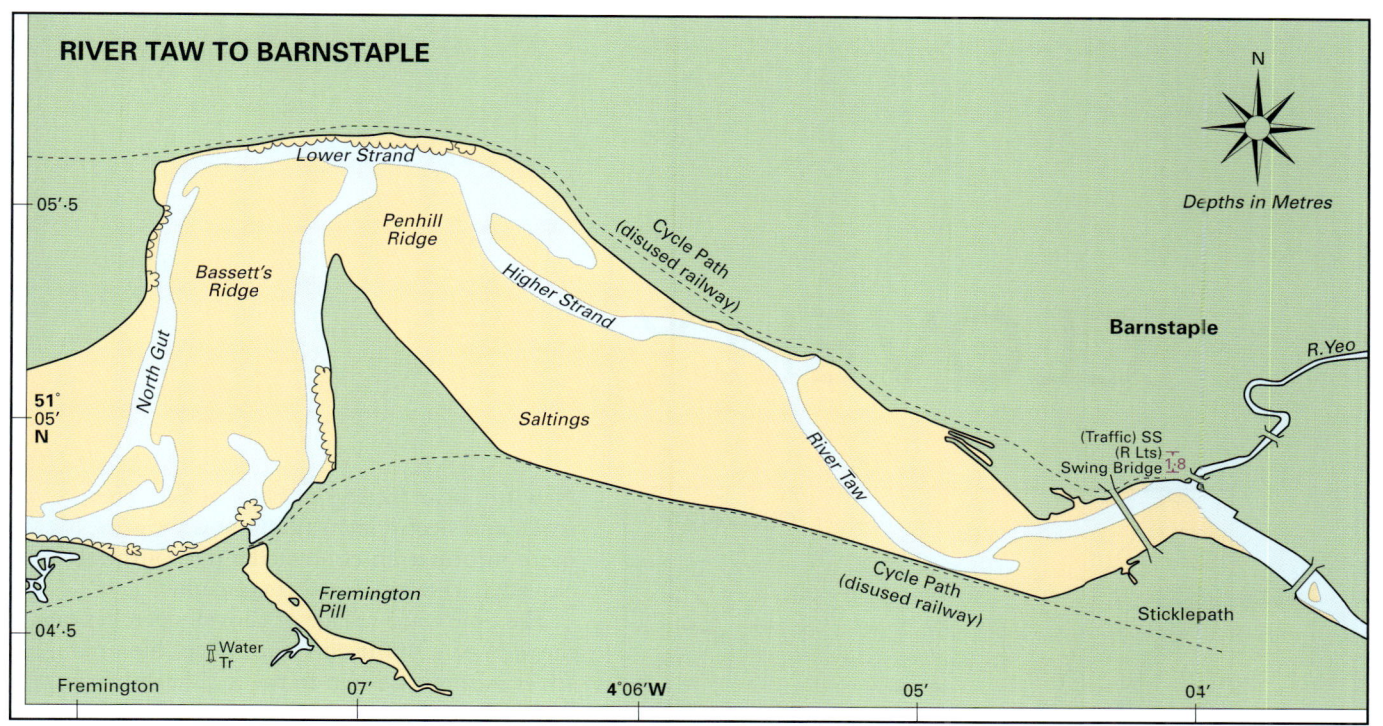

There's an active gig rowing club at Appledore

Bristol Channel and Severn Cruising Guide • 157

CLOVELLY

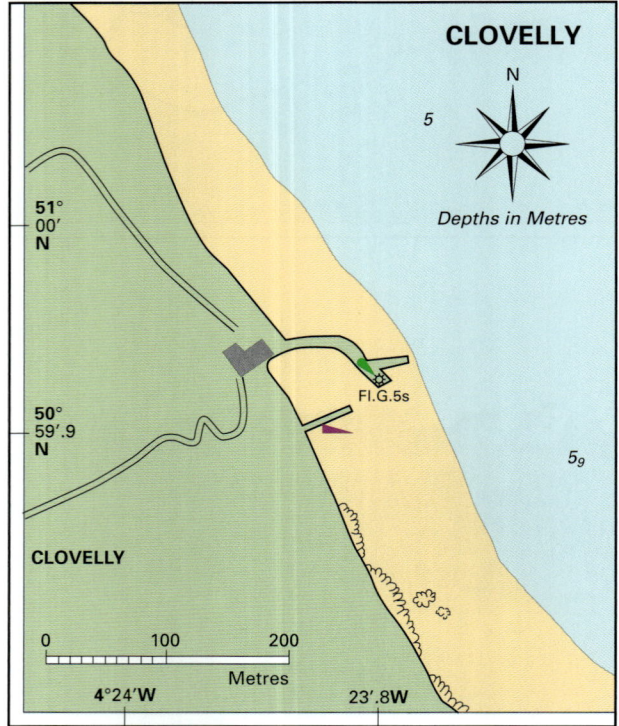

Clovelly looks like everyone's idea of a North Devon fishing village, huddled under dramatic high ground five miles east of Hartland Point. A stone pier protects the miniature drying harbour and in quiet weather or offshore winds you can anchor off the entrance against a spectacular coastal backdrop. Even in due westerlies, Clovelly is fairly well protected by the land curving up towards Hartland Point. Just over a mile east of the harbour, a drying rocky ledge known as The Gore juts out northwestward from the coast for about three quarters of a mile. Be careful of this hazard if you are following the shore round from the mouth of the Torridge.

The Clovelly harbourmaster, ☎ 07975 501830, welcomes visitors and for a couple of hours each side of high water you can lie alongside any part of the harbour quay so long as the landing steps are kept clear. You'll eat well at the Red Lion Hotel near the quay or at the New Inn near the top of High Street. There is water and electricity available and showers, for more information contact the harbourmaster, clovellyharbourmaster@gmail.com.

The time warp village of Clovelly perches on the side of a 400ft cliff and its cobbled main street meanders down to the tiny harbour and lifeboat station past picture-book cottages and narrow winding alleys. The harbour is protected by an ancient stone breakwater that curves out to keep out the worst of westerly weather. Clovelly remains undeveloped largely because it is blissfully free of cars, thanks to the foresight of the Hamlyn family that has owned and managed the village and its surrounding estates since 1738.

From Elizabethan days, herring fishing was the staple livelihood and Clovelly prospered until the huge shoals started mysteriously to move away in the 1830s. Times were then harder for a while until, towards the middle of the 19th century, the writer Charles Kingsley returned to this idyllic spot where he'd grown up when his father was rector. Inspired by boyhood memories and the atmosphere of Clovelly, Kingsley wrote *Westward Ho!* and *The Water Babies*, which both became best-sellers. These two books and the growing Victorian taste for seaside holidays produced a tourist boom for this corner of the North Devon coast. Old photographs show paddle-steamers from around the Bristol Channel arriving off Clovelly at the end of the 19th century to put trippers ashore in small boats.

Clovelly owes its survival from 20th-century invasion to Christine Hamlyn, who managed the restoration of the old village cottages, kept motor traffic corralled at the top of the hill and ensured that crass commercialisation wasn't allowed to spoil the natural grandeur and calm atmosphere of this special place. The Clovelly Estate Company, still run by the Hamlyn family, owns all the village buildings and the surrounding acres, and has managed to protect the character of this unique community against all the odds.

The old quay at Clovelly

SOUTH COAST

LUNDY ISLAND

Less than three miles long from north to south and little more than half a mile across, the windswept plateau of Lundy Island lies out in the fast tides of the Bristol Channel, 10 miles northwest of Hartland Point. Owned by the National Trust, Lundy has a fine collection of old buildings, including a notable Victorian church and the moody 13th-century ruins of Marisco Castle. Lundy is well worth a visit in settled weather and Ilfracombe is a good jumping off point with your own boat. Alternatively take the elegant island ferry *MS Oldenburg*, which runs regularly to Lundy from Bideford and Ilfracombe.

Lundy is high, steep-to and surrounded by tidal races and overfalls, so pick a quiet day and approach near slack water – whether high or low it doesn't much matter, although at low water slack the sea around Lundy is generally at its quietest. The usual anchorage in westerlies is in the snug bay off the southeast landing jetty, just north of Rat Island and the Lundy south lighthouse. It's a long haul up the cliff path to the top, but the views down to the anchorage and across to the Devon mainland are spectacular. The Marisco Tavern is a welcome port of call after the climb. If there's any east in the wind you can anchor on the west side of Lundy at Jenny's Cove, provided there's no swell, though landing from here is tricky. Lundy has some dramatic cliff walks, with spectacular views back across to Hartland Point and the Devon coast. The Marisco Tavern serves Lundy ale and good pub grub.

Although Lundy has strong tides, no harbour and rather uneasy waters, it's nevertheless fascinating to sail out to the island for a day, starting from Ilfracombe, Appledore or perhaps the anchorage off Clovelly. Ideally

The Lundy anchorage on a calm day
Landmark Trust / Jill Tate

SOUTH COAST

choose a period when the tides are about halfway between springs and neaps, and taking off. This will give you a convenient morning and evening high water, a fairish stream to Lundy and back, and overfalls that are not too savage.

At night

Strangers are advised not to approach Lundy at night, but the two powerful lights at either end of the island are important marks for navigating in the vicinity – Lundy North West Point Fl.15s17M and Lundy South East Point Fl.5s15M. The end of the southeast landing jetty is also lit Fl.R.3s3M.

The steps down to the lighthouse on Lundy *Landmark Trust / Jill Tate*

Top: St Helen's church, Lundy *Landmark Trust / Jill Tate*

Middle: The Marisco Tavern is a popular draw on Lundy *Landmark Trust / Jill Tate*

Bottom right: The classic *MS Oldenburg* brings visitors to Lundy from Ilfracombe or Bideford *Landmark Trust / Stu Leavy*

The magic of Lundy

Visiting Lundy is a fascinating experience. Some people suggest it is like stepping back in time but in fact Lundy is a unique place. Now owned by the National Trust the many fine old buildings on the island are managed by the Landmark Trust and you can rent one of these peaceful retreats to escape the 21st century for a while. You could choose to stay in Castle Keep, Government House or the original lighthouse on the southeast side of the island, which at 167m high is a useful daymark. The Castle is still known as Marisco Castle after the rather piratical 12th and 13th century lords of the island who spent much of their time menacing shipping in the Bristol Channel.

Later owners include William Hudson Heaven, a wealthy Gloucestershire businessman whose fortunes sadly took a turn for the worse in the mid-19th century. He leased part of the island to a granite company but that business only lasted about five years. Appropriately William's son, the Rev Hudson Heaven, had the church built in 1897 using money bequeathed to the family but his heir, Walter, finally had to sell Lundy in 1917 when his creditors foreclosed. It was bought by Augustus Christie, a rather more astute businessman, who leased the farm to a North Devon farmer and set about building on the tourist potential of the island. He established tea rooms and a regular boat service for both passengers on day trips and supplies for residents. Lundy rapidly became an active community again and a viable business.

The last family to own Lundy were the Harmans. Martin Harman had visited the island as an 18 year-old in 1903 and fell in love with it. In 1925 he had the chance to buy the island and the supply boat, MV *Lerina*. Martin Harman was a keen naturalist and an early conservationist, setting the trend for the long term future of the island. After he died in 1954 his son, Albion, continued running the island on the same principals. When Albion died in 1968 his wife and sisters could no longer run the island so had to offer it for sale. As a result of a generous donation from a philanthropist the National Trust was able to buy Lundy in 1969 on the understanding that the Landmark Trust would run it.

The name Lundy comes from the Norse for puffin island and there are said to be 15 times as many puffins as people here. One of Martin Harman's legacies to the island is its stamp, the Puffin, which you can buy at the well-stocked general store where you can send post to the mainland. Another is the Lundy Field Society which was inaugurated in May 1946 with Martin Harman as its first president. The Society was the brain-child of Leslie Harvey, a zoology lecturer at what is now Exeter University. The initial plan was for a committee of the Devon Bird Watchers and Preservation Society to establish a station to monitor bird migration but Martin Harman wanted to ensure the island's independence was maintained so a separate society was formed.

The LFS is still very active today and volunteers continue to monitor the populations of puffins, guillemots, Manx shearwaters and storm petrels which breed on Lundy every year. There are also Soay sheep, feral goats Highland cattle and Japanese sika deer that were introduced to the island by Martin Harman. A large colony of grey seals lives around the island and on terra firma there are several rare and endangered species of plant. The Lundy pony has now become a recognised breed although it too was brought to the island by Martin Harman and comes from New Forest, Connemara and Welsh stock. The seas around Lundy have been protected since 1973 and are now a Marine Protected Area.

In summer, visitors arrive on Lundy in gracious style aboard *MS Oldenburg* from Bideford or Ilfracombe. Built in 1958 in Bremen, *Oldenburg* worked as a ferry around the German Frisian Islands. Her original panelling and brass fittings have been restored and two new Cummins engines give her a comfortable cruising speed of 13 knots. The winter helicopter service from Hartland is rather less romantic.

Further information: **www.landmarktrust.org.uk** or **www.lundyisland.co.uk**

Shipwrecks and rescues

Facing the full might of the Atlantic the funnelling entrance to the Bristol Channel was the downfall of many a sailing vessel and the massive tides and shifting sands can still be treacherous. On the Swansea Docks website is a list of vessels wrecked in the area between 1687 and 1983, ships of many nationalities, sizes and types, and it is quite staggering how many are there. The Ship Aground pub at Mortehoe, north of Barnstaple, has maps of the North Devon coastline and Lundy showing known wrecks, almost too many to count.

The Mixon Shoal, the Scarweather Sands and the Nash Sands are just three notorious locations of groundings on the Welsh coast and the Wolves, a group of rocks near Flat Holm, also features in many accounts of wrecks. As a result of the grounding on the Nash Sands of the *Frolic*, a paddle steamer on passage from Haverfordwest to Bristol, and the loss of 80 passengers and crew, Trinity House erected two lighthouses on Nash Point, the High light and the Low light. The function of the Low light was replaced by red sectors in the High light in the 1920s. Other important lighthouses are on Caldey Island, Flat Holm, two on Lundy, and many headlands on either shore of the Bristol Channel.

The original lighthouse on Lundy was on the top of the island. It had an upper rotating light and a lower fixed light but at a distance these could appear as just one fixed light. In 1828 *La Jeune Emma*, en route to Cherbourg, thought this was the fixed light on the west coast of Ushant and foundered on the rocks off Lundy with the loss of thirteen lives. The old lighthouse was so high up that it could be obscured by fog when the weather was clear at sea level so in 1897 it was replaced by two lighthouses lower down, one on the north end of the island and the other at the south.

The introduction of new lights caused at least one wreck when the Master of the *Brechin Castle* probably mistook the Helwick Light for the Mumbles, as he would have been unaware of the position of the newer light. The vessel was on passage from Port Adelaide to Swansea with copper ore and wool and there were two families on board. The ship broke up on Mixon Shoal with part of the hull washing up in Oxwich Bay and other wreckage came ashore at Limeslade. There were no survivors.

Although wrecks caused the loss of many lives there are also numerous reports of heroic rescues with captains, pilots, and local people putting their own lives at risk to save crews and passengers from these disasters. One such rescue was in January 1839 when a brig, the *Thomas Piele*, bound from Swansea to Dublin went aground some way offshore. One of the crew swam ashore to get help as she was breaking up. Captain Jones of the *Two Sisters* took the

Haydn Miller, the Tenby lifeboat *RNLI*

ship's boat and with two other captains and Pilot Jenkins rowed out to help the stricken vessel. People watching from the shore thought the rescuers had been lost but twice they were washed out of their boat and, luckily, back to shore. Captain Foley then took the boat with Pilot Jenkins and three others and they managed to rescue the master and four crew, though three others had already drowned. The rescuers were all recognised for their bravery by the RNLI. This is just one of so many stories of quite amazing rescues.

The fate of cargoes from shipwrecks may be the other side of the coin. The idea of wreckers deliberately obscuring, moving or showing lights to lure ships to disaster, often associated with the north coast of Cornwall, may well have been over dramatized for the sake of a good yarn, though no doubt there were instances of it happening. The more realistic explanation is that in areas where life was pretty hard the spoils from a wreck were a welcome perk. When the *John Lilley* went aground on Saunton Sands in 1843 the captain and crew were rescued by the lighthouse keeper, the Appledore customs officer and a local man. Customs and Excise Officers were not quite so successful at rescuing the cargo, which was mostly rum and tobacco, and the Barnstaple Customs Collector had to admit that most of the cargo disappeared, despite many local searches.

On both coasts of the Bristol Channel the RNLI maintain lifeboats that have rescued numerous people and saved many lives. Tenby, Padstow and Clovelly are just three important lifeboat stations where local volunteers regularly put their own lives at risk when they receive 'the shout'. There has been a lifeboat at Tenby since 1852, the first one was a 28ft, 10-oared self-righting boat that was housed in Penniless cove in one corner of Tenby harbour. In 1905 a lifeboat house and slip were built off Castel Hill and a new building was opened here in 2006 with a new Tamar class lifeboat, the *Haydn Miller*.

Tenby's lifeboat houses

Clovelly's diminutive harbour has had a lifeboat since 1870 when the first boat was a 33ft traditional wooden sailing lugger with a crew of 15 and 10 oars. The current Atlantic 85, *Toby Rundle*, has been on station since 2014 taking over from the *Spirit of Clovelly*, an Atlantic 21. The station was closed from 1988 when it was felt that the Appledore and Padstow boats could safely cover the area and from 1990 to 1997 the Clovelly Trust operated a privately funded inshore lifeboat. The RNLI reopened the station in 1998.

Down the coast at Padstow the lifeboat station has been in Mother Ivey's Bay since 1967. The new lifeboat house and slip were opened in 2006 when the *Spirit of Padstow* came into service. There has been a lifeboat in Padstow since 1827 and the RNLI took control of the station in 1856 when the boat was stationed at Hawker's Cove, on the west shore just into the Camel Estuary. To commemorate the move to the new location in 1967 Matthew Arnold wrote the 'Padstow Lifeboat March' but it wasn't heard until June 1976 at the Royal Festival Hall as part of the BBC International Festival of Light Music.

BUDE HAVEN

Summary

Bude Haven lies 11 miles south of Hartland Point and its outer part consists of a narrow drying channel on the west side of a shallow river estuary. A long Atlantic swell often breaks over the outer shoals and strangers should only enter in quiet weather, during daylight and near high water. A few local moorings are protected from the west by a breakwater running out from the shore to Chapel Rock. The old Bude Canal joins the sea in the south part of the estuary and yachts can lock into the canal basin on a reasonable spring tide. Given calm conditions the approaches to Bude are straightforward, with two sets of leading marks indicating the deepest water.

Tides HW Bude is at HW Milford Haven −0040 or HW Dover −0540. HW heights above chart datum: 7.7m MHWS and 5.8m MHWN. There are no published LW heights.

Port Control Bude Haven is managed by Cornwall Council. For the Harbourmaster ☎ 01288 353111, mobile 07816 077755 or call *Bude Harbour Office* on VHF 6/12. 48 hours' notice is required for access through the lock.

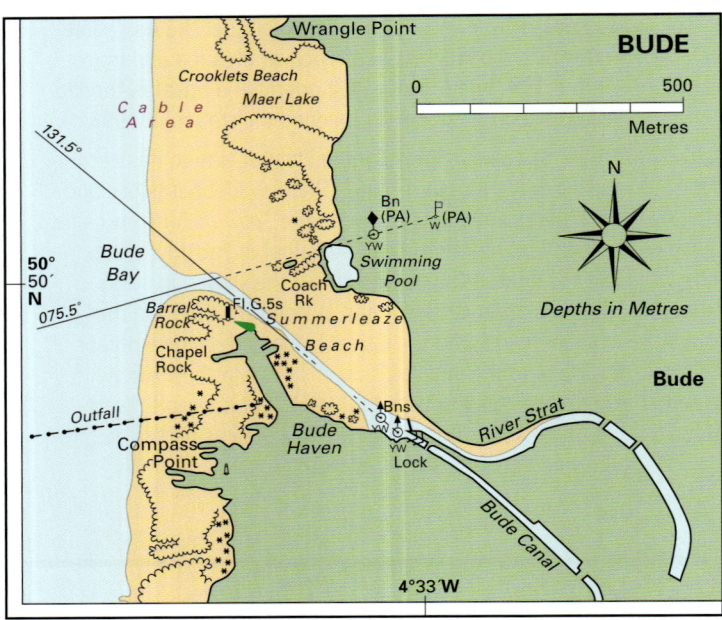

Tidal streams and currents Once you have 'turned the corner' and are well south of Hartland Point, you avoid the main, powerful flow of the Bristol Channel. The streams therefore tend to be relatively weak along the north Cornish coast.

Description

Not many boats visit Bude, but its old barge canal provides one of the snuggest hideaways in the Bristol Channel – once you are safely in! Bude is an amiable Cornish seaside town, the first place you reach cruising south from Hartland Point. Although the coast around Hartland is high, Bude itself is fairly low-lying and 'Bude Haven' consists of the comparatively sheltered west side of a shallow river estuary, which faces northwest and dries out to firm sand. A breakwater jutting out to Chapel Rock protects the narrow river channel where local moorings are laid. A long Atlantic swell often rolls in from seaward, breaking over the outer shoals on the north side of the estuary. The beach here is a favourite with surfers. Local boats approach Bude Haven from the southwest, leaving these breakers to port and Chapel Rock to starboard.

In quiet or offshore weather, intrepid strangers can enter Bude Haven near high water and lock into the old canal basin half a mile southeast of Chapel Rock. This peaceful waterway was built between 1819 and 1825 to carry shell sand inland to improve the acid soil, but now the lower stretch below the road-bridge makes an attractive retreat for a few yachts and fishing boats, sheltered from the Atlantic with views across the beach and estuary. Bude's friendly town centre is not far from the canal quay. Locking can take place within two hours of high water at springs but needs to be almost right on high water at neaps because a minimum depth of 2.5m is needed just outside the lock.

There is currently a regeneration project in progress to improve the amenities for visitors to Bude Haven. Boats up to 24m LOA, 7.5m beam and 2m draught can be accommodated. The quayside has been sympathetically developed with a shower block, craft studios, restaurants and cafés making this an attractive place to visit.

Approach and entry

Imray chart *C58 Trevose Head to Bull Point* is best for this stretch of coast, with its useful inset plan of Bude Haven. Strangers should only approach Bude near high water on a reasonably high spring. The outer approaches to Bude are clear of dangers and the passages south from Hartland and northeast from Padstow are both straightforward. In westerly winds, though, you should keep a safe offing from this rather craggy and unforgiving lee shore. Conspicuous just over three miles north of Bude Haven are the large, rather eerie radar dish aerials up behind Lower Sharpnose Point. Even if you are arriving from the southwest, from the direction of Padstow, these aerials are often the most obvious landmarks on this stretch of coast. Lower Sharpnose Point is also a favourite with rock climbers so you may see some activity on the cliffs.

Compass Point, a little way south of Bude entrance, can be identified by a prominent tower with a flagstaff on its north side. You approach Bude Haven from the WSW having first reached a position about six cables northwest of Compass Point. From here, pick up the outer set of leading marks which are above the low cliffs on the north side of the estuary, behind the swimming pool at the north end of Summerleaze beach. The front outer mark is a white spar with a yellow diamond topmark and the rear outer mark is a white flagstaff. Approach the estuary with these two in transit bearing 075°, a line which leaves Chapel Rock at the end of the breakwater well to starboard and puts you in position for the final approach.

Peaceful moorings on the Bude Canal

SOUTH COAST

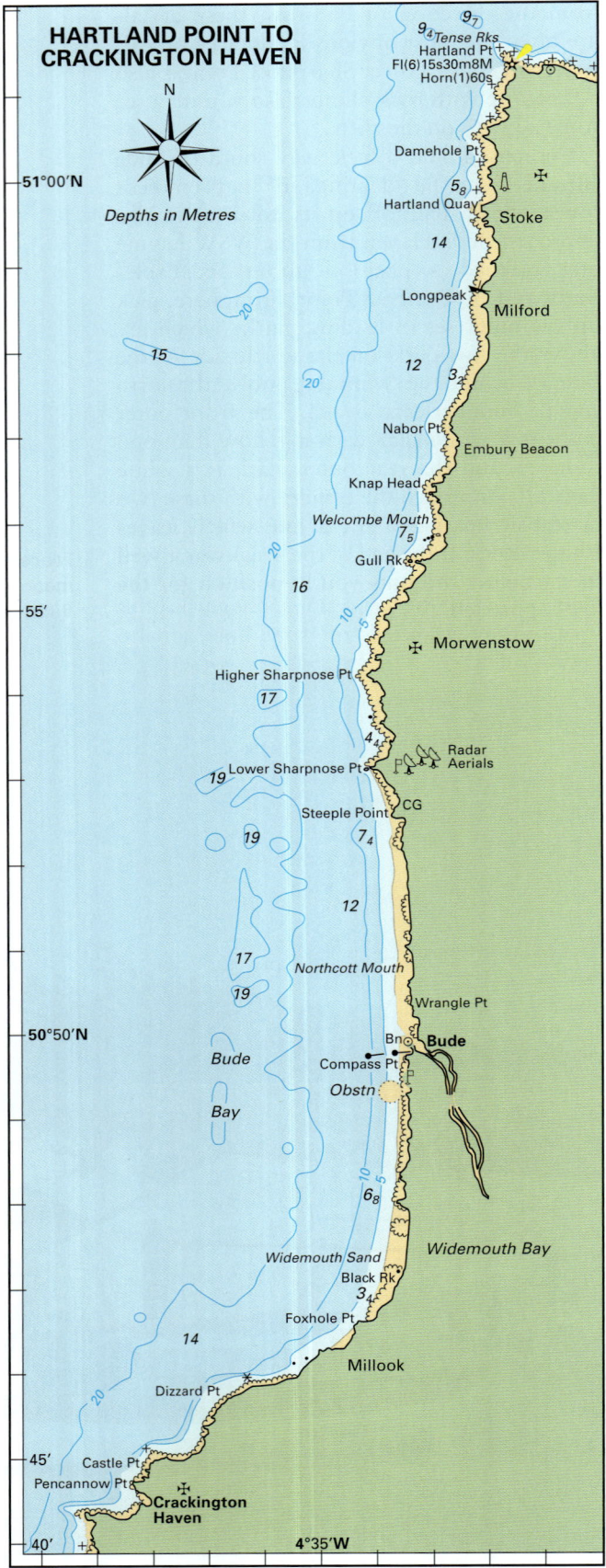

Keep a close eye to the southeast for when the next set of leading marks come into line. They stand just outside the lock leading into the Bude Canal – the front inner mark is a white pile beacon and the rear inner mark a white spar, both with yellow triangular topmarks. These two in transit bearing 131° take you up to the lock entrance, leaving Barrel Rock green beacon (with its barrel topmark) and then the east side of Chapel Rock close to starboard. A green post beacon just outside the lock marks the end of a low wall that covers at high springs. Bear in mind that, while the lock can operate within two hours of high water at springs, you would need to arrive almost dead on high water at neaps because a minimum depth of 2.5m is needed just outside the lock for it to open. It's important to have contacted the harbourmaster well in advance, preferably 48hrs beforehand, to make sure the lock will be ready. Inside the canal yachts can moor alongside the north bank to bollards and rings, a snug and very attractive spot overlooking the beach.

When approaching Bude, follow both sets of leading marks carefully and don't be tempted to come in directly from the northwest straight onto the second pair. Strangers should never approach Bude if a heavy ground swell is running, when in any case the lock may not be able to operate. In calm weather there's usually sufficient depth to enter or leave within two hours of a reasonable high water, but approaching an hour before high is prudent to give you the last bit of flood in hand.

Entry at night

Not recommended and no lights are shown.

Berths and anchorages

Bude Canal The canal basin provides the only safe berth for visitors and is quiet, sheltered and handy for the town. Fresh water is available from a quayside unit for water and electricity on a pay-as-you-go basis. There is a shower and amenities block and a choice of eating places on the quay or it's a short stroll into town. Just opposite the canal basin is the Falcon Hotel which has a good restaurant.

Small boats stay on moorings outside the Bude lock

The imposing lock gates

SOUTH COAST

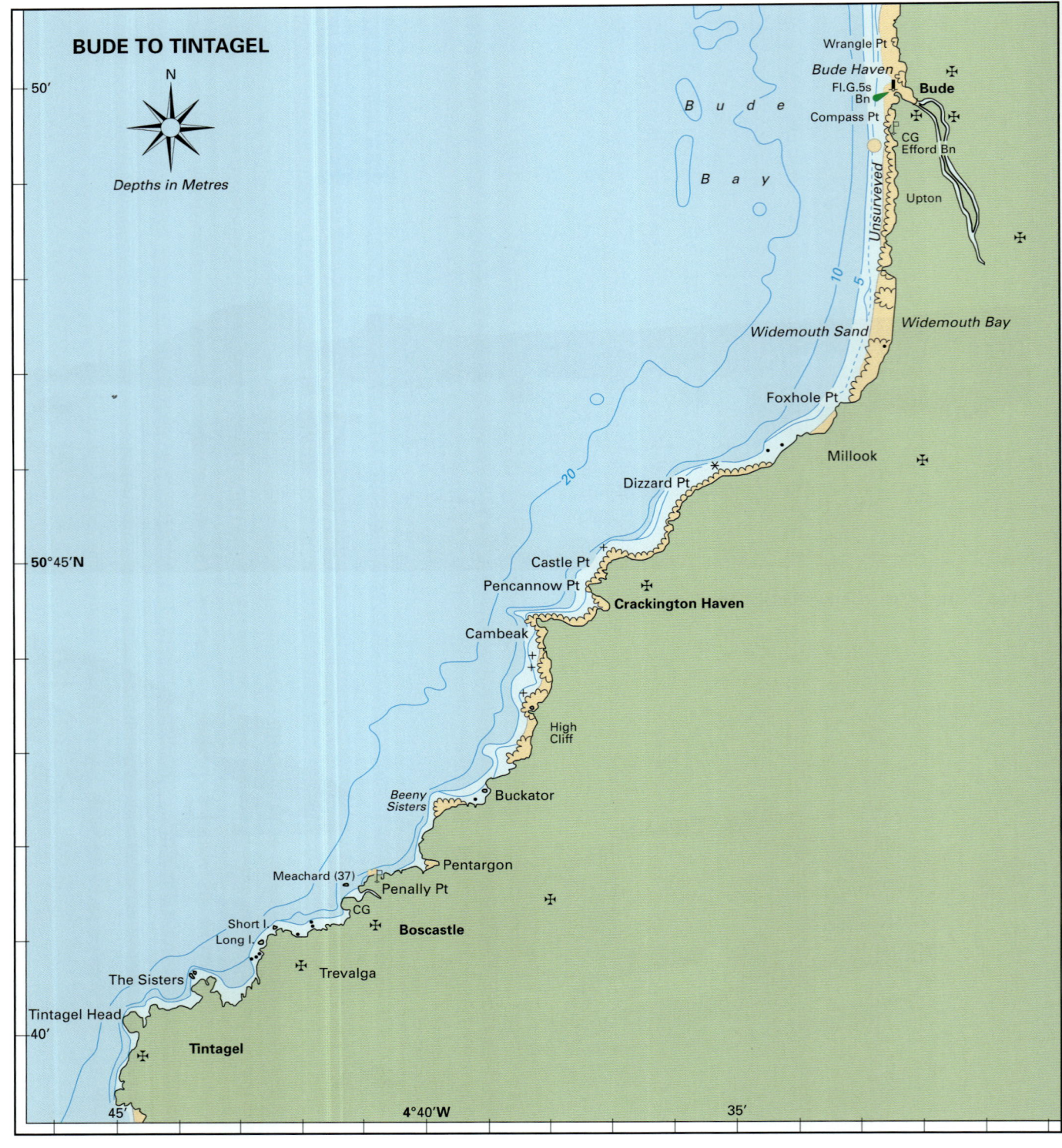

The old Bude canal

Although Bude now seems an unlikely port of call for cargo ships, it was and still is a very snug haven on a rather forbidding coast where safe harbours are few and far between. Vessels were trading into Bude from at least the Middle Ages and in the busiest days of sail sizeable ketches, schooners and barges arrived from the South Wales ports and from further up the Bristol Channel, bringing in coal and limestone and taking out local grain and oak bark for tanning. When the Bude Canal was completed in 1823, Bude Haven began to flourish and profits were beginning to be made. In 1838 a violent storm destroyed the original breakwater which had been built as part of the Canal & Harbour works. The Canal Company persuaded HM Government's Inspector to grant a loan to rebuild the breakwater to its present design, the loan was repaid by not paying dividends after running costs had been covered.

The Bude Canal was originally built to carry shell sand inland in order to reduce the acidity of the local farmland. The waterway comprised two distinct sections – a traditional barge canal for two miles from the sea lock to Helebridge wharf not far below Marhamchurch and then an extensive tub boat system that penetrated well inland to serve a wide area of North Cornwall and West Devon. The tub boats each had four wheels, allowing them to travel up and down inclined planes on rails by being attached to a continuous-loop chain driven by water power, instead of using the more common system of locks.

The total length of this waterway was over 35 miles, with branches reaching surprisingly far into the hinterland towards Holsworthy and Tamar Lake. Following the long Tamar Valley the tub boats could even reach Druxton Wharf near Launceston. The Bude canal system was notable for its six inclined planes at Marhamchurch, Hobbacott Down, Vealand, Merrifield, Tamerton and Werrington. Water to supply the Bude Canal system came along an aqueduct fed from a reservoir now known as Lower Tamar Lake.

As with many British waterways, the coming of the railways sounded the death knell for barge traffic. The London and South Western Railway reached Bude in 1898. Trading on the Launceston Branch had already ceased in 1891 when it was abandoned by Act of Parliament. The main line of the Canal continued until 1902 when it was purchased to provide a potable source of drinking water by the then Stratton & Bude Urban District Council. A water treatment works was constructed at Vealand taking the water from the reservoir. Bude Haven continued as a small port until after the Second World War. Not far into the canal, just above Falcon Bridge, you can see the original Bude lifeboat house dating from 1865. In those days the lifeboat was either launched through the canal and its lock if the tide was high enough, or carried down to the beach on a horse-drawn carriage.

Bude was once a busy port

BOSCASTLE

This tiny gem of a haven lies 10 miles southwest of Bude and is almost invisible from seaward. You enter via a narrow dog-leg gully hewn from natural rock. The inner part is protected by two short breakwaters. Owned by the National Trust, Boscastle was originally built by Sir Richard Grenville in 1584 and was once Launceston's main port for importing coal and shipping out slate and corn. Sailing coasters and barges once working in here to discharge and load, heaven knows how.

In quiet weather you can nose into Boscastle near high water, having identified Meachard Rock (37m high) one and a half cables offshore. A white coastguard hut stands on the south arm and there's a flagstaff on the hill above the north arm, Penally Point. Pass outside Meachard and steer for the coastguard hut until the harbour opens up between the cliffs to port. Then head straight in, staying in mid-channel. Leave the outer breakwater to port and come to starboard round the inner breakwater. The tide won't let you linger long inside and there's precious little space to moor, but it's fun just to have been into Boscastle by boat. The attractive village at the head of the harbour was badly damaged by flash floods in 2004, but the restoration has been well done.

If you do decide to stay for a tide in Boscastle and take the ground, don't go too far into the harbour, where the bottom is rocky and unsuitable for drying out, but stay close to the inner mole where you can settle on stony sand and mud. It's best to moor bow to the quay like the local fishing boats, with an anchor out astern. Watch out for the onset of any swell, which can set you bumping as you dry.

Boscastle village is very picturesque, although busy with tourists during the season. Fresh water is obtainable at the head of the harbour.

Evening light on Boscastle entrance

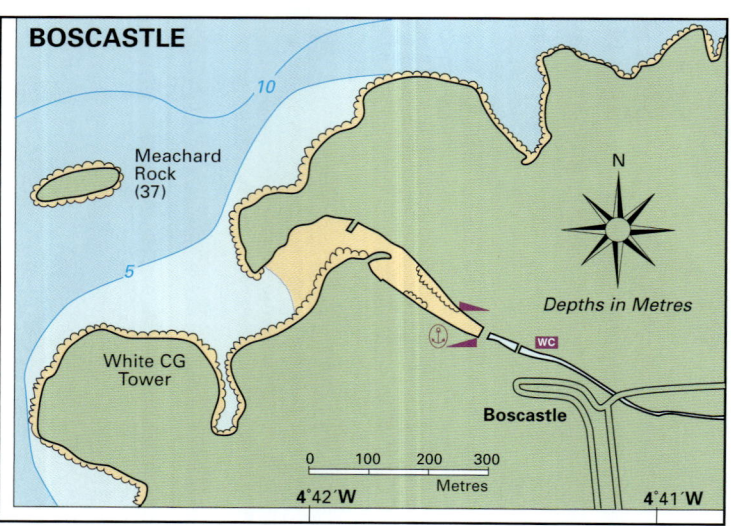

Small boats at high water in Boscastle harbour

PORT GAVERNE

A narrow inlet half a mile east of Port Isaac, Port Gaverne faces northwest and dries to a stone and pebble bottom. Although only suitable for small local boats to dry out, in settled summer weather or offshore winds the mouth of the bay can provide a pleasant lunchtime anchorage above half-tide. The convivial Port Gaverne Hotel is at the head of the inlet and it also runs Pilchards, a charming beach café.

The beach and slip at Port Gaverne

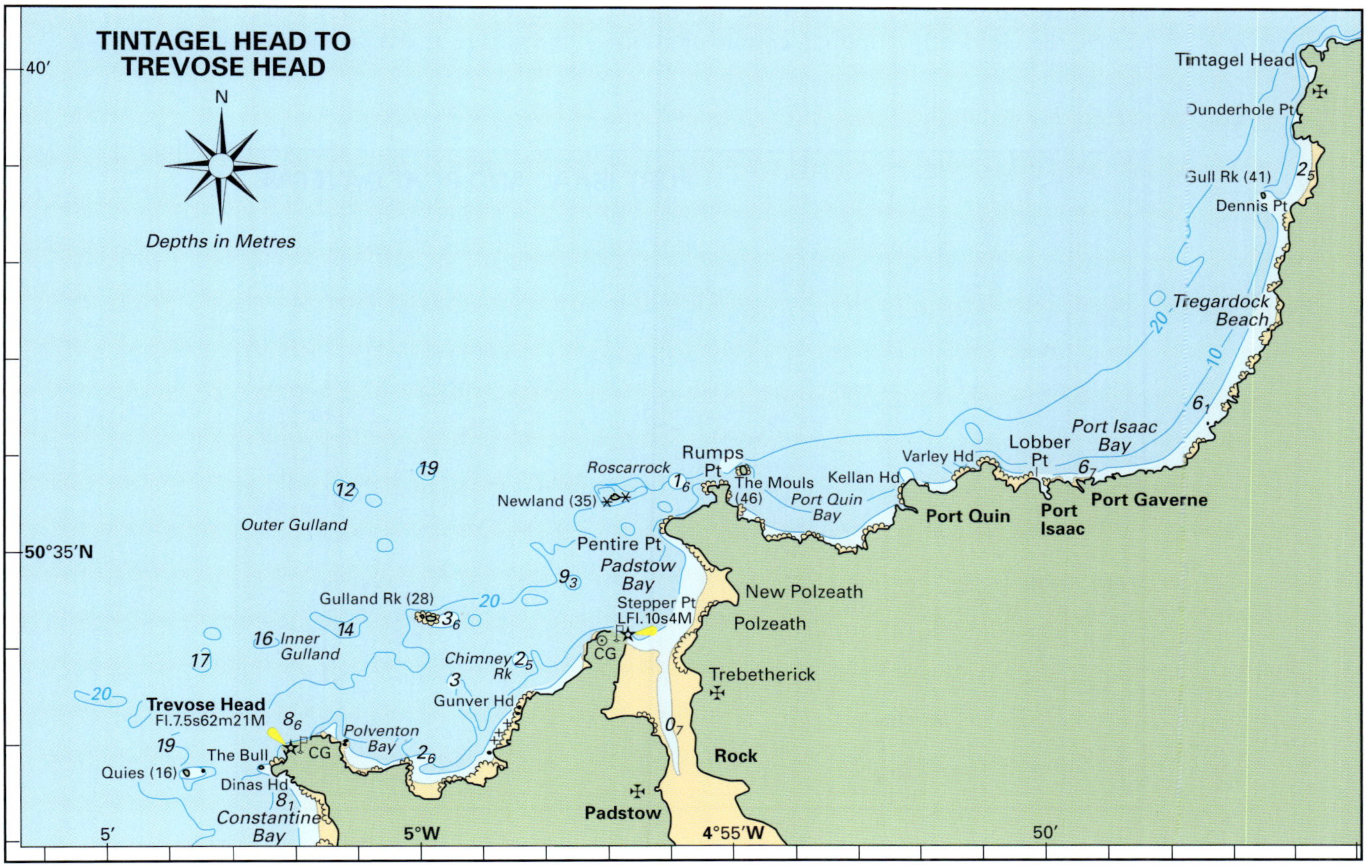

Bristol Channel and Severn Cruising Guide • 173

PORT ISAAC

The entrance to this picturesque drying harbour lies half a mile ESE of Varley Head and about five miles SSW of Tintagel Head. Port Isaac can be located from seaward by steering a shade east of south towards St Endellion church tower, conspicuous a little way inland. When entering the inlet, keep over towards Lobber Point and make for the head of the west breakwater to avoid Kenewal and Warrant Rocks, two drying ledges lurking due north of the east breakwater.

Port Isaac faces due north and dries to firm sand at about half-tide. There is very little protection in onshore winds, when a nasty surge can find its way into the harbour. It's a good idea to take local advice before committing yourself to drying out. Moor stern-to the beach with an anchor out ahead, but keep well clear of local boats. Port Isaac has some shops, the Golden Lion pub, a couple of good fish merchants and some rather expensive restaurants. The harbour and its beach is a very pleasant spot in quiet settled weather or when the wind is anywhere from the south.

Don't attempt to enter Port Isaac at night. The whole of this stretch of coast is unlit between Stepper Point LFl.10s4M and Hartland Point Fl(6)15s25M, a distance of over 30 miles.

As a result of the TV series 'Doc Martin' (2004–2019) and the success of the shanty group Fishermen's Friends with its subsequent film, Port Isaac is now very much on the tourist trail and gets very crowded. Visiting yachts are not encouraged and you may receive a less than enthusiastic welcome. There are now just a couple of working fishing boats in the harbour and recent problems with the east breakwater could put the harbour and the bottom part of the village at risk from flooding.

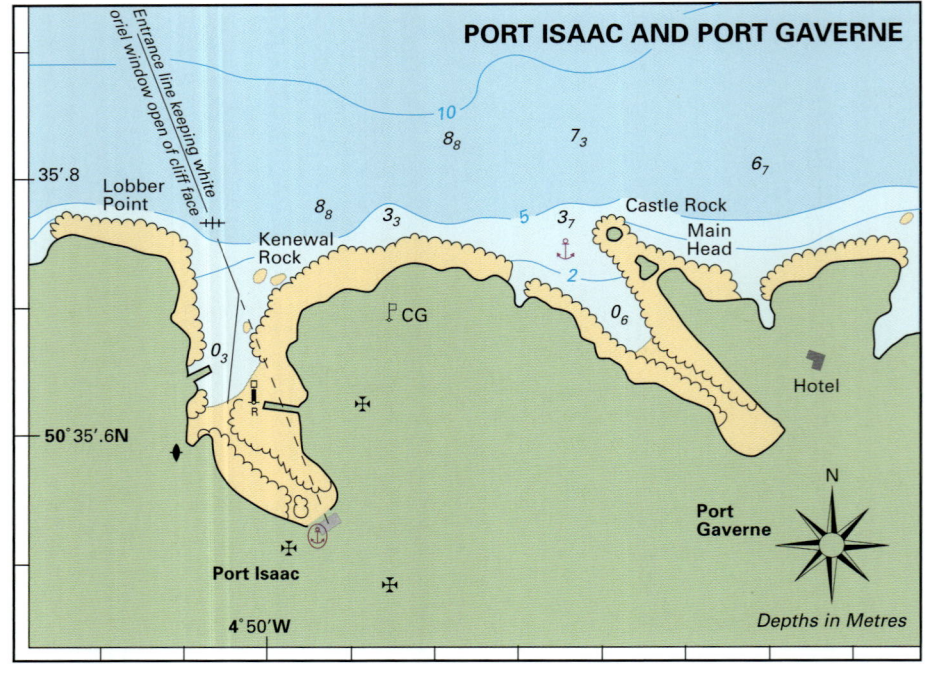

Looking out to the Bristol Channel from Port Isaac

The beach and inner moorings at Port Isaac

SOUTH COAST

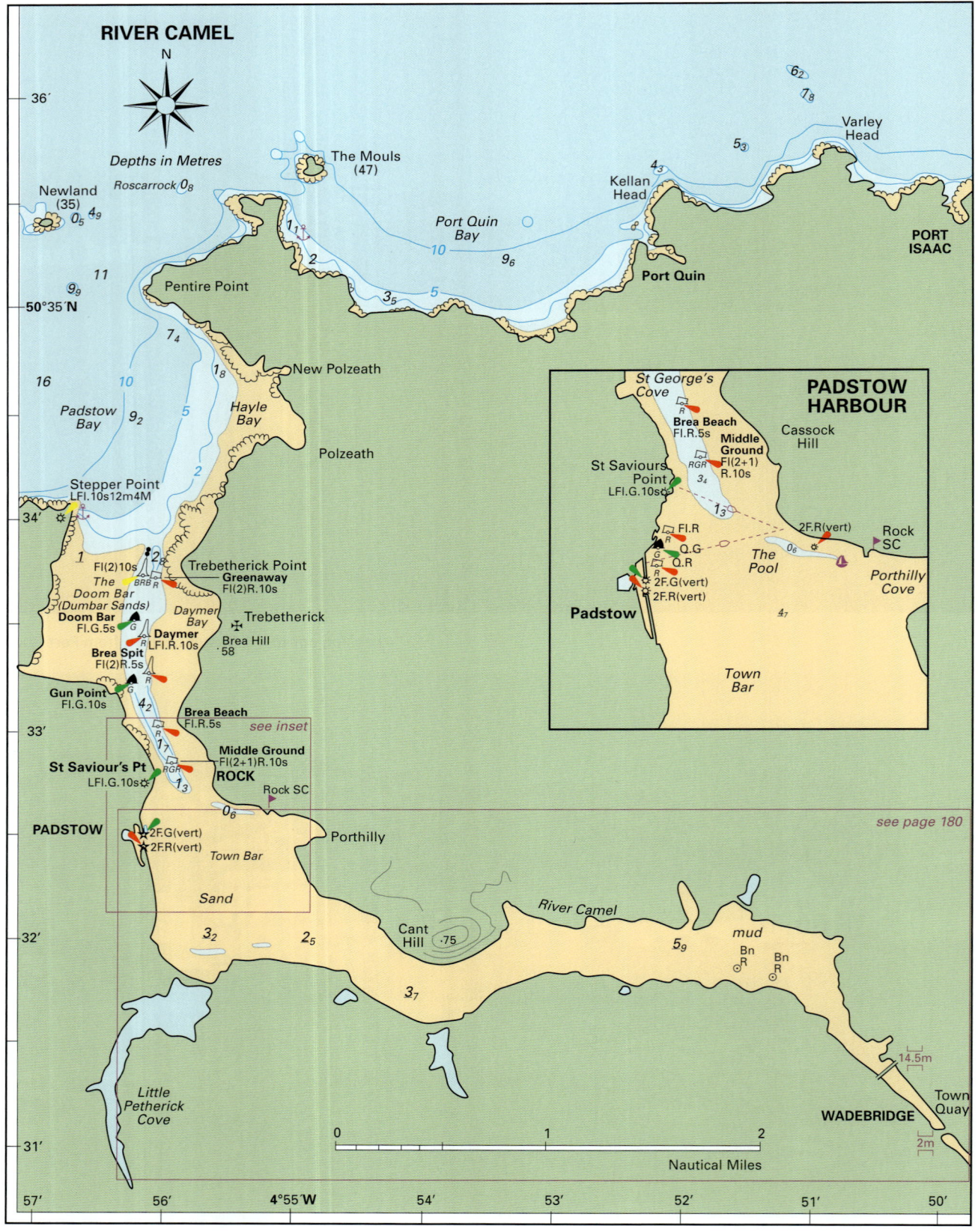

PADSTOW AND THE RIVER CAMEL

Summary

The mouth of the Camel River faces northwest between Stepper and Pentire Points, about four miles ENE of Trevose Head. The broad sandflat known as Doom Bar extends across the entrance from the west side towards Trebetherick Point, leaving only a narrow channel at low springs. Strangers shouldn't approach the estuary until two hours before high water. Although Doom Bar has a certain reputation and the sea breaks heavily over the sands in strong winds from between north and west, in most moderate summer weather the Camel is perfectly straightforward to enter on the tide. Padstow's sheltered locked basin is one of the most attractive and picturesque berths in the West Country. You lie alongside the north or south quays in traditional fashion, just as the old trading coasters would have done, or there are now pontoon berths attached to the quay opposite the gate. The berthing master is on duty for two hours each side of high water, which is usually the period for which the lock gate is open. Slight variations may occur between springs and neaps, so don't cut things too fine, especially when arriving.

Tides HW Padstow is at HW Milford Haven −0050 or HW Dover −0555. Heights above chart datum: 7.3m MHWS, 0.8m MLWS, 5.6m MHWN, 2.6m MLWN.

Port Control Padstow Harbour Commissioners ☏ 01841 532239. Approaching yachts should call *Padstow Harbour* on VHF 12, Monday–Friday 0800–1700 and two hours each side of high water. The harbour office can be contacted on padstowharbour@btconnect.com

Tidal streams and currents The streams off Padstow reach about two and a half knots at springs. In Padstow Bay the SW-going stream starts three quarters of an hour after local high water and the NE-going stream starts just before local low water.

Sailing out of Padstow into the Camel Estuary

Description

The dramatic north coast of Cornwall, facing the casual power of the Atlantic, has always been regarded as rather hostile to seafarers. You can't help noticing the number of wrecks marked on the chart between Pendeen and Lundy Island. Yet a friendly haven can do much to change the perception of a cruising area, and the charming locked basin at Padstow has made this whole coastline a much more attractive and feasible proposition ever since the gates were installed back in the late 1980s to turn the inner harbour into a soothing retreat which one soon becomes reluctant to leave.

Although Padstow Bay is open between west and north, and prolonged onshore gales can make the entrance look spectacular, for most of the time the restful estuary of the River Camel is perfectly easy to get into within a couple of hours of high water. The notorious Doom Bar sounds more dire than it usually is. The word 'Doom' actually derives from dun or dune meaning 'sand' or 'sandy', but perhaps this gloomy name still keeps some visitors away from Padstow.

Strangely, the dunes and green slopes on the east side of the Camel have a slightly foreign flavour in high summer. In the warm light of a Cornish afternoon, gazing across the estuary towards Cassock Hill, you may recall odd corners of southern Biscay, or parts of South Brittany near Quiberon Bay. There are also sleepy fjords in Jutland that strike a sandy chord of similarity.

The Channel marker off St Saviour's Point

PADSTOW AND THE RIVER CAMEL

The village of Rock, just opposite Padstow, has a nostalgic atmosphere of long summer holidays by the sea and this timeless estuary was one of John Betjeman's favourite places. Some of his best known seaside lines were inspired by family summers spent at Trebetherick. Betjeman fans should certainly take the ferry across to Rock and follow the path downstream to St Enodoc's church where he is buried. The ferry trip also takes you past the Camel sand banks and mud flats which are such a haven for migrating birds.

Padstow inner harbour is a picturesque place for yachts to lie, with convivial pubs and good food close to hand. The Old Custom House Inn is on the waterfront and nearby are the famous seafood eateries run by Rick Stein. The shops, restaurants and cottages are jumbled together in narrow streets, many built in the distinctive Cornish style of slate hung over granite. Padstow's colourful mix of pastel shades contributes to the slightly continental feel of the town. The inner harbour is very much the focus of daily life, with local cruisers, small fishing boats and visitors all enjoying the conviviality of the waterfront. When the harbour gates are open, tripper launches come in and out.

The harbourmaster and staff are welcoming and very helpful to visiting boats. Diesel is available alongside just outside the lock gate to the south so it may be best to check with the berthing officer before you arrive if you want to fill up on your way in. For petrol you can leave cans, marked with the boat's name, at the harbour office and they will be replenished at a local garage and returned later in the day, check out arrangements at the office.

Strolling south from the inner basin, you pass the lower drying harbour where there's often a small coaster or sand dredger alongside, the crew busy at some obscure mechanical activity. On certain tides, quite a busy fishing fleet uses Padstow as a base, though sadly a large proportion of the catch is promptly exported by truck to France, Spain or Portugal. On the Riverside at South Quay is Rick Stein's famous Seafood Restaurant, and among the Padstow back streets you'll also find the Stein café and delicatessen.

Before Rick Stein, Padstow was most famous for its 'Obby 'Oss, the strange traditional dance around the town with its origins in ancient pagan fertility rites. The markings on both the Old 'Oss and the Blue Ribbon 'Oss are distinctly Celtic and the May Song accompaniment to the dance is familiar to many who have never seen the real thing. This colourful event takes place on May 1st, unless this falls on a Sunday in which case the 'Oss dances on May 2nd.

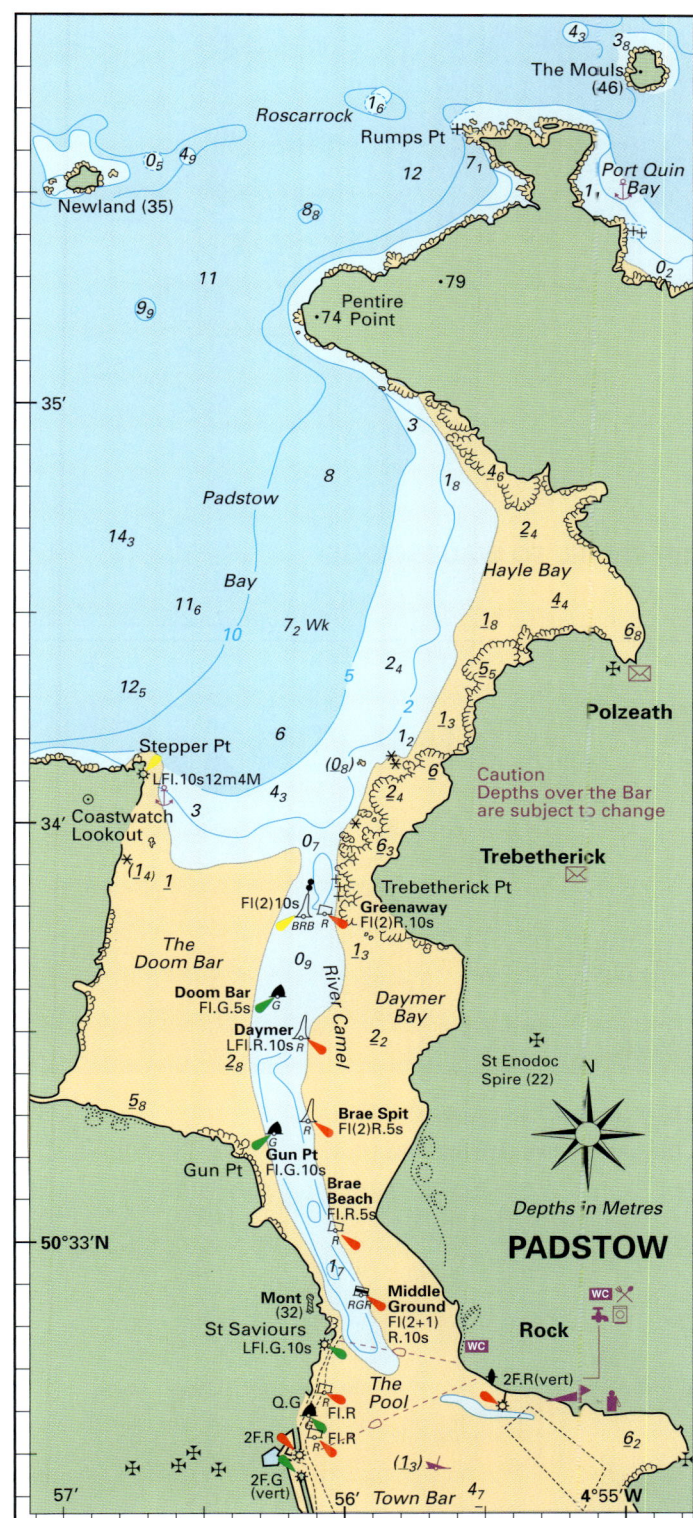

The present 'Obby 'Oss regalia is a fearsome head mask let into a body-covering costume supported by a circular wooden hoop about six feet in diameter. The 'Oss processes swirling and dancing through the town, accompanied by a Teazer and his retinue. The event is colourful and striking, but there's also something slightly sinister about the pagan gaiety and rustic music.

Bristol Channel and Severn Cruising Guide

SOUTH COAST

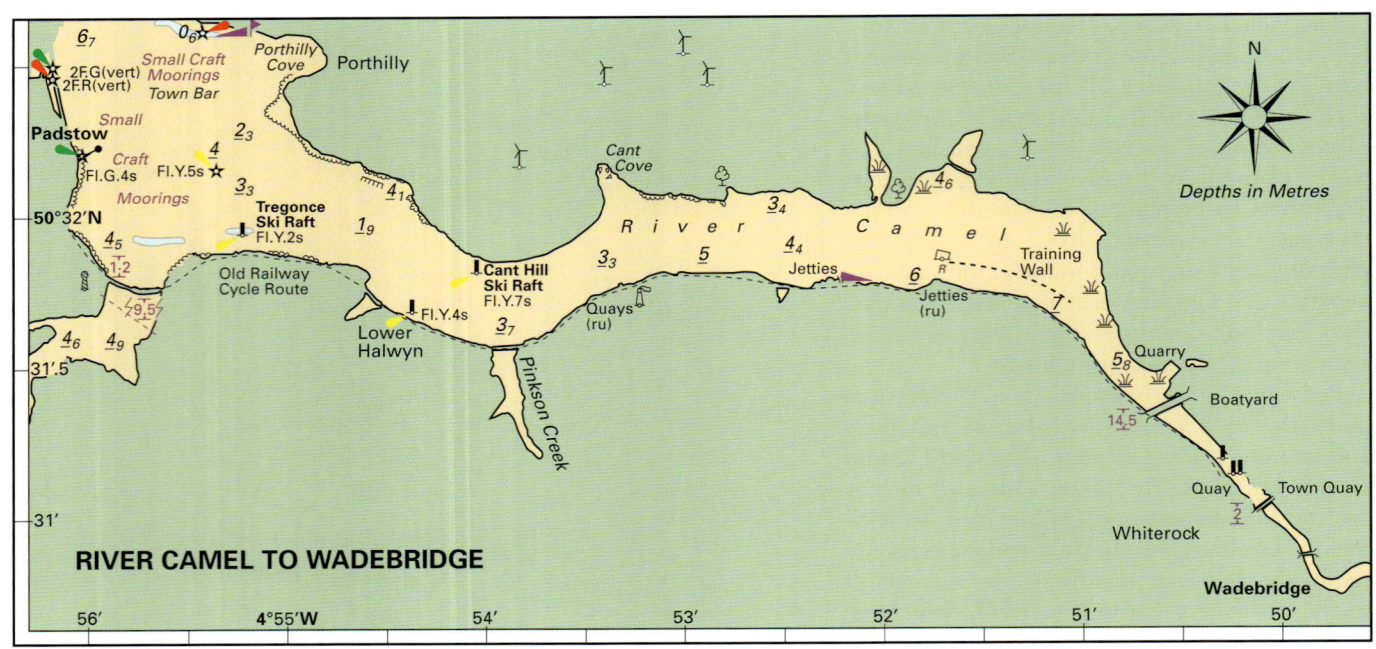

RIVER CAMEL TO WADEBRIDGE

Above: Who can resist Padstow's shellfish?
Below: The gated inner harbour at Padstow

Approach and entry

Coming from the NE Pass outside Newland Rock (37m high), which lies just over half a mile northwest of Pentire Point. Then turn into Padstow Bay and head SSE towards Stepper Point, which has a conspicuous white daymark on its north side. Padstow Bay is clear of dangers.

Coming from the SW Having rounded Trevose Head and its off-lying rocks known as the Quies, make for Stepper Point by passing inside Gulland Rock (28m high), but outside Gurley Rock (with 2m depth over it) and Chimney Rock (with 2.3m over it).

Strangers should only enter the Camel estuary within two to three hours of high water. From a position three cables northeast of Stepper Point, head southeast at first towards Trebetherick Point and then turn due south to leave Greenaway red buoy close to port. Continue south towards St Saviour's Point on the west side of the river, leaving the green Bar buoy to starboard and then heading for the red-green-red Channel buoy just off St Saviour's. For Padstow harbour, leave this buoy close to port and then keep close to the west shore, leaving another green buoy to starboard and a red buoy to port. Keep close to the north breakwater so as to leave the Town Spit bank, just off the entrance, safely to port. In heavy weather from the west, it's best to enter the Camel near high water and round Stepper Point close to, hugging the west side of the river until you are abreast Trebetherick Point. Then cut straight across to the buoyed channel and proceed as above.

Anyone new to visiting Padstow would do well to spend time looking at the video produced by the harbour office which shows clearly what to expect as you enter the Camel estuary in a boat, www.padstow-harbour.co.uk. The site also provides information on berthing, facilities and local engineers, mechanics etc. and contact details.

Up to Wadebridge Above Padstow the Camel River is navigable for four miles up to the market town of Wadebridge. The channel is always shifting, but the Padstow harbourmaster will supply up-to-date information. Wadebridge has a sailing club and a boatyard, but there's nowhere very convenient to dry out. It's therefore best to go up and back on one tide, just for a look see. Along the south side of the river, a pleasant cycle path follows the old railway route up to Wadebridge, the Camel Trail.

Entry at night

This is quite feasible for strangers so long as there's not too much sea running in the outer estuary and provided the visibility is not less than about three miles. The two outer lights are Trevose Head Fl.7.5s21M and Stepper Point LFl.10s4M, and these should be used with GPS to confirm your position as you approach

The ferry coming back from Rock

The gates are left open for free flow for +/-2hr around high water

SOUTH COAST

A cruise out to Doom Bar is very popular

Padstow Bay. It's important to avoid Newland Rock and Gulland Rock which are unlit.

The channel up to Padstow is lit as follows: Isolated Danger Marker Fl.(2)10s; Greenaway red buoy Fl(2)R.10s; Doom Bar green buoy Fl.G.5s; Daymer LFl.R.10s; Brea Spit Fl.(2)R.5s; Gun Point Fl.G.10s; Brea Beach Fl.R.5s; Channel Marker Fl.(2+1)R.10s; green beacon just south of St Saviour's Point LFl.G.10s; harbour approach green buoy Q.G; harbour approach red buoy Q.R; Padstow north breakwater head 2F.G(vert) and south breakwater head 2F.R(vert).

Berths and anchorages

Padstow inner harbour Visitors berth in the inner harbour as directed by the harbourmaster. The retained depths in the basin are something over three metres. Water and electricity are available at various outlets around the harbour. There are excellent showers, loos and laundry facilities at the harbour office on the river side of South Quay, and in the red brick building at the river end of North Quay which is an attractive converted warehouse. The access key fob code for showers is available from the harbour office where you will also find the tourist information office.

Anchorage in the Pool As a result of shifting channels, commercial moorings and ground tackle, anchoring is not encouraged in the Pool. The tide runs hard through the Pool – up to four or five knots on both the flood and ebb at springs. There is a least depth of about three metres here.

Anchorages outside the estuary

Hawkers Cove If you arrive early on the tide for Doom Bar you can anchor on the west side of the estuary mouth close SSE of Stepper Point, taking careful soundings as you draw south of the point. There is good shelter here in any winds with some south in them.

Port Quin Bay If you are approaching Padstow from the northeast and are early on the tide, you'll find a good anchorage in westerly winds on the east side of Rumps Point and about a quarter mile SSW of The Mouls rock (conspicuous 46m high).

Trevose Head If you are approaching Padstow from the southwest, there's a snug anchorage on the east side of Trevose Head in Polventon Bay. Fetch up about a cable southeast of the lifeboat slip and you'll be sheltered in winds from between northwest through south to southeast. Note that Trevose Head itself is high (71m) while the land behind it is not. This can make the Head look like an island from a distance, especially from the west.

Historic Padstow

The port of Padstow has been used by travellers and traders for thousands of years as it is really the only natural harbour on the north coast of Cornwall. What is now called The Saints' Way is an ancient route across Cornwall linking the Camel and Fowey valleys, which was used for centuries to enable trade between Brittany and Ireland. In the 6th century St Petroc established a monastery at Padstow, then travelled to Brittany and Rome before returning to establish a Priory in Bodmin, as a result of which the route became a pilgrims' way. This trail has now been reopened, and you can join it at the Padstow end near the parish church of St Petroc.

It's astonishing now to realise how much early trade was conducted across land and sea between Cornwall, Brittany and Ireland and the Celtic link is still strong, especially in music. During the 1st century BC, Venitii settlers arrived in North Cornwall from Brittany, building forts on the coastal headlands. In medieval times, trading continued between the Celtic countries and a kind of chamber of commerce – the Guild of St Petroc – was set up until the 16th century on the North Quay of Padstow harbour in Abbey House, thought to be the oldest house in the town.

In the mid-16th century, Sir John Hawkins sheltered in Padstow while returning from the West Indies. Whether he was making for Bristol at the time, or missed the English Channel, no one is quite sure. Sir Martin Frobisher also called in after his search for the Northwest Passage in 1577. You can see from the chart that strong southerlies or southwesterlies make Padstow quite a sheltered port-of-call, especially once you've rounded Trevose Head fairly close in. However, in the days of sail, those same southerlies could easily set ships north of the entrance to the English Channel by mistake, leaving them vulnerable on the 'wrong' side of Cornwall. Just into the estuary the Doom Bar was particularly treacherous for sailing ships as the steep cliffs of Trevose Head could suddenly cut off the wind and the ship would lose steerage and be swept onto the bar.

During the 17th century, when Cornish mining was expanding, copper ore, tin and lead were shipped from Padstow to Bristol and slates were exported from the Camel quarry. By the 19th century many people left England from Padstow to emigrate to America, Canada or Australia and several ship-building yards were prospering in the estuary. The *Empress of China* was a three masted ship built in Padstow that took hundreds of people to Australia. The Cornish herring industry was also at its height and cured fish of all kinds was being exported from Padstow.

There are still several fishing boats working out of Padstow but there has been a huge increase in leisure boating and the convivial harbour is a popular port of call. The town has become a busy tourist destination, not least as a result of its reputation for good restaurants. A big draw to the town on May Eve is the 'Obby 'Oss festival, the origins of which go back to pagan times.

Padstow in its trading history *Photo courtesy of Padstow Museum*

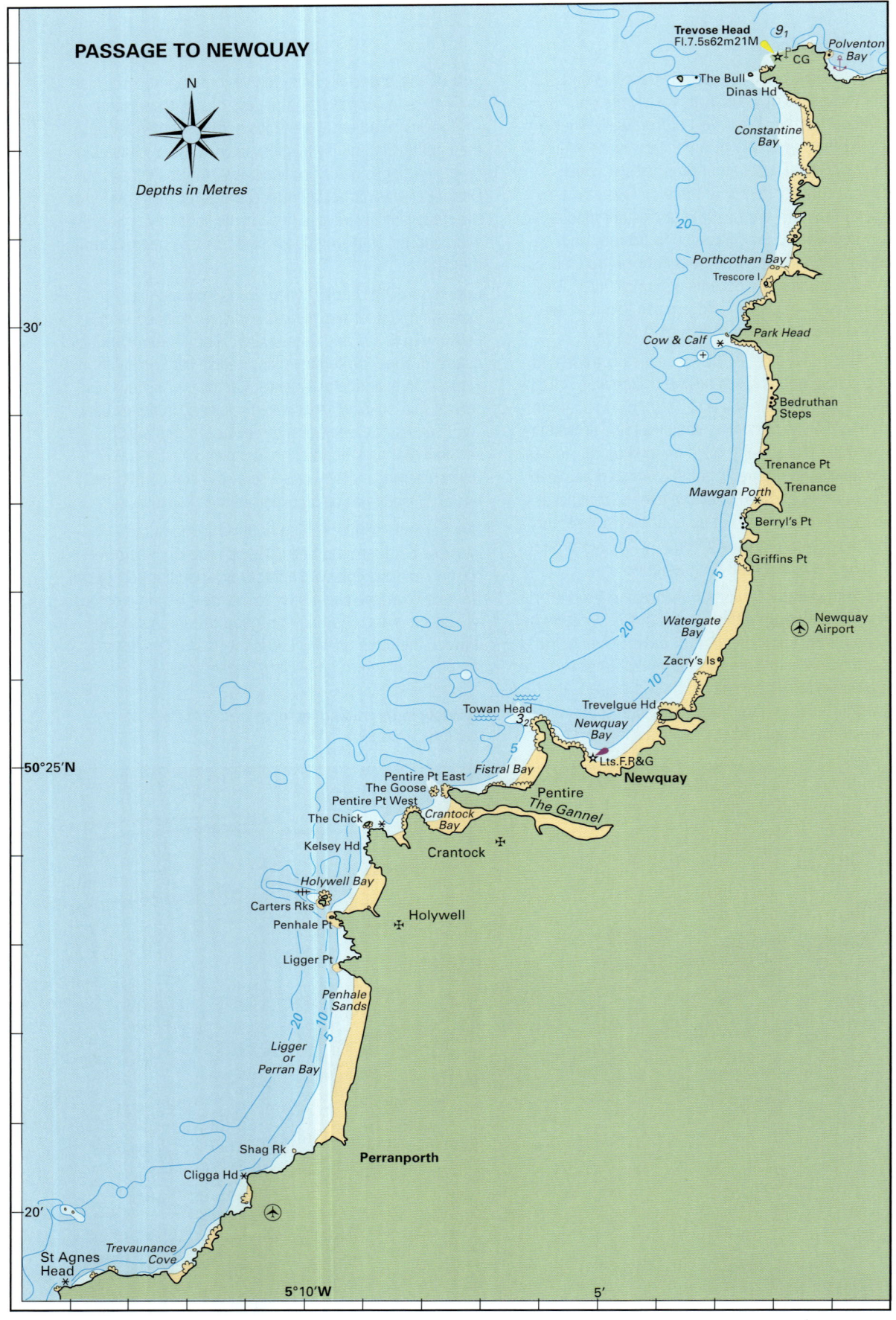

NEWQUAY

This rather quaint and timeless drying harbour is tucked into the southwest corner of Newquay Bay not quite eight miles south of Trevose Head. Space is very limited amongst all the local boats, but the harbourmaster can usually find room for a visiting yacht to take the ground. Tucked well under the crook of Towan Head promontory, Newquay harbour is very well protected from westerly weather, but northeasterlies send in a swell and you shouldn't try to enter in any strong onshore winds when a heavy surge into the harbour will make drying out difficult.

In any moderate summer weather you can enter Newquay within two hours of high water, making the final approach from the northeast. If arriving from the west round Towan Head, keep two cables offshore around the Atlantic Hotel headland until the harbour entrance opens up, to avoid Old Dane Rock just north of this headland and a couple of shoal patches, including Listrey Rock, off its northeast side. Entering Newquay at night is not advisable except in very calm conditions, but the breakwater heads are lit (2F.G and 2F.R). In quiet weather there's an anchorage in Newquay Bay on the east side of Towan Head, just opposite an old disused slip in an area known as the Gazzle.

The harbour is sheltered by two stone breakwaters. There are good berths alongside and the bottom is firm sand. Contact the harbourmaster in advance or as you arrive, calling *Newquay Harbour* on VHF 12 or ☎ 01637 872809. Newquay comes under Cornwall Harbours and 'officially' they have

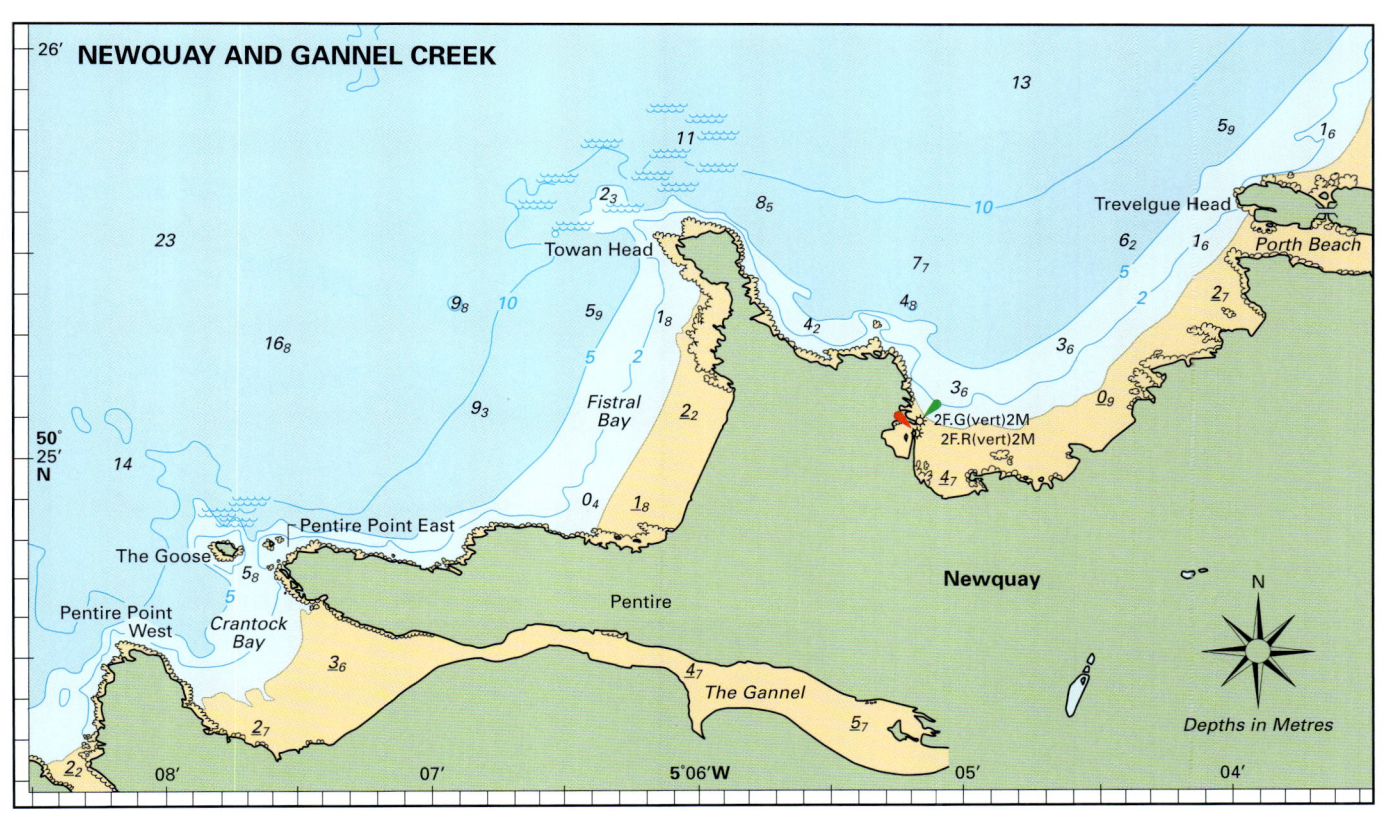

Bristol Channel and Severn Cruising Guide • 185

Left: The beach and drying harbour at Newquay

Right: One of Newquay's many trip boats

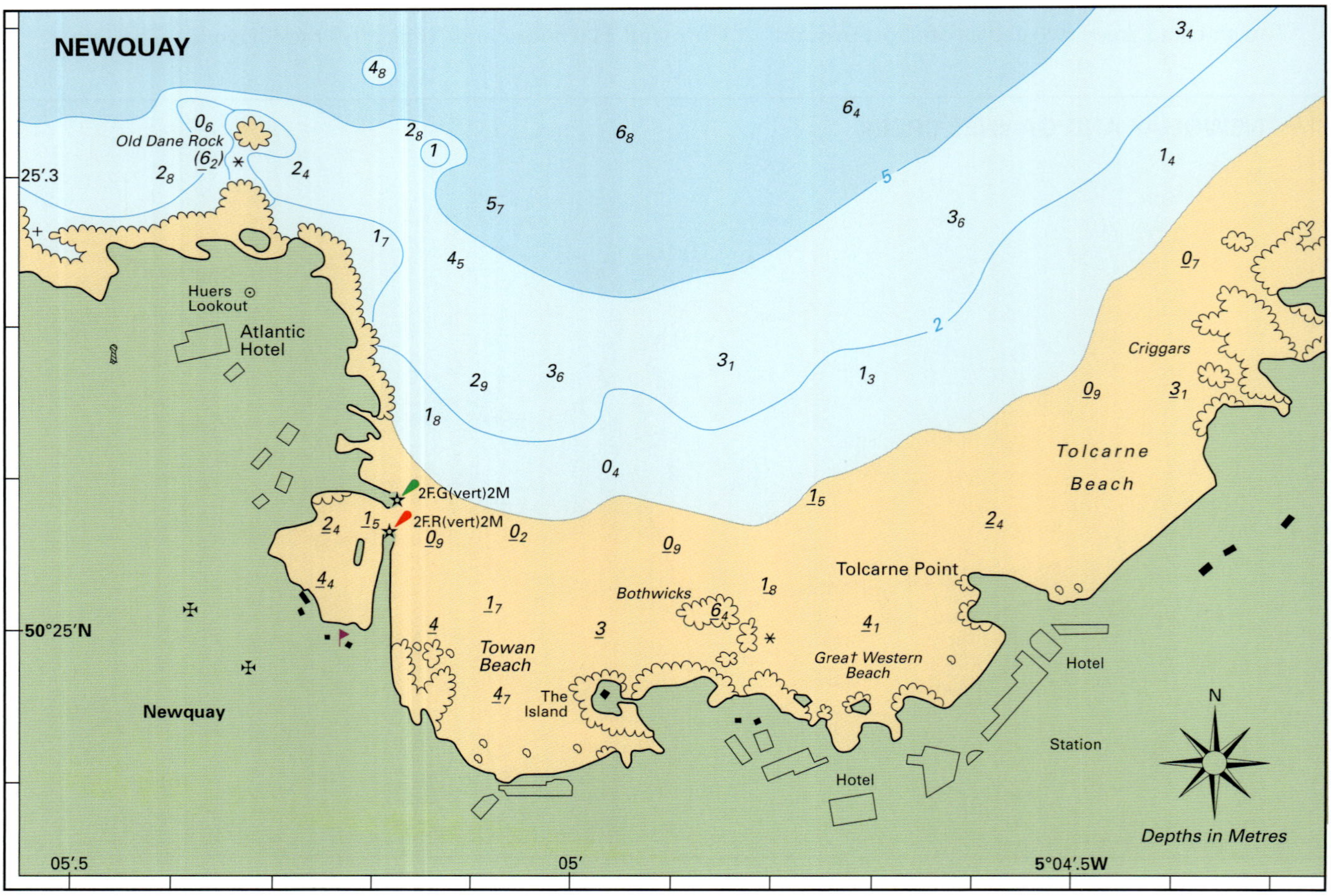

two drying visitor berths on the quay for boats up to 10m. An old embankment 'island' divides the harbour and is normally left to starboard going in, but visitors can sometimes dry out on the beach to the west of the embankment, laying an anchor out astern and taking lines ashore. You'll find a water tap on the quay.

Newquay is a lively and now very trendy resort, famous for its beaches, surf and youthful chilling out. Visiting yachtsmen, however, can experience the more traditionally salty side of Newquay, which changes little over the years. In quiet summer weather there's nothing more relaxing than being moored in the harbour just watching the world go by. Fishing boats come and go near high water, or are being worked on when the tide is out, so there's always some gentle activity in this pleasant little haven. You'll find shops, pubs and bistros a short stroll from the quayside. There have been vague plans for a marina at Newquay for as long as anyone can remember, but hopefully this may never happen.

Fishermen's Mission

The life of a deep-sea fisherman is not easy today but in 1881, when the Fishermen's Mission started, it was very tough indeed. In its 140 year history the Mission has brought help to countless fishermen and their families of both a practical and spiritual nature. In the late 1800s Mission workers actually went out in boats to the fishermen at sea, taking food and medical supplies as well as ministering to their religious needs.

As the fleet and working practices changed the Mission adapted its support. Initially it provided accommodation ashore as fishermen often landed many miles from home and transport was much harder then and expensive on a fisherman's limited wages. These hostels offered a safe and warm place for the men to stay between trips and in the largest fishing ports provided beds for up to 100 fishermen. In more recent times the larger boats have bunks on board and many work out of their home ports so now the Mission provides smaller centres around the UK with year round support.

Fishing is probably the most dangerous peacetime occupation and safety at sea is crucial. The Mission has been actively involved in providing lifejackets, (PFDs – Personal Flotation Devices) and in the development of lighter, less bulky PFDs which are easier to wear when you are working. Health and well-being are very important when you spend a lot of time far from medical services and quite often on your own. It can be very difficult to arrange appointments so the Mission runs harbour side events, the SeaFit programme, offering dental check-ups, contact with physiotherapists, medical staff and mental health advisors for fishermen and their families.

The Fishermen's Mission is frequently the first on the scene after an emergency and they help families with financial and emotional support when there is an accident at sea. All of this work is funded by donations from incividuals and corporate supporters which enables Mission Port Officers to be on hand 24 hours a day. The service is not just for active fishermen but helps their families and retired fishermen as well.

Next time you are admiring fishing boats in a harbour, buying a lovely fresh plaice or tucking into fish and chips spare a thought for the fishermen and their families and consider supporting the Fishermen's Mission, it does amazing work. For more information the website is **www.fishermensmission.org.uk**

The Fishermen's Mission offers help and practical support in ports around the country *The Fishermen's Mission*

GANNEL CREEK

This peaceful, fascinating backwater not far south of Newquay is entered by way of Crantock Bay. Gannel Creek dries to firm sand and shoal-draught bilge-keelers can find good and unexpected shelter by tucking well up towards its head. You should choose a period of calm, settled weather for visiting the Gannel, when the tides are making well towards springs. Come out of Newquay harbour an hour and a half before high water, round Towan Head by at least a quarter of a mile and then steer southwest across Fistral Bay towards East Pentire Point. Give the off-lying Goose Rock (18m high) a wide berth, particularly on its south side.

You enter Crantock Bay between West Pentire Point and the Goose, keeping in the middle of the bay but near the top of the tide broadly following the line of the south shore round towards the narrow mouth of Gannel Creek. The creek is not well charted and local boats usually follow a more recent gully into the creek close along the north shore past Point Noe. Going through the outer entrance narrows you start by keeping towards the north shore, then curving over towards the south shore at the narrowest part before returning to the north side of the creek just as it starts to widen out again past a boat-house and slipway. After half a mile you emerge into the wide inner part of the creek, opposite a short tributary which branches off to starboard. Not far beyond this spur, on the north side of the creek, is a low causeway used by pedestrians to cross the residual stream at low water. There's a good spot to dry out just short of this causeway, near one or two local moorings. It's best to anchor fore-and-aft and take the ground close to the north shore. There are no facilities here and the nearest shops are a fair climb back over towards Newquay.

Never try to enter or leave the Gannel in onshore winds, at night, or more than one and a half hours each side of a spring high water. If conditions deteriorate while you are there, edge further up the creek if necessary to avoid any swell which the flood might bring in. Once the ebb has started falling away though, the effect of the sea outside is soon shut off and you are left in perfect tranquillity on a bed of golden sand.

It's interesting to reflect that, until the late 19th century, the mouth of the creek was used a good deal by sailing ketches and coasting barges that brought coal, fertilizer, limestone and pottery into the Gannel when the tide and weather served. Drying out on the firm sand inside the creek, these vessels unloaded their cargoes into shallow-draught barges for the two-mile passage up the creek to Trevemper, which in those days was quite a busy trading centre for the surrounding country.

It's difficult now to imagine the business of sailing or warping cumbersome vessels into

Local boats moor well up the Creek

GANNEL CREEK

Gannel Creek is a well-kept secret

this shallow natural haven at the top of the tide. The shipping activity declined here after Newquay harbour was built and over the years the narrow entrance channel has gradually silted up with encroaching sand.

Severe storms in recent years have changed the course of the river at its mouth across Crantock Beach and reduced the depth of water available. Quite a few local boats, mostly shallow draught bilge keelers, still moor in the upper reaches but currently waterborne visitors come in kayaks or on paddleboards. The ferry that used to take visitors from Newquay across the mouth of the river to the beach from Fern Pit café may run during high season.

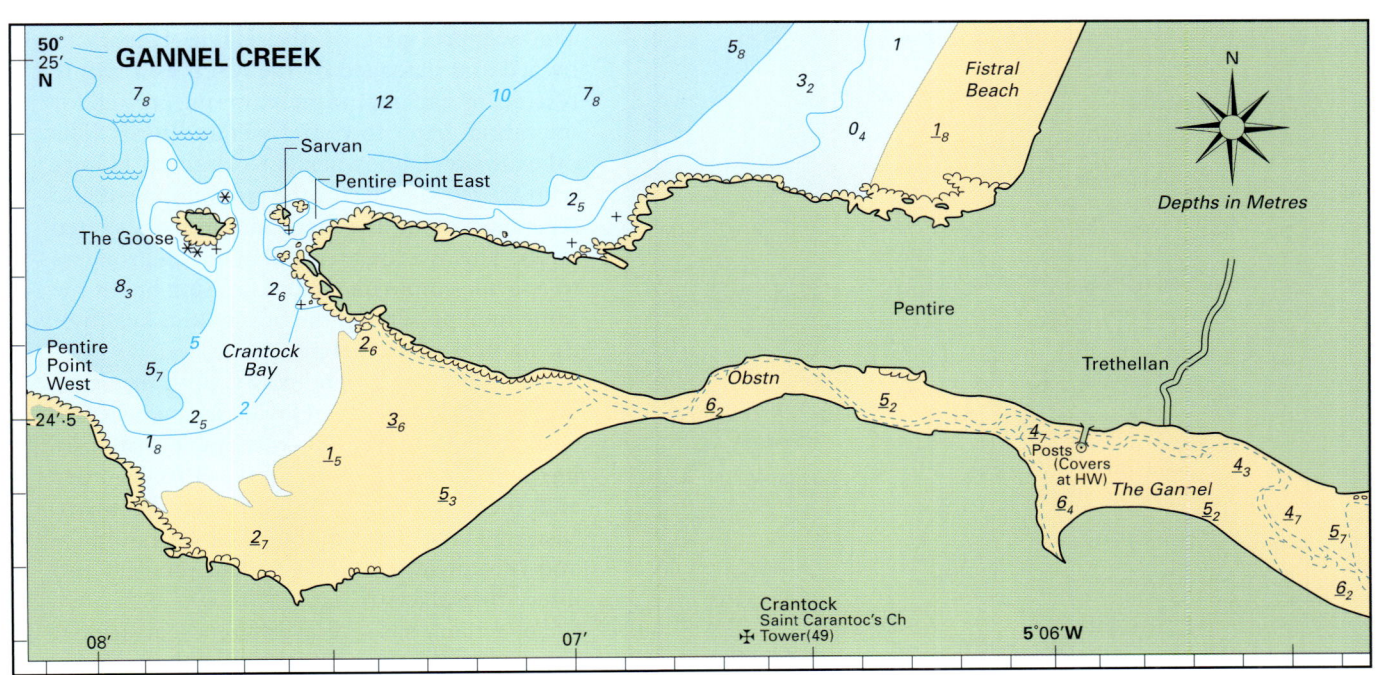

HAYLE

Summary

Hayle has had a varied history over many years. Once a busy little commercial port with coasters regularly bringing in metal ore and shipping out machinery, its harbour approaches gradually silted up and by the 1980s there was little to attract visiting boats. In the following decade various bold plans to build a sizeable marina and develop waterside properties were put forward but nothing materialised. The present North Quay development is pressing ahead as far as real estate goes but there appear to be limited aspirations on the boating front.

Hayle does in fact offer excellent shelter once you have negotiated the broad drying flats which form the outer bar and then found your way up to the town quays, which dry to soft mud and sand. Anyone wishing to visit Hayle should call the harbourmaster to establish the present state of the Hayle channel before setting off across St Ives Bay. Adventurous types with shallow draught boats can feel their way in an hour or so before high water, during daylight and provided that conditions are calm in the bay with no underlying swell.

Tide HW Hayle at HW Milford Haven –0100 or HW Dover –0605.

Port Control Hayle Harbour Authority. For the harbourmaster ☏ 01736 754043, 07500 993867 or call *Hayle Harbour* on VHF 18/14.

Tidal streams and currents Situated in the south of St Ives Bay the streams are fairly weak but at low water the approaches dry ½ mile offshore.

Description

The western part of the Hayle Estuary is owned and managed by the RSPB as a nature reserve. It is an important wintering ground for migrating water fowl and wetland birds. The other major landowner is Corinthian Homes who are responsible for the redevelopment and regeneration of the harbour and associated lands. This is a long term plan which promises to provide employment and housing but at the same time preserving the beauty and health of the natural environment.

The town has a rich history, both maritime and industrial and the Hayle Heritage Centre tells the story well. It was an enormously important mining port in the 19th century and there were two foundries in the town. Visiting Hayle now you feel a sense of purpose and enterprise with independent retailers and interesting places to eat.

The estuary has several different recreational user groups with over 200 boats in the harbour,

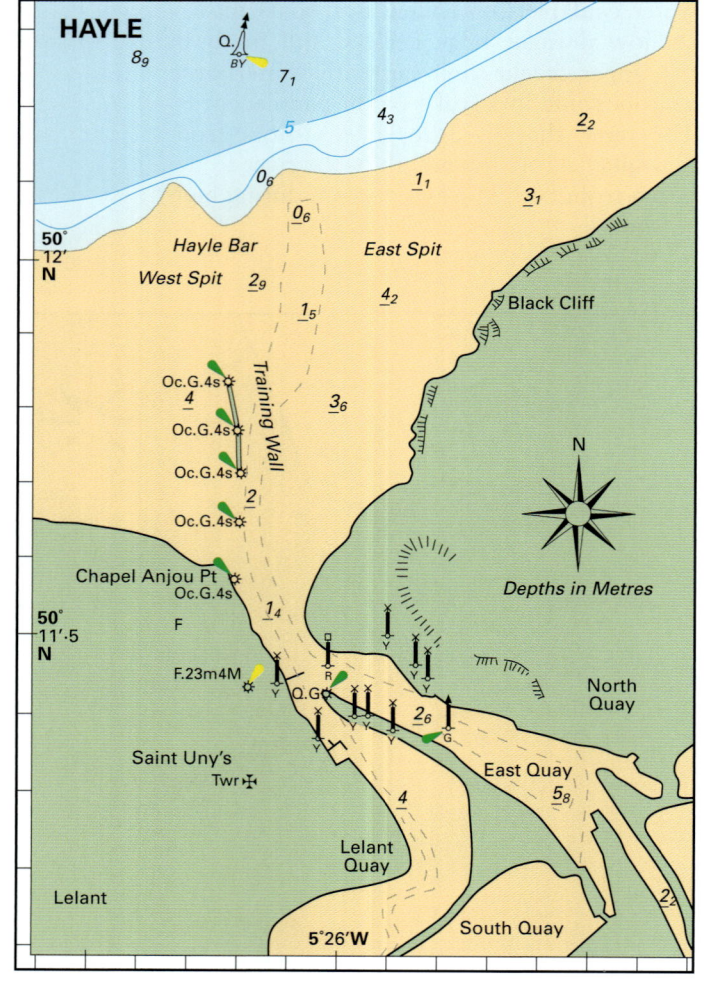

HAYLE

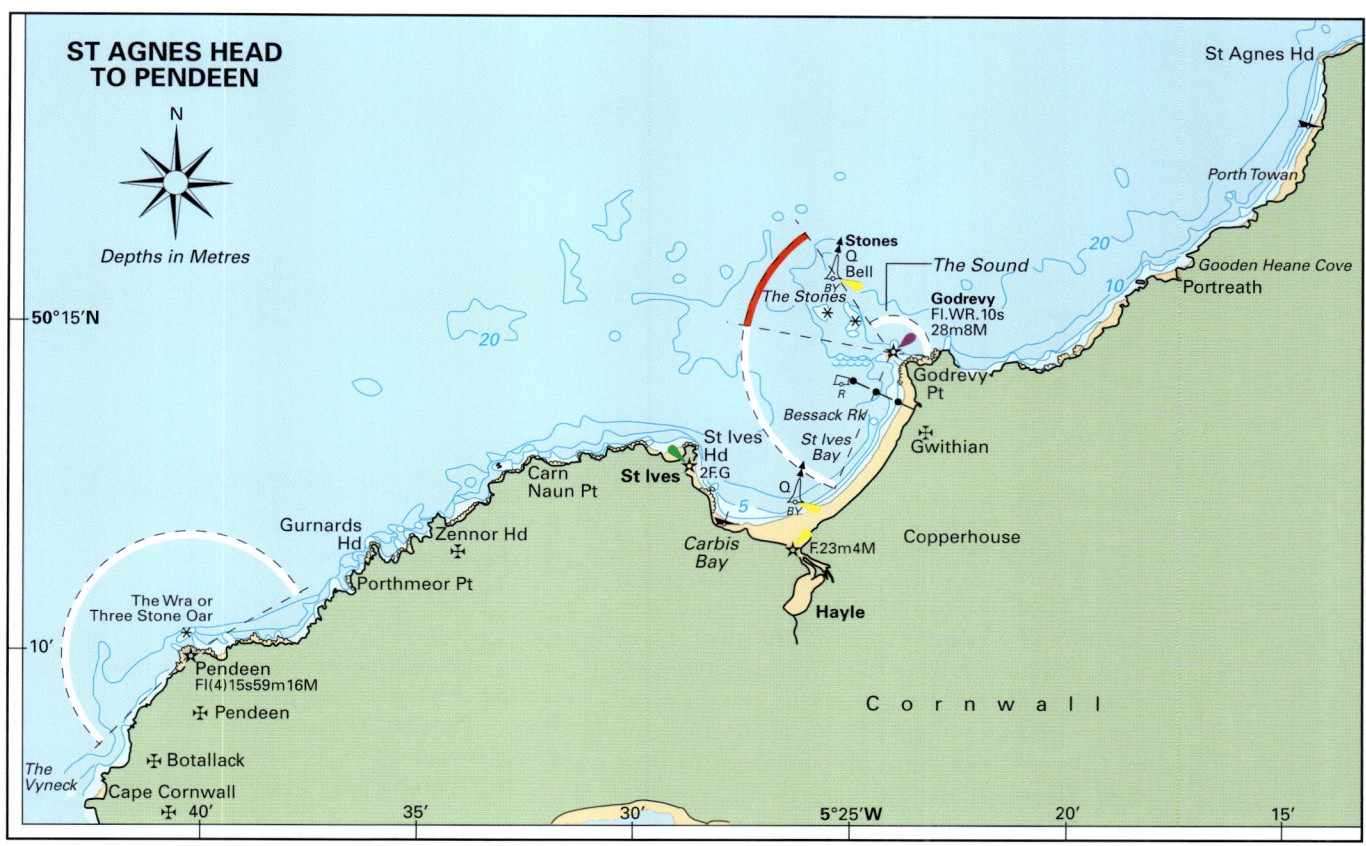

both leisure and commercial, with waiting lists for both types of moorings. The increasing use of the estuary by both residents and visitors requires delicate management to maintain harmony between different user groups and to prevent damage to the natural and historic environment. Good co-operation between the groups is creating a balance between conservation, tourism and leisure activities contributing to an optimistic future for Hayle.

Outer approaches

Hayle entrance lies right in the south of St Ives Bay with St Uny's church tower visible just behind Chapel Anjou Point. You should approach from due north, steering for the church tower initially on a bearing of 180°. The approach is accessible 2 hours either side of HW with offshore wind and no ground swell but it is best to enter about 1 hour before HW. From the N cardinal buoy on the edge of Hayle Bar follow the harbourmaster's instructions to the first green beacon, Oc.G.4s, on the training wall.

Entry

Having passed the fifth starboard hand G beacon turn slightly to port and leave Q.G beacon ahead to starboard. This marks the N end of a steep shingle bank, called the Middle Wear, which separates the River Hayle from the channel to port which leads to North Quay. Cockle Bank now lies ahead, so keep to the port side of the channel.

Berths and anchorages

You can moor alongside the North Quay where a floating pontoon has been installed below the new apartment building. There is also a mooring ladder or you can moor alongside another vessel. The harbourmaster may be able to direct you to a vacant mooring if you can take the ground.

The first phase of the new development at Hayle

Bristol Channel and Severn Cruising Guide • 191

ST IVES

Summary

This picturesque and rather famous Cornish fishing harbour is protected from seaward by St Ives Head and by the long stone breakwater, Smeaton Pier, which extends southwards from it. You approach from the northeast, avoiding an old ruined breakwater guarded by the New Pier green buoy (unlit). The harbour area can be entered above half-tide and dries to firm sand. Bilge-keel boats may use the drying fore-and-aft visitors' buoys towards the west side of the harbour. Keelboats can anchor between the main pier head and Porthminster Point to stay afloat but be aware of the risk of picking up ground tackle here so buoy your anchor.

Tide HW St Ives at HW Milford Haven –0100 or HW Dover –0605. Heights above chart datum: 6.6m MHWS, 0.8m MLWS, 4.9m MHWN, 2.4m MLWN.

Port Control Cornwall Harbours, www.cornwallharbours.co.uk

For the harbourmaster ☎ 01736 795018, 07816 077755 or call *St Ives Harbour* on VHF 16, working on 12.

Tidal streams and currents Streams are fairly weak immediately off the harbour but reach up to three knots at springs off St Ives Head and Godrevy Point. For passage-making round Land's End you should take into account that, two miles off Pendeen, the NE-going stream starts four and a half hours before local low water and the SW-going stream about two hours after local high water. Rates here can reach two and a half knots at springs.

Just off St Ives harbour near the New Pier green buoy the stream is south-going for the first two and a half hours of flood, but then a clockwise eddy sets in around St Ives Bay to give a north-going stream past New Pier buoy for most of the tidal cycle.

Description

St Ives lies almost at the far Atlantic end of the North Cornish coast and its attractive drying harbour was once important to the pilchard fishery. The town has steep, winding cobbled streets and is invaded by tourists virtually all

St Ives harbour dries to firm sand

ST IVES

APPROACHES TO ST IVES AND HAYLE

year. For well over a century it has also been a popular retreat for artists and the Tate St Ives gallery should not be missed during a visit here.

In practical terms, St Ives can be a useful passage haven for yachts at this remote end of the Cornish peninsula, offering good shelter in southwesterly gales. However, unless conditions are especially calm and settled, only bilge-keeled boats should dry out in the harbour. Taking the ground with a keelboat on legs is not recommended because ground swell can be difficult and dangerous on this coast, sometimes rolling in from the Atlantic even when the weather is quiet. In particular, winds from between northwest and northeast can make it difficult for yachts to settle down safely. There are no longer visitor moorings outside the harbour so to stay afloat a keel boat would need to anchor but beware of the numerous moorings laid SSE of the harbour between the main pier head and Porthminster Point.

As you would imagine with such a popular tourist destination the choice of pubs and restaurants is extensive. There are numerous galleries but a visit to the Barbara Hepworth Museum should not be missed and there is also the Tate. In the town there are some gems of shops in amongst rather a lot of dubious merchandise, not least a wonderful independent bookshop.

SOUTH COAST

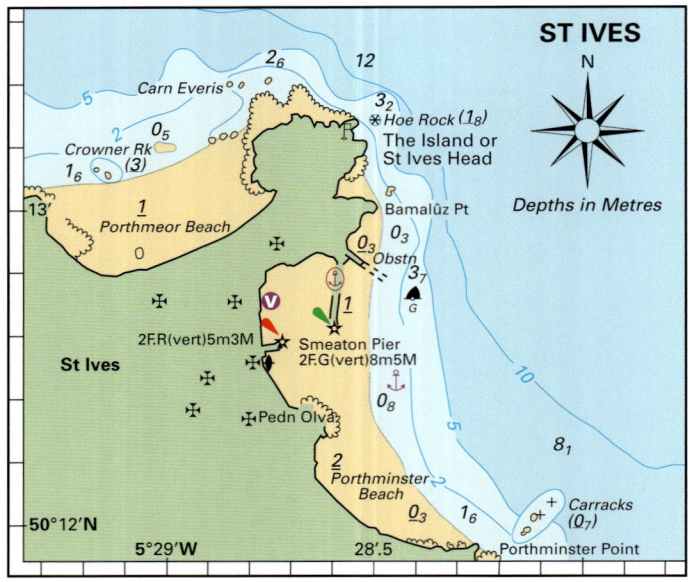

Outer approaches

Coming from the NE The main hazard when approaching St Ives from further up the coast, say from Padstow, is the extensive area of rocks known as The Stones, drying up to 5.4m and lurking between three quarters and one and a quarter miles northwest of Godrevy Point. This dramatic headland forms the east arm of St Ives Bay, jutting out three and a half miles northeast of St Ives harbour. Close off Godrevy Point is Godrevy Island and its lighthouse Fl.WR.10s, with the red sector shining northwest over The Stones.

With care, in fair weather near slack water, you can cut between The Stones and Godrevy Island through The Sound, a clear passage half a mile wide. Keep within a quarter of a mile of the Godrevy Island side as you go through, to be sure of staying well off The Stones. However, in fresh winds with a weather-going tide the whole area off Godrevy Point is affected by overfalls and you should then pass seaward of The Stones N cardinal bell buoy Q.

Having rounded The Stones buoy or passed through The Sound, make for St Ives Head, sometimes known as 'The Island', conspicuous on the far side of St Ives Bay. If arriving via The Stones buoy, steer west for half a mile before turning inshore for St Ives Head, to be sure of avoiding Hevah Rock (dries 1.3m), which lies just over half a mile south and a touch west of the buoy. If you have come through The Sound and are tacking inshore towards St Ives, watch out for two drying dangers round the shore of St Ives Bay – Bessack Rock (dries 2.3m) a mile south by west of Godrevy Island, and the Carracks, four cables southeast of St Ives harbour entrance off Porthminster Point.

Coming from the SW Round St Ives Head by at least two cables to avoid Hoe and Merran Rocks, and then steer southwards to leave a green conical buoy (unlit) well to starboard. This buoy marks the end of the old ruined breakwater. All dangers in this approach from northward are avoided by keeping Knill's Monument, 166m high and prominent three quarters of a mile inland, just open to the east of the conspicuous Tregenna Castle Hotel and bearing no less than 197°.

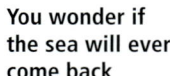
You wonder if the sea will ever come back

Artists in St Ives

When the Great Western Railway reached St Ives in 1870 it opened up the far west of Cornwall and in particular this remote fishing village. Among the visitors from London and the Home Counties were several artists, members of the Royal Academy, who discovered the clear light and stunning seascapes of this extremity of Britain. In the 1890s the St Ives Art Club was started, where resident and visiting artists could meet, including well-known figures in the London art scene such as Whistler and Sickert.

The popularity of St Ives for Victorian artists fortuitously opened up a new source of income for the area as it coincided with a decline in both the fishing and mining industries. Local people began to rent out accommodation and studio space and the better off artists employed them as models and servants. The attraction of St Ives to artists continued into the early 20th century, with exhibitions at Lanham's Gallery in High Street. Artists also hung their paintings in local pubs such as the Sloop Inn.

In 1927 the St Ives Society of Artists was formed by marine artist George Fagan Bradshaw (1887-1960). With the huge influx of painters to St Ives, Bradshaw was concerned that the image of the artistic population could suffer because of a surfeit of dubious amateurs. The St Ives Society of Artists was established to promote the best professionals and raise the standards of the colony. The society was initially based at Lanham's Gallery, but in 1928 moved to Julian Olsson's former studio in Back Road West, near its present site in Norway Square. Many of the artists' studios were in old sail lofts or pilchard stores left empty after the shoals diminished in size. This part of the town, with its narrow cobbled streets and granite cottages is called Downalong.

In 1945 the society took a tenancy on the Mariners Church, which had been built in 1905 for the fishing community but had fallen into disuse. Despite various personality clashes and breakaway groups over the years the St Ives Society of Artists has weathered financial storms and is a strong and active community nearly 100 years later.

The website **www.stivessocietyofartists.com** gives a fascinating insight into the St Ives artistic scene and you can view paintings by society members. If you are visiting the town, be sure to have a look round the galleries in the former Mariners Church, an imposing building in the heart of the old quarter overlooking the harbour. The Main Gallery is in the upper floor of the church and is a spacious, airy, light exhibition area where three exhibitions a year are held of members' work, at other times invited artists exhibit here. Below, the Crypt Gallery can be rented by individual artists or groups to show and sell their work. A fascinating range of styles, media and concepts are on show all year round and work by both established and up-and-coming artists can be bought, you might be discovering a new talent.

At the start of the Second World War, Barbara Hepworth and her husband Ben Nicholson moved to St Ives. After the war they spearheaded a new group of abstract artists who found inspiration in the Cornish land and seascapes.

After her death in 1976, Dame Barbara Hepworth's studio and garden became part of the Tate Gallery. Here you can see her sculptures in bronze, stone and wood. Her original studio, now the Hepworth Museum, displays her paintings and drawings.

Top: St Ives artists exhibit in the old Mariners Church
Bottom: The narrow streets of the artists quarter

There are lots of local boats in St Ives but visitors are a rarity

Entry

You finally approach the harbour from the east, once you are well south of the old pier green conical buoy. Head for the main breakwater head and then curve northwest between the main breakwater and the shorter west pier, steering towards the conspicuous white building towards the centre of the seafront and the four, fore-and-aft drying visitors' buoys just opposite. Alternatively, in quiet weather, make for the deepish water SSE of the harbour between the main pier head and Porthminster Point and anchor. Yachts should only go alongside the main breakwater for fresh water or by arrangement with the harbourmaster, because Smeaton Pier is reserved for fishing boats and commercial vessels.

Entry at night

Strangers can approach St Ives at night with care. Godrevy Island is the key light in the outer approaches. Arriving from further up-Channel is fairly straightforward in good visibility, because you should pick up the St Ives pier head lights as soon as you enter St Ives Bay – the main (east) pier head 2F.G(vert)5M and the shorter west pier 2F.R(vert)3M.

Arriving from the southwest, use Pendeen light Fl(4)15s16M and then Godrevy light Fl.WR.10s12/9M to keep a safe distance offshore. Continue east in the white sector of Godrevy until you can see the St Ives breakwater lights opening up behind St Ives Head, and then turn south into St Ives Bay. When making the final approach to the harbour, be sure to pass well outside the unlit green conical buoy.

Berths and anchorages

St Ives harbour Bilge-keel boats can use the drying fore-and-aft visitors' buoys towards the west side of the harbour. In strong northerly wind the swell in the harbour can make it quite uncomfortable. You have to speak to the harbour master to get the key for the showers. With the number of commercial boats here chandlery is available but fuel is not easily accessible. You may be able to moor alongside the west pier but it is best to contact the harbourmaster first.

Anchoring outside the harbour If waiting for sufficient rise of tide to enter St Ives, you can anchor outside the harbour a cable or two southeast of the main pier head.

Carbis Bay There's an attractive fine weather anchorage in Carbis Bay, about a mile SSE of St Ives harbour entrance. Be sure to avoid the Carracks, a drying ledge extending nearly two cables offshore between St Ives and Carbis Bay, and the obstruction and old wreck right on the drying line in Carbis Bay.

APPENDIX

Key to plans

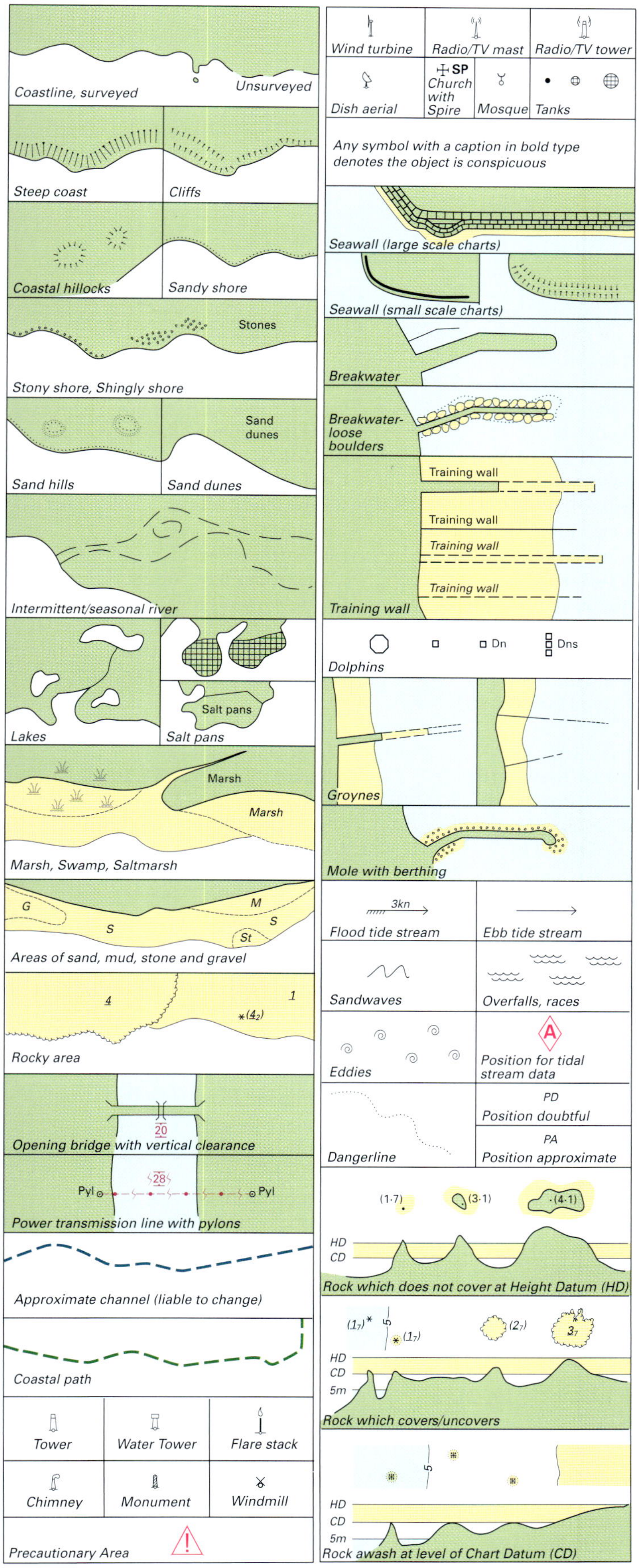

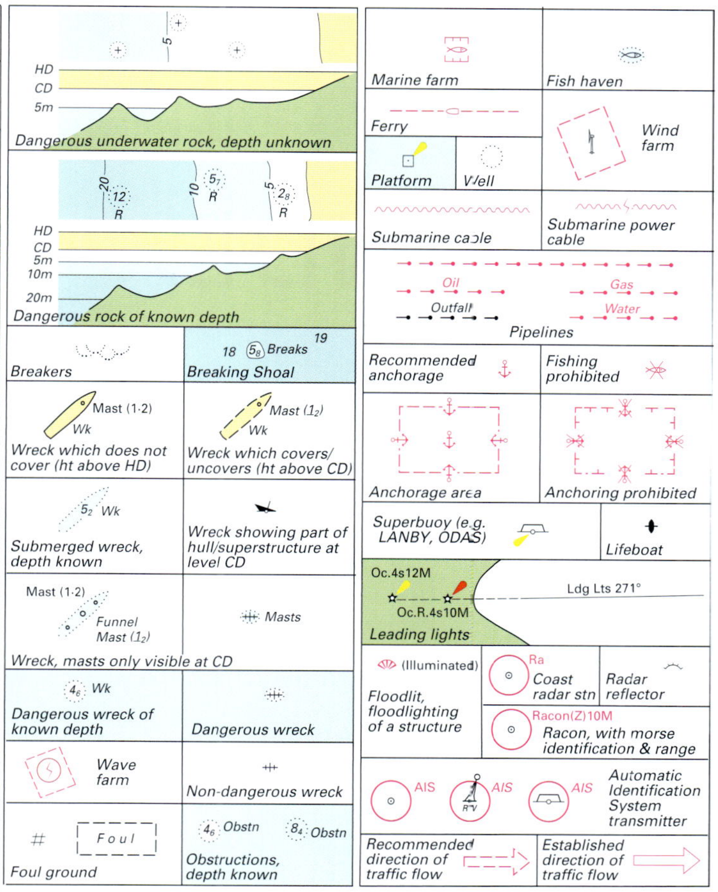

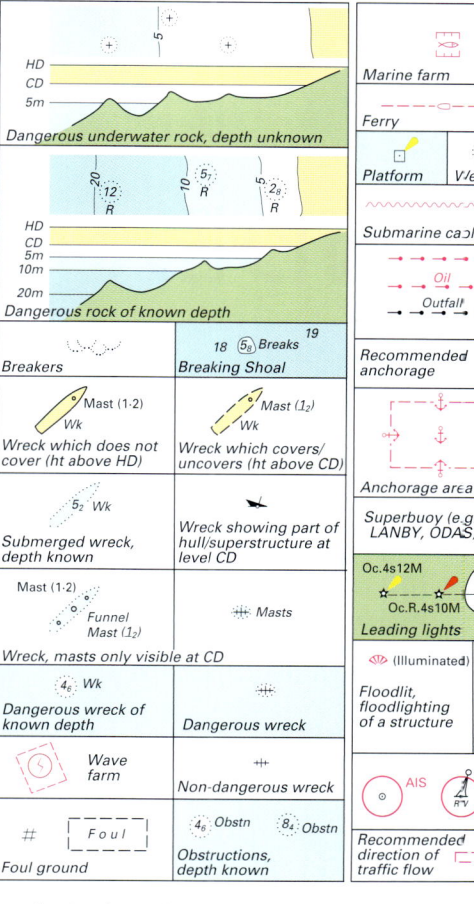

Admiralty Charts

Admiralty have announced the withdrawal of their paper charts by 2026.
- 1076 Linney Head to Oxwich Point
- 1149 Pendeen to Trevose Head
- 1151 Bristol Channel – Bridgwater Bay
- 1152 Bristol Channel – Nash Point to Sand Point
- 1156 Trevose Head to Hartland Point
- 1160 Plans on the Coast of Somerset and Devon
- 1161 Swansea Bay
- 1164 Hartland Point to Ilfracombe including Lundy
- 1165 Bristol Channel – Worms Head to Watchet
- 1166 River Severn – Avonmouth to Sharpness
- 1168 Harbours on the North Coast of Cornwall
- 1169 Approaches to Porthcawl
- 1176 Severn Estuary – Steep Holm to Avonmouth
- 1178 Approaches to the Bristol Channel
- 1179 Bristol Channel
- 1182 Barry and Cardiff Roads with approaches
- 1478 Saint Govan's Head to Saint David's Head
- 1859 Port of Bristol
- 2878 Approaches to Milford Haven
- 3273 Entrance to Milford Haven
- 3274 Milford Haven
- 3275 Milford Haven – Milford Dock to Picton Point

Imray charts

- 2600 The Bristol Channel – Trevose head to St David's including the River Severn
- C7 Falmouth to Isles of Scilly and Trevose Head
- C58 Trevose Head to Bull Point
- C59 Bristol Channel – Worms Head and Bull Point to Sharpness
- C60 Gower Peninsula to Carmarthen
- Y26 Milford Haven

Electronic Charts

ID30 West Britain and Ireland for Imray Navigator

Bristol Channel and Severn Cruising Guide

INDEX

Afan BC 44, 45
Afan River 44–5
Anchor Head 117, 118, 119
Angle Bay 11
Apperley 92
Appledore 151, 152, 154, 156
   Pool 154, 155–6
Arnold, Matthew 165
Ashleworth 84, 92
Avon Gorge 102, 107
Avon River (Bristol) 82, 100–6, 110
   hobblers 105, 107
Avon River (Tewkesbury) 92
Avonmouth 82, 91, 100
Axe River 120–2

Baggy Point 152, 155
MV Balmoral 58
Banwell River 116
Barnstaple 154
Barnstaple Bay 149, 150, 151, 152, 155
barrage schemes 64
Barry 50–4
Barry Island 50, 51, 52
Barry Roads 51
Barry YC 50, 51, 54
Beachley 81
Beachley Point 75, 84
Bendrick Rock 53
Berkeley Castle 99
Berkeley Pill 84
Berkeley Power Station 80
Betjeman, John 179
Bevere Lock 95
Bewdley 96
Bideford 152, 154, 156
   Bar 151, 152
Birnbeck Island 117, 118, 119
Black Nore Point 103
Black Pool 29
Black Rock 120, 121
Black Rock Point 74
Black Tar Point 15
Blackstone Rocks 112, 115
Blue Anchor Road 130
Blue Book, The 115
Boscastle 172
   2004 floods 140
Braunton Burrows 152

Braunton Pill 154
Breaksea Power Station 51, 54
Brean Down 64, 117, 118, 119, 120, 121–2
Brent Knoll 124, 125
Bridgnorth 96
Bridgwater Bay 123–7
Bridgwater Bore 127
Bridgwater Marina 127
Bristol 100–107
   Arnolfini Arts Centre 102, 105
   Cumberland Basin 105
   Docks 102, 103, 107
   Floating Harbour 102, 105, 106, 107
   Marina 102, 105
   SS Great Britain 102, 107
   St Augustine's Reach 102, 105
Bristol Channel Yachting Association 115
Bristol Channel YC 35, 40
Bristol Deep 68, 101, 103
Briton Ferry 42–3
Broad Pill (Avon) 107
Brue River 123, 126
Brunel, Isambard Kingdom 107
Bude Canal 166, 168, 171
Bude Haven 166–71
Bull Point 148, 151, 155
Bull Rock 84
Burnham-on-Sea 123–6
Burnham-on-Sea Motor Boat and SC 123, 124, 125, 126
Burrow Nose 143, 145
Burry Holms 30, 31–2
Burry Inlet 30, 31–3
Burry Port 30–3
   Marina 33
Burry Port Marine Services 30–1
Burry Port YC 30

Caldey Island 17, 19, 21, 23, 164
Caldey Roads 22
Caldey Sound 19, 21
Camel River 176–82
Canal and River Trust (CRT) 91
Capstone Point 148
Carbis Bay 196
Cardiff Bay 56–63

Barrage 56, 58, 60
Cardiff Bay YC 56, 58–9, 61
Cardiff Flats 59
Cardiff Grounds 59, 68
Cardiff Marina 56, 57, 59, 61
Cardiff and Penarth Roads 59
Carew River 14
Carmarthen 27
Carmarthen Bar 28
Carmarthen Bay 26, 28
Castlemartin Range 9
Chaceley Stock 92
Chapel Anjou Point 191
Chapel Rock (Bude) 166, 167, 168
Chapel Rock (Severn) 74, 83
Charlcombe Bay 111
Charston Rock 72, 74, 84–5
Charston Sands 72, 74
Chepstow 75
Chepstow BC 75
Chepstow and District YC 72, 73–4
Chilton Trinity 124
Cleddau River 6, 12, 14–15
Clevedon Pill 112–13
Clevedon SC 112
Clifton Suspension Bridge 102, 107
Clovelly 155, 158–9
   lifeboat 165
Combe Martin 141–2
Combwich 124, 125
   Pill 127
Combwich Cruising Club 127
Compass Hill 147
Compass Point 167
Copperas Rock 142
Crantock Bay 188
Cresswell River 14
Crockerne Pill 100, 102–3, 105–6
Crow Point 152, 154, 156
Culver Sand 53, 118, 125, 129

Dale 11
Dale Roads 10
Dale YC 11
Diglis Canal Basin 89, 94–5
Doom Bar 177, 178, 183
Dunball Wharf 123, 124

INDEX

Ely River 56, 57, 58–9, 60–1
English Grounds 68, 69, 101, 112

Farley 111
Ferryside 27, 29
firing ranges 9, 28, 116
Fishermen's Mission 187
Fistral Bay 188
Flat Holm 54, 60, 62, 117, 164
flatners (boats) 76–7
floods 140
Foreland Ledge 137
Foreland Point 132, 134, 137
Frampton-on-Severn 91
Fretherne 90

Gannel Creek 185, 188–9
Garron Pill 14
Gelliswick Bay 12
Ginst Point 27, 28, 29
Gladder Brook 96
Gloucester 84, 89, 91
  Docks 92, 97
  National Waterways Museum 92, 97
Gloucester and Sharpness Canal 84, 87, 89, 91–2, 96
Gloucester Harbour Trustees 85
Gloucester Pilots Partnership 85
Godrevy Island 194, 196
Godrevy Point 194
Gore Point 136
Gore Sand 123, 125
Gore, The 158
Gower Peninsula 34–5
SS Great Britain 102, 107
Green Castle 29
Greenleigh Point 132

Ham Green 107
Hamlyn family 159
Harman, Martin 163
Hartland Point 151, 155, 158, 166, 168
Haverfordwest 15
Hawker's Cove 165, 182
Hayle 190–1, 193
Helwick Channel 32, 34
Helwick Pass 34, 35
Hepworth, Barbara 193, 195
Hinkley Point Power Station 124, 125
historic boats 76–7, 97, 102, 105, 107, 154, 161, 163, 171
hobblers (Avon longboats) 105, 107
Hobbs Point 12
Holt Lock 95
Hook 15
Hurlstone Point 134, 136
Hutchwns Point 48

Ilfracombe 146–9
  passages from 151
Ilfracombe YC 146, 148
Instow 152, 154, 156

Jackson's Bay 54
Jones Bay 22

Kempsey 93
Kingsley, Charles 158
Kitchen, The 32
Knightstone Harbour 117, 119

Landmark Trust 116, 154, 163
Langford Grounds 113, 114–15
Langford Swatch 114–15, 116
Lantern Hill 147, 148
Lark Spit 125
Laugharne 27, 28, 29, 41
Lavernock Point 53, 59, 60, 64
Lawrenny Quay 14
Lee Breakwater 45
lifeboats 81, 164–5
lighthouses 23, 62, 164
Limekiln Point 32
Lincomb Lock 95
Linney Head 9
Llangwm Pill 15
Llansteffan 27
Lobspound Point 126
Loughor River 30
Lower Sharpnose Point 167
Lundy Field Society 163
Lundy Island 150, 151, 160–3
  lighthouses 164
  MS Oldenburg (supply ship) 154, 161, 163
Lydney Dock 78, 78–80, 85
Lydney YC 79
Lydstep Haven 22
Lyn Rivers 138, 140
Lynch Pool 33
Lynmouth 138–40
  1952 *floods* 140
Lynton 138

Maisemore 90
Manorbier Range 9
Mathern 73
Mathern Oaze 74
Meachard Rock 172
Milford Haven 6–16
Milford Marina 10, 11–12
Minehead 131–3
Minsterworth 90
Mixon Shoal 32, 164
Monkstone Cruising and SC 42, 43
Monkstone Marina 42, 43
Morte Point 151, 155
Mother Ivey's Bay 165
Mumbles Bay 35, 40
Mumbles Head 35, 39
Mumbles YC 35, 40
museums 92, 95, 97, 129, 142, 156, 193

Nash 67
Nash Passage 37, 39–40
Nash Point 37
Nash Sand 37, 39, 164
National Coastwatch Institution (NCI) 55

National Trust 161, 163, 172
National Waterways Museum 92
nature reserves 14, 62, 123, 190
Neath River 42–3
Nell's Point 52
Nelson Point 105
Newport 67–70
  transporter bridge 71
Newport and Uskmouth SC 67, 69–70
Newport Deep 68, 69
Newquay 184, 185–6
Neyland Yacht Haven 6, 12–13
North Devon Maritime Museum 156
North Devon YC 154, 156
Northam Burrows 154, 156

oil spill (Sea Empress) 16
Old Quay Head 147
Oldbury-on-Severn 98
Oldbury Pill 98
Oldbury Power Station 98
MS Oldenburg 154, 161, 163
Over Bridge 90
Oxwich Bay 34–5

Padstow 176–83
  lifeboat 165
Panthurst Pill 84
Parrett River 77, 123, 124–5, 126
  tidal barrage 124
Pembroke Haven YC 12
Pembrokeshire YC 12
Penally Point 172
Penarth 58, 59, 63
  Marina 56, 57, 58, 60
Penarth YC 63
Pendine Range 28
Pennar Gut 12
Pentire Point 177, 180
Petrockstowe Basin 154
Picton Point 15
Pilgas 27
pilots 50, 54, 85, 105, 107
Polventon Bay 182
Porlock Bay 134–6
Porlock Weir 134–6
Port Eynon 34–5
Port Eynon Point 34
Port Gaverne 173, 174
Port Isaac 174–5
Port Quin Bay 182
Port Talbot 43, 44–5
Portbury Docks 100, 101
Portbury Pier 101, 103
Porthcawl 47–9
Porthcawl Point 37, 47
Porthminster Point 192, 194, 196
Portishead 108–10
  Marina 82, 101, 103, 108, 109–10
Portishead Cruising Club 103, 105
Portishead Point 103, 108
Purton 91

INDEX

Pwllcrochan Flats 10

Quedgeley 92

Rhoose Point 51
Rhymney River 65–6
Rhymney River Motor Boat, Sail and Angling Club 65
Rillage Point 143, 145, 148
River Towy YC 27, 28
Rock 179
Rockham Shoal 148, 155
Royal National Lifeboat Institution (RNLI) 50, 164–5
Royal Portbury Docks 100, 101

St Ann's Head 6, 9, 10, 17
St Clears 28
St Govan's Head 9, 17
St Ives 192–6
   artists 195
St Ives Head 194
St Ives Society of Artists 195
St Julian's Pill 67, 70
St Margaret's Island 23
St Pierre Pill 72
St Saviour's Point 181
St Thomas's Head 115, 116
Sand Ridge 137
Sandy Haven 11
SARA (Severn Area Rescue Association) 81
Saul Junction 91–2
Saundersfoot 18, 24–5
Saundersfoot SC 24
Scarweather Sands 37, 39, 164
Sedbury 84
Severn Area Rescue Association (SARA) 81
Severn Motor YC 94
Severn River 82–98
   barrage schemes 64
   bridges 75, 86, 91
   maximum boat dimensions (upper river) 96
   Severn Bore 90
   trows 76
Severn Valley Railway 96
Sharpness 72, 82, 84, 87–9, 91
   Docks 89, 91
   Locks 84, 89
   see also Gloucester and Sharpness Canal
Sharpness Marine 84, 87, 89
Sheep Island 9, 10
Shepherd's Patch 91
shipwrecks and rescues 164–5
Shoots, The 72, 74, 83–4, 103
Skern Point 154, 155
Skokholm Island 7, 9
Skomer Island 4–5, 7, 9
Slimbridge Wildfowl and Wetlands Centre 91
Slime Road 80, 84
Spear Rocks 112, 113
Spry (trow) 76
Steep Holm 62, 117, 119, 125
Stein, Rick 179

Stepper Point 177, 180, 181
Stert Flats 123
Stert Island 123, 124, 126
Stonebench 90
Stones, The 194
Stourport Marina 95–6
Stourport-on-Severn 89, 91, 95–6
Stourport YC 96
Stroudwater 92
Summerleaze Beach 167
Swansea 36–41
Swansea Bay 36–7, 39
Swansea Yacht Haven 36, 38, 40
Swash Channel 101, 103, 105

Taf River 27, 28, 29, 41
Taw River 152–6
Tawe River 36
Tenby 17, 18–22
   Harbour 22
   lifeboat 165
   Roads 18, 21, 22
Tenby SC 19
Tewkesbury 84, 91, 92–3
   Marina 93
Thomas, Dylan 28, 41
Thornbury SC 98
tidal energy generation schemes 64
Torridge River 151, 152–6
Towan Head 185, 188
Towy BC 27, 28
Towy River 27–9
Trebetherick Point 177, 181
Trevemper 188
Trevose Head 177, 181, 182, 183
trows 76
tub boats (Bude Canal) 171
Turbot Bank 6, 9
Tusker Rock 48
Tywyn Point 27, 28

Uphill 120, 121
Uphill Pill 120–1, 122
Uphill Sands 120
Uphill Wharf Marine Centre 121, 122
Upper Cleddau 14–15
Upper Lode Lock 92
Upton Marina 93
Upton-upon-Severn 84, 91, 93
Usk River 67–70
Uskmouth Power Station 67

Vale of Berkeley 91

Wadebridge 181
Wain's Hill 112, 113
Wales International Coastal Centre 24
Walton Bay 111
Warren Point 132
Watchet 77, 128–30
   Boat Museum 129
   Marina 128, 130
Watermouth Cove 143–5

Watermouth YC 145
Welsh Grounds 68, 69, 101
Welshpool 91
West Somerset Steam Railway 128–9, 132
Weston Bay 117–22
Weston Bay YC 120, 122
Weston-super-Mare 117–19
Whitmore Bay 52
Widmouth Head 143, 145, 148
wind farms, floating 20
withy boats 77
Woodspring Bay 114, 116
   Priory 116
Worcester 84, 89, 94–5
Worcester and Birmingham Canal 95
Worms Head 32, 34
Wrach Channel 60
wreckers 165
Wye River 75

Yeo River 115, 116